Fighting the Devil

Fighting the Devil

A True Story of Consuming Passion, Deadly Poison, and Murder

Jeannie Walker

ISBN: 1-4609-233-4
ISBN-13: 9781460992333

In memory of Sheriff Jake Bogard, who inspired and encouraged me

Contents

List of Illustrations

Author's Note

A lot of people have said, "This story needs to be told."

I was given a huge responsibility, and I'm hoping I got it right. For a long time I have felt the "presence" of my ex-husband, who was murdered in an unthinkable and horrendous way. I owe him a voice because he no longer has one.

So here I am writing the words, telling you the blood-curdling details. Recollections, observations, police records, court transcripts, news articles, medical reports, and memories of lives touched are all dimensions to this story. It is about a family forced to endure more than any family should have to endure.

I lived though the trials and tribulations. I am honoring a commitment foisted upon me, which led me to become a sleuth and follow a sinister trail wherever it led. No one could have predicted the aftermath with its strange twists and unexpected results.

This is a true story, depicted the way it really happened.

Introduction

There was a time when the millionaire rancher, Jerry Sternadel, gave all the orders. No one dared to tell him times were a-changin'. When he discovered in May of 1990 that his wife, Lou Ann, and his bookkeeper, Debbie Baker, had stolen thousands of dollars from him, he demanded the money back by Memorial Day, threatening to have them arrested for embezzlement if they did not. He also told his wife he was going to divorce her.

A week before Memorial Day, Jerry ate lunch with Lou Ann and Debbie as he often did. Soon after consuming his taco salad, he became violently ill, with nausea, vomiting, and severe diarrhea. He was admitted to the hospital on three different occasions between May 23 and June 12.

Doctors were mystified as to what was causing this otherwise healthy forty-nine-year-old man to become so deathly ill. Jerry did not smoke or drink, and he exercised daily. During his final stay in the hospital, toxicology tests showed 4,895 mcg of arsenic in his system. Even while he was a patient in the hospital, the arsenic levels had continued to climb!

Jerry told nurses and anyone within earshot that his wife and bookkeeper were killing him. Lou Ann insisted that his medications were making him hallucinate.

Jerry Sternadel became a virtual prisoner in the hospital when hospital security strapped him to his hospital bed to keep him from leaving the hospital. Lou Ann and Debbie were constantly at his bedside, keeping visitors at bay. In the last days of his life, Jerry screamed out that the two women were killing him and begged for someone to help him.

On June 12, 1990, Jerry died a horrific, painful death while still strapped to the hospital bed with restraints on his hands and feet. Soon after, police received an anonymous tip about the suspicious death. An autopsy proved Jerry had died from extreme arsenic poisoning. The death certificate read, "Patient was given arsenic over a period of time until lethal amounts finally killed him."

Jerry's widow was the sole beneficiary of a $350,000 life insurance policy and estate.

During the investigation, it was learned that a teenager had visited the ranch just before the millionaire's death. The boy had become violently ill immediately after drinking juice from the refrigerator. Toxicology tests showed 278 mcg of arsenic in the boy's system.

The statements Jerry's widow gave to the sheriff and Texas Ranger investigating the case raised the hairs on the backs of the investigators' necks. Lou Ann seemed to have a lot of dirty laundry. Her story did not wash at all.

A thought lingered in the minds of the investigators: if the widow was not responsible for the arsenic poisoning of her husband, then who was? The sheriff and ranger believed that they knew the answer but would have to prove it and that the widow's modus operandi (MO) just might be the means by which they would get their murderer. They were going to live with this homicide investigation night and day.

A couple of years after Jerry Sternadel's death, investigators got a much-needed break in the case when a bottle of arsenic was discovered in a storage locker. The locker had been rented several months before Jerry's death by the bookkeeper under an assumed name.

Sheriff Jake Bogard had plenty of sleepless nights thinking about this case. The dedicated lawman felt he would not sleep well until he was able to put the murderers behind bars. He would work on and live with this case until his untimely death from lung cancer.

The names of some individuals related to this case have been changed. An asterisk (*) indicates such names the first time each appears in the book.

Jeannie Walker sad that her ex-husband, Jerry Sternadel, had died

Calling the Police

C alm and collected, I was able to handle anything thrown at me. But at this moment, I was an emotional wreck. My stomach was in knots. All I could think of was the devastating news.

It was six o'clock in the afternoon. Hesitantly, I walked to my office and picked up the telephone. My hand was trembling as I dialed the long-distance number. The phone rang three times.

"Homicide."

My usual ability to stay calm in the face of disaster deserted me. I cleared my throat and took a deep breath. My voice was quivering.

"I'm calling to report a murder."

"Did you say someone was murdered?"

"Yes, sir, a man died at Bethania Hospital. He was poisoned. Please send an officer over to the hospital right away."

"Lady, try to calm down! I need some information. What's your name?"

"My name is Jeannie Walker."

"What is the name of the person who was murdered?"

"Jerry Sternadel. He was a patient at Bethania Hospital. He died a few minutes ago. His widow is saying he died from natural causes. But he was murdered with arsenic poison. The widow's name is Lou Ann Sternadel."

"How do you know all this?" the detective questioned.

"My daughter called me from the hospital. I just got off the phone with her. She said she heard the doctors say something about her dad dying from arsenic poison."

"Is the person who died related to you?"

"Yes, he is my ex-husband."

"Ma'am, where are you calling from?"

"I'm calling from Long Island, New York."

"You're in New York? And you're calling about a man who died here in Wichita Falls, Texas?"

"Sir, I live on Long Island. I'm calling to tell you my ex-husband was poisoned to death. Can you please send an officer to the hospital right away? His death needs to be investigated. The widow is saying she won't allow an autopsy."

The police officer responded, "Ma'am, we already received a call. Officer Ritchie has been dispatched to the hospital. Just for the record, if it is determined that a crime has been committed, the dead man's wife won't have any say as to whether there will or won't be an autopsy. Did you say the dead man was your ex-husband?"

"Yes, sir. He was my ex-husband and the father of my two children. They were at the hospital when he died. They're over at the hospital right now."

"Ma'am, I need your phone number and address for the record."

After giving the officer the information he needed and hanging up the phone, I said a prayer before sitting down to make another call.

My twenty-six-year-old daughter was standing by a pay phone in the hospital in Wichita Falls. She grabbed the receiver on the first ring. In between sobs, Becky told me that two police officers had just arrived at the hospital. She said her brother had broken down and was given a sedative.

"Honey, I'm so sorry about your dad. I know how devastated you are. But you need to be strong so you can help your brother. I'm calling American Airlines right now for a flight to Wichita Falls. Lord willing,

I'll be there tomorrow. The good Lord will help you and your brother get through this terrible time. Honey, just hang on!"

Relatives and friends of my ex-husband were gathered in Bethania Hospital just steps away from the critical care unit. They had just been told of his passing and were bewildered and grief-stricken.

My twenty-four-year-old son was devastated by the news of his dad's death from arsenic poisoning. He was on the verge of collapse.

Becky used a tissue to wipe away her tears. She had overheard a couple of nurses talking about arsenic the day before but had not been able to believe what she was hearing. Now she knew that it was true, but it was too late for her to help her father. She tenderly wrapped her arms around her younger brother, who had just been given a tranquilizer by one of the doctors.

Becky looked over at her stepmother, Lou Ann, and screamed loudly, "I'll tell you one thing. There's no way Daddy would poison himself."

She pointed at the woman who had married her father after our divorce. "Look at the way she's acting. She and Debbie Baker are laughing and joking, like this is all a big party. She's not sad Daddy died. I think she poisoned Daddy."

My daughter's comment about her stepmother was the first time anyone said openly that Lou Ann might have poisoned Jerry.

When I made that long-distance call to the Wichita Falls Police Department, I did not know that an anonymous caller from the hospital had already tipped them off. Officers had immediately gone to the critical care unit in the hospital where they had produced identification and begun questioning hospital personnel. The detectives had learned that Jerry had been diagnosed in the hospital as having had acute gastric enteritis. They also learned that toxicology tests had revealed high levels of arsenic in his system.

Right away, homicide investigators determined that the death was a probable homicide and promptly gave the order for an official autopsy to be performed. The officers knew it was highly unlikely that anyone would have chosen such an unpleasant and painful method of suicide.

The investigators also learned that Jerry's behavior during his hospitalizations was inconsistent with that of a person self-administering poison. Hospital personnel said he had fully cooperated with doctors and nurses. He had made it known to everyone that he wanted to get better and didn't want to die. He had even begged the nurses and doctors to save his life and not let him die.

Toxicology tests performed at the hospital proved that the arsenic poisoning could not have been accidental because of the continuous arsenic administration and the extreme amount of arsenic in the body at the time of his death.

The corpse was taken from the hospital and transported to the coroner's office in Dallas for a postmortem examination. The forensic pathology examination would determine the exact cause of death and whether or not the death was a homicide.

Neighbors, friends, and relatives believed Lou Ann Sternadel to be a loving wife. They thought they saw an affectionate and considerate woman who would do anything to help her husband. But the police saw the widow in a different light. They believed the marriage had grown stale and that a divorce was in the offing. They had an idea that Jerry's wealth had given Lou Ann a taste for a more exciting lifestyle and that she needed him out of the way in order to retain it. They saw her as someone who wanted to dispose of her husband and believed she may have used at least one accomplice to achieve that goal.

When detectives questioned Lou Ann, she said she had no idea how arsenic could have entered her husband's body. She said she didn't think her husband had any enemies who would want to see him dead.

The murder case was within the jurisdiction of the Clay County Sheriff's Office in Henrietta. Sheriff Jake Bogard had been in law enforcement for twenty-five years and had been sheriff for sixteen of them. His longevity in office gave him a confident manner.

Texas Ranger Bill Gerth was called in to help with the homicide investigation. When Bogard and Gerth questioned the widow, they both felt she provided pat answers. She came up with different answers to the same critical questions. They knew the widow's habit of repeating verbatim answers was a typical defensive pattern.

This wasn't a typical murder or an ordinary homicide investigation. It wasn't an open-and-shut case like one in which the victim is shot or stabbed to death. This was a murder the perpetrator had planned on getting away with. It was going to be a hard case to investigate and prove. Death caused by arsenic poisoning could easily mimic or appear to be a natural death caused by some unknown disease. In essence, murder by arsenic could be a perfect murder.

Karma

Good and evil fortunes fall to the lot of pious and impious alike ...
—Spinoza

Wednesday, June 13, 1990, at 8:10 AM Eastern Daylight Time, I sat looking out the small window of the commercial jet. Thinking about the murder made me a bundle of nerves. Jerry Sternadel had been, after all, the father of my children. He had always been in excellent health, but now he was dead from arsenic poisoning at the age of forty-nine.

My mind flashed back to Memorial Day weekend when my daughter called to tell me her dad had been admitted to the hospital. Becky had said she drove to Wichita Falls from Dallas to visit her dad at the hospital on May 23. The doctors thought he was sick with a stomach virus.

"Daddy looked pale and weak. But he told me he felt better after he was admitted to the hospital. I told him I wanted to go to the horse races in Louisiana and asked him if he thought it would be okay. Daddy said for me to go ahead to the races. Mother, do you think I should go to the horse races or stay with Daddy?"

Knowing my daughter was miserable spending time around her stepmother, I advised her to go to the races but to call often and check on her dad. "If your dad is still in the hospital next week, make sure you go to Wichita Falls and visit him."

Becky called me on Monday, May 28, around six o'clock in the evening. She said her dad had been released from the hospital. When she had called the ranch, her stepmother had said her dad was asleep.

"I told Lou Ann I wasn't going to hang up until I talked to Daddy, so she finally put him on the phone. Daddy said he was glad to be out of the hospital. He said he would be up and around and back to checking on his men. Mother, Lou Ann did not want me talking to Daddy. Do you think Daddy told Lou Ann he didn't want to talk to me? You know Daddy and I have been arguing lately every time we talk."

"Becky, believe me, if your dad did not want to talk to you, he wouldn't have picked up the phone. How did he sound?"

"He sounded kind of weak, but he said he was feeling better. He asked me when I was coming down to see him. He said, 'Becky, I've been sick, real sick, and I want you to come visit me.'"

"What did you tell your dad?"

"I said I would come visit him as soon as I could."

"Well, then, go see your dad as soon and as often as you can. You can't visit me very often, but your dad is right there in Texas. Wichita Falls is not that far a drive from Dallas."

"I know," Becky said. "But Lou Ann makes me feel like I'm not welcome. She hates it when Daddy shows me any attention. Lou Ann is always putting me down."

An air pocket made the plane ride a little bumpy, bringing me back to reality, but left me feeling a little melancholy. Gazing out the small window, I recalled telephoning the ranch on the afternoon of June 3, a Sunday. My ex-husband had answered the phone. He sounded weak but seemed glad to hear my voice. I asked him how he was feeling.

"I'm tired, and my stomach is bloated."

"Are you constipated?" I questioned.

"Hell, no!" he replied. "I've been having real bad diarrhea but I can't urinate."

"What have you been drinking and eating?"

"I've been drinking 7UP this morning, but I don't feel like eating. I don't really feel like eating or drinking anything."

"You should be drinking iced tea—it's good for your kidneys," I responded. "A doctor told me that a long time ago."

"I don't give a shit what your doctor said. I've been drinking 7UP and Cran-Apple juice."

"Are you okay? Who is at the ranch with you? Where's Lou Ann?"

"Lou Ann went to town for something."

"What did your doctors say?"

"Hell, the doctors don't know what the hell is wrong with me. Lou Ann and Debbie keep pouring Cran-Apple juice down me. They keep telling me I've got to drink lots of fluids or I'll get dehydrated."

"Cran-Apple juice is good for you. By the way, who is Debbie? Is she a good friend?"

"Hell, Debbie works for me. She's my bookkeeper. She's only worried about getting a paycheck. Debbie practically lives here. She and Lou Ann stick together like glue. And don't tell me what the hell I should drink."

It was easy to tell Jerry was getting agitated. It also sounded as though he was having trouble breathing. My suggestion was that he try to eat something to build up his strength.

"I sure hope you get to feeling better."

"Mother is making some soup and bringing it out this afternoon," Jerry replied. "Look, I'm tired. I'm gonna hang up now."

It seemed that the phone call had been only yesterday. But Jerry didn't get better, and now he was dead from arsenic poisoning.

I began thinking about the early morning phone call I had received from my son on June 5. From the tone of his voice, I could tell Sandy was worried. He said he had argued with his stepmother in order to get his dad to the hospital.

"Mother, I thought I was going to have to knock Lou Ann out just so I could get Daddy to the hospital. She kept standing in between the door and me. Daddy was gasping for air just to keep breathing. I was afraid he was going to die. I went next door and got the neighbors to help me carry Daddy to the car. Lou Ann kept grabbing my arm saying, 'Your dad is fine. He don't need to go to the hospital. He's doing just fine right where he is. You're not taking him to the hospital. The doctors can't do anything for Jerry anyway.' I told her to get out of my way before I knocked the living daylights out of her.

"I told her Daddy was going to the hospital, and when he got to feeling better there were going to be some changes made out here. I told Lou Ann I was going to take charge until Daddy got well. I was tired of Lou Ann not caring that Daddy was getting worse all the time. I told her I was calling Becky to come down here and then Becky and I were going to get some good doctors for Daddy. Mother, the doctor at the emergency room told me that if Daddy hadn't been brought to the hospital, he would have been dead before morning. I don't understand why I had to fight Lou Ann. She knew how sick Daddy was. I don't understand why Lou Ann didn't care if Daddy lived or died."

A sudden drop in cabin pressure inside the airplane ended my flashback. But I couldn't quit thinking about Jerry's death. I remembered Becky telling me her dad was strapped down in the hospital.

"Daddy's hands and feet were tied down to the hospital bed. It looked like Daddy was a prisoner."

The thought of the agony and terror my ex-husband must have felt being strapped down to the hospital bed brought back a very unpleasant memory. It was the summer of 1970. My two small children were playing outside. Jerry drove up and walked into the house. It was lunchtime. I quickly fixed a couple of ham sandwiches. Jerry sat down at the kitchen table. He took a bite of the sandwich. "Umm, this is good. But dessert is going to be a lot better."

After finishing my sandwich, I went into the master bathroom to wash my hands and brush my teeth. Jerry followed me into the bathroom.

Before I realized what was happening, he grabbed one of my hands and wrapped a short piece of white nylon rope around my right wrist.

"What are you doing? Is this a joke?"

Jerry glanced at me. Without saying a word, he quickly grabbed my other hand and wrapped the nylon cord around it. "I didn't come home for a damn sandwich. I came home to knock you up."

"Okay, you're scaring me! Untie me please," I said as I held my hands out. "This is not funny. Please cut me loose."

He ignored what I was saying and pushed me down onto the bed. "I'm not going to cut you loose. I don't know why I have to rape my wife just so I can have sex with her."

He walked over to the bedroom dresser, opened a drawer, and pulled out a long length of nylon cord. I was becoming very frightened of my husband. I rolled off the bed and tried to run out of the bedroom.

Jerry raced over, quickly closing the bedroom door. He grabbed the ropes on my hands, pushed me backward onto the bed, and tied my hands to the bedpost with the nylon cord. I started tossing and kicking as he pulled my skirt up past my waist.

"Kick, you bitch. That'll just make it more fun!"

"Please! Please! The kids are outside. They'll come into the bedroom."

"No, they won't. I locked the outside doors. Wouldn't you like another brat to go with those two?"

He grabbed my foot as I kicked and wrapped the cord around it. He tied my right foot to the right bedpost at the foot of the bed. Then he wrapped the nylon cord around my other foot and tied it tightly to the left bedpost at the foot of the bed, spreading my legs out.

Somehow I managed to get the nylon cord from my right hand loose. I started slapping at him. He grabbed my hand and quickly tied it to the head of the bed. "You're a real fighter. Hell fire, you're making me hot! What's the big deal! Hell, this is going to be the best sex you ever had."

I was helpless and spread out on the bed like a pig about to be slaughtered. All I could do was beg my husband to quit. He had always liked rough sex, but he had never, ever hinted that he would rape me someday. Even though we had been married for several years, this was a man I did not know. I begged and pleaded with him to stop. I could hear our two children outside yelling for us to let them come inside the house.

"Jerry, please let me up. The kids don't understand why I won't let them in."

"Oh, shuddup! All you ever think about is those fucking brats." He pulled a pocketknife out of his pants pocket.

Oh, my God! I thought. *He's going to kill me!*

He took the knife and cut my panties off and tossed them to the floor. He laid the knife down on top of the table beside the bed. He pulled his jeans and underwear off and started to climb on top of me.

"Oh, I forgot! You're going to have to wait a little longer. I just remembered how clean I have to be to have sex with you. I gotta go wash up. It won't take but a minute. I'll leave the door open, so you can watch me take a piss and wash my hands."

I lay on the bed helpless and begging, "Please, Jerry! Don't do this! Please don't do this!"

He came out of the bathroom, stripped naked, with a strange look on his face. He crawled on top of me. His penis was enlarged and rigid.

I pleaded, "Please don't do this. Please don't do this."

My emotional pleas were ignored. He penetrated me with his manhood, plunging deeper and deeper inside me. He pounded his flesh against mine, all the while professing his love for me. It culminated with his having multiple orgasms. Exhausted, he lay on top of me in a tired heap. Finally, he climbed off of me and walked slowly into the bathroom. "Hell, I sure worked up a sweat."

The mental pain over the shameful, degrading way I was being treated by my husband was far greater than the physical pain I felt. It was all I could do to keep from bursting into tears. I pulled and fought against the restraints holding my hands and feet tightly to the bedposts. I begged, "Jerry, please untie me. Please cut me loose and let me up."

"Hey! You're staying right there. I know you want to get up and wash out. No, you're staying right there. There's no damn way you are going to douche my sperm out of you."

"The kids," I said. "I hear them crying. I've got to check on them. Please cut me loose."

"I'll check on the damn kids. I'm sure they're just fine. I'm sending them over to the neighbor's house. You're sick and need to stay in bed. The bedroom door will be locked so they can't come in. I'll pick them up when I come home from work. See you later, bitch."

I was helpless and strapped to the bed until Jerry came home later that afternoon. He walked into the bedroom and reached for the pocketknife on the nightstand. The knife slipped from his hand and cut his fingers. He picked up the knife from the floor and slowly began cutting the ropes that bound my hands and feet. When he finally cut me loose and let me up off the bed, he said, "I guess we'll have another little bundle of joy in nine months."

"What do you mean?" I asked.

"I just got you pregnant. This is the wrong time of the month for you. I looked at the calendar yesterday. You always mark an X on the wrong days of the month to have sex. So that's how I know I got you pregnant. You can go wash out now, but it won't do you any good!"

"I can't believe you would treat me this way. Someday you're going to pay for what you did. Someday you'll be strapped down and helpless just the way you strapped me down. Nobody will help you either, just like you didn't help me. You'll be strapped down, and nobody will take pity on you," I sobbed as I ran to the bathroom, slammed the door, and locked it behind me.

"Well, I see you're all stirred up. I've got some jobs to check on. I'll be back later. Maybe you'll be calmed down by then."

I stayed in the bathroom until I was sure Jerry was gone. Then I got dressed and went looking for the children. They were outside playing on the swings. When they saw me, they ran over, "Mommy, why did you lock us out?"

I looked at them, "Mommy didn't know the door was locked."

"Mommy, we knocked on the door and hollered. But you wouldn't let us in the house. We saw Daddy. He wouldn't let us in. Are you sick, Mommy?"

"I was a little sick, but I'm okay now. I'm sorry I didn't hear you. Let's go clean up, and then I'll fix you something to eat."

After the children ate some hot soup, I let them watch cartoons while I took a long, hot shower trying to wash away the horrible memories of that afternoon. I was in bed and pretended to be asleep when Jerry came home late that night and went straight to bed.

The flight attendant's question as to what I wanted to drink brought me back to reality. But I couldn't help but think of the possibility that when Jerry was strapped down to the hospital bed, he might have realized the terror I had experienced when he had strapped me down and raped me. I had forgiven him a long time ago for the heartless act he committed that day, but I never forgot.

For some reason, all of a sudden I felt humiliated and angry all over again. And I had the notion that maybe Jerry had deserved to be strapped down and helpless. Maybe it was bad karma. I believe that every action you take eventually returns to you with equal impact. Good will be returned with good; evil will be returned with evil. What Jerry did to me was brutal. But what was done to Jerry was wicked and cruel. The people who poisoned him to death were evil and merciless. I believe Jerry's motivation in what he did to me was out of twisted, distorted love and fear of possibly losing me. The motive of the people who poisoned Jerry to death was an evil, greedy desire for power and control. I was sure fear and terror were Jerry's dominant emotions when he was strapped down and helpless in the hospital. Jerry did not want to die.

In a way, it was my fault that Jerry was murdered for his money. If I had taken my half of all the community property we had when I divorced him, he might still be alive. In my heart, I felt Jerry hadn't deserved to be poisoned to death.

I wondered who could have poisoned Jerry without his knowing it? Who was that close? Only one person: Lou Ann. As I sipped my coffee, I started thinking about some of the interactions I'd had with her. I recalled when Lou Ann took my children out of school. I remembered the school principal telling me that another woman had picked up my children. The teachers said that the woman had produced a note that they thought had been written by me giving her permission to pick up the children. They said my children knew the woman and called her Lou Ann. When I asked for the note, the teachers said they had let the woman keep it. I remembered being scared, worried, and mad all at the same time. I could not understand why the teachers were so lax in letting a strange woman take my children from school. Instantly, I drove over to the house where Jerry lived with Lou Ann. I kept knocking on the door until Lou Ann finally appeared. I confronted her.

"Lou Ann, I know you picked up my kids from school. I want to know where they are."

Lou Ann responded, "I don't know where your brats are. You need to talk to Jerry."

"Where can I find Jerry?"

"At work where he belongs," she said with a big smirk on her face. "Goodbye!"

I was almost hysterical with fear and immediately drove to the police station.

The officers said nothing could be done until my children were missing for twenty-four to forty-eight hours.

"It's Friday afternoon," one officer said. "You need to go home in case the kids show up. Maybe the kid's dad had someone pick them up to get an early start on the weekend. He does have visitation rights, doesn't he? Or did you take that away from him too."

It was painstakingly clear the officers had no sympathy for me or for my dilemma. I drove straight home, watched the clock, and waited. That night was the longest one of my life. The next morning, I drove to Jerry's house and parked in the driveway. I noticed Lou Ann's car parked in the back of the house behind some bushes, as if she was trying to hide it from view. I got out of my car and walked up to the back door of the house. As I was knocking on the door, I thought I saw a curtain on one of the side windows move.

Lou Ann finally came to the door.

"Lou Ann, I want to know where my kids are. I know you took them from school. Where are my kids?"

"You're crazy! I don't know where your fucking kids are. You need to talk to Jerry."

"I will talk to Jerry," I quickly responded. "Just tell me where Jerry is."

"I just called him. He's on his way right now. And so are the cops. Good-bye!" She slammed the door shut.

At that moment, the curtain on the side window inside the house was pulled aside, and I saw my daughter Becky, then only nine years old, standing at the window. She was crying, "Mommy, don't leave. Please, Mommy, don't leave. Mommy, please, I want to go home."

When I saw my daughter and heard what she was saying, I jumped onto the porch. I could see Lou Ann through the window in the door. She was laughing. She glared at me with her bug eyes and then turned and walked away.

I jumped off the porch and walked over to the window where my daughter was standing inside the house with her hand up against the windowpane. "I'm not leaving, sweetheart!" I said, putting my hand up against the glass. Glancing through the window, I saw Lou Ann race into the room. I watched in horror as she grabbed my daughter by the hair, slapped her in the face, and screamed at her.

"You little bitch! I told you to stay away from the window."

I jumped back onto the porch and rammed my fist through the windowpane in the door. I reached inside the broken window and unlocked the door latch. Blood gushed from my right hand as I raced through the back door and into the house to the room where I saw Lou Ann hitting my daughter.

Lou Ann met me in the doorway of the bedroom. She lunged at me, screaming. "Get the fuck out of my house. Take your fucking brats and get out now!"

Pushing Lou Ann aside, I rushed toward my young daughter. Lou Ann lunged at me again and grabbed a handful of hair. In a split second, I turned and hit her.

Lou Ann screamed, "You bitch! Now I'm gonna beat the shit out of you."

I doubled up my fist and struck Lou Ann smack in the face. She moaned and grabbed another handful of my hair with her left hand. I quickly grabbed her arm and twisted it behind her back. Both of us fell to the floor. I seized her head and started banging it on the wood floor. She let go of my hair and started clawing and scratching at me.

I heard someone walking on broken glass directly behind me and quickly glanced toward the sound. I saw Jerry. My immediate thought was that he was going to pull me off Lou Ann. But he just stood in the middle of the room with his arms folded.

Lou Ann reached up and grabbed another handful of my hair. I boxed her ears and held her down on the floor. When she finally stopped pulling my hair, I let go of her and pushed myself off the floor. I looked over at Jerry. He was laughing.

Lou Ann lay sprawled out on the hardwood floor crying and howling, "Jerry, you sorry bastard. Why didn't you pull her off me? That bitch was trying to kill me!"

Jerry looked over at me. "Looks like you beat the shit out of Lou Ann. Too bad I wasn't here to see the whole thing. I don't think Lou Ann will ever tangle with you again."

A voice yelled out. "Police. What's going on in there? We got a call about a disturbance. The back door is busted up with glass all over the place."

"Oh, these two women were fighting over me," Jerry replied. "My ex-wife won the fight, but she was just leaving."

"Not without my kids," I responded.

"Take your fucking brats!" Lou Ann yelled. "Jerry, I told you she was crazy!"

Jerry glanced over at Lou Ann. "She sure put you in your place, didn't she?"

Lou Ann raced over to the policeman. "Officer, this woman tried to kill me. I want her arrested."

My son and daughter were peeking out from behind a nearby door. They were crying as they ran over and grabbed my hand. I bent down and hugged them.

"Mommy is so sorry all this happened. It's okay now. A police officer is here to help us."

Lou Ann's two little girls were standing in the doorway of a nearby bedroom sobbing.

Lou Ann turned toward her young children and screamed, "Shut the hell up!"

The police officer looked at me. "Ma'am, you need to step outside."

I walked out of the house with my children. Once outside, I explained to the police officer that Lou Ann had taken my children from school without my permission or knowledge.

"I saw my children inside the house begging for me to take them home, so I rammed my fist through the window to get inside the house."

Jerry walked over to the police officer. He said it was all just a misunderstanding and everything was his fault. "Lou Ann told me she doesn't want anyone arrested. My ex-wife just got a little excited. As for the broken window, that was broken by a baseball when I was playing catch with my son."

The police officer looked over at me, "Ma'am, your hand is bleeding. Looks like you cut it up pretty bad." He looked over at Jerry. "Are you going to press charges?"

"What for?" Jerry asked with a laugh. "I'll fix the window." He looked over at me. "Your hand is bleeding. It needs to be bandaged. I'll drive you to the emergency room."

"I'll bandage it when I get home. I'm taking Becky and Sandy, and that's where we're going."

"No, I can't allow that," Jerry responded.

"I'm not leaving my kids here. Officer, can't you do something to help me?"

Jerry said, "I have paperwork showing the kids are in my custody. They are staying here with me."

"Officer, I have full custody of these children," I responded. "I can show you the court papers. I have the right to take them home with me."

"You two will have to sort this out in court," the officer replied. "Ma'am, could you step over to the squad car?"

I walked over to the police vehicle.

"What's your name?"

"Jeannie," I replied.

"Jeannie, I feel for you, but I can't do anything. Technically, you are guilty of trespassing and destroying private property. He could file charges against you if he wanted to, and I would have to haul you off to jail. You need to go home and take care of your hand. I'm sure everything will work out."

The announcement on the plane brought me back from my trip to the past.

"Thank you for flying American. We hope you had a good flight."

When I was assigned my seat, 13C, I felt it was a good omen because the date was June 13.

"I thought you might be staying with us," the flight attendant said.

"I'm just always the last passenger off the plane."

"Well, thanks for helping me by folding your blanket."

"You're very welcome," I replied as I continued walking down the narrow corridor of the airplane. I saw the pilot coming out of the cockpit. "Thanks for getting us here safely."

"Thank you for flying with us!" the officer responded. "Enjoy your stay in Dallas."

As I approached the doorway to the airport terminal, I saw a young woman running toward me, "Mother, you're here! I can't believe it. You're actually here!"

My daughter had grown into a beautiful young lady. She was tall and slender with wavy brown hair and brown eyes that sparkled like diamonds. A young man dressed in a uniform walked up and stood next to her.

"Oh, I forgot about you! Mother, this is Ron. He's with airport security. It's been a hectic and crazy day. You won't believe what happened! I was almost arrested."

"What!" I exclaimed. "Arrested? Arrested for what?"

Matter-of-factly, Becky said, "I was in such a hurry that I left my wallet with my identification inside the car. Anyway, I didn't think I would need to prove who I was. See, when I went through the gate, I had a gun in my purse. It's only a stun gun. I forgot to leave it in the car. Security was called. They didn't believe me when I told them I was a parole officer. So that's why Ron is here. He's going with us to the car to look at my ID. I told him about Daddy being murdered and you coming here to help us find the killers."

The security guard walked with us to the airport parking lot. He checked Becky's identification and admonished her. "You are a parole officer—you should know better. But with your dad being murdered and all, I realize it was just an honest mistake on your part. They will catch those criminals. Only somebody who's got the devil in them would do something that horrible. Just keep your faith strong and remember: what goes around comes around."

The Funeral Home

The sprawling mesquite-laden countryside stretched as far as the eye could see as Becky and I drove down Texas Highway 287, listening to the soft music floating from the radio. An impressive and iridescent shade of blue radiated from the sky as the sun appeared and disappeared behind floating clouds that seemed to be playing peek-a-boo with the warm rays of sunlight. Over the horizon the small town of Henrietta, Texas, was just coming into view.

Our plan was to stop off at the sheriff's office to see if anyone knew anything about Jerry's murder and then drive straight to the funeral home to find out if Jerry's body had been returned from the autopsy. I took the next exit and headed toward Henrietta and parked in front of the sheriff's office.

Sheriff Bogard had rugged good looks and appeared to be in his fifties. "Well," he said in a Texas drawl, "I never expected the first person to come forward in this investigation would be the murdered man's *ex*-wife."

"Sheriff, this is my daughter, Becky," I said. "Becky is Jerry Sternadel's daughter."

"Well, I'm glad to see both of you." He looked at Becky. "Young lady, I'm so sorry about the loss of your dad."

"Thank you," Becky muttered.

"Have either of you been to the funeral home yet?"

"No, Sheriff, we haven't. I just arrived from New York. Becky picked me up at the airport, and we drove straight here. We didn't know when the body would be returned from Dallas."

"Sternadel's body arrived a couple of hours ago at the Hampton Vaughn Funeral Home in Wichita Falls.

"We have ruled his death a homicide, but we're waiting on the autopsy results to make it official. I'm a little rushed for time today, but if you come back to my office tomorrow, I might have some more information. Maybe you can help us fill in some missing pieces."

We left and then drove straight to Hampton Vaughn Funeral Home. After looking at the cars in the parking lot, Becky exclaimed, "We're in luck—Lou Ann is not here!"

"How do you know she's not here?" I asked.

"Because I don't see Daddy's Lincoln Town Car. Daddy put a phone in it so he could keep track of his jobs. Lou Ann would be driving it in order to keep in touch with Debbie Baker."

I responded, "That is good news."

"Mother, I think Lou Ann and Debbie murdered Daddy."

"Becky, please don't say anything like that to anyone inside the funeral home. Let's just view your dad and then leave."

"Okay, I won't say anything. I don't know if I can look at Daddy. I can't believe he's dead. Mother, I've got knots in my stomach."

"I've got knots in my stomach too," I replied. I got out of the car and walked around to the passenger side to open the door for my daughter. I gave her a big hug and took her hand. "Come on, let's go see your dad."

Our pace quickened as we approached the front door of the funeral home. The insistent sound of our stiletto heels hitting the pavement sounded like the clickety-clack, clickety-clack of a train. We reached for the brass handle of the door simultaneously, as if in concert with each other.

An attractive middle-aged man wearing a tailored charcoal-gray suit and starched white dress shirt stood just inside the doorway. "Good afternoon," he said, politely ushering us into a high-ceilinged foyer. The scent of candles infused the air. "Whom do you wish to visit?"

"Jerry Sternadel," we said in unison.

"Oh, I'm so sorry. There is no viewing for Mr. Sternadel. However, you can sign the register."

"You mean we can't see him!" Becky exclaimed.

"No, I'm afraid not. The widow left explicit instructions that no one is to view Mr. Sternadel, at least not until she comes in later."

"How long has the body been here?" I asked.

"I believe Mr. Sternadel arrived around eleven this morning."

Glancing at my watch, I saw it was almost three-thirty.

"Has Lou Ann Sternadel been here today? Has anyone else been here to view the body?"

"The widow hasn't come in yet, but some friends of the deceased came by and signed the register. They weren't allowed to view the body. Mrs. Sternadel left us instructions that no one was to view the body without her permission."

Without hesitation, Becky stated emphatically, "Well, I'm not just anyone. I am Jerry Sternadel's daughter! That's my daddy in that coffin!"

"Oh, I am so sorry," the man replied, seeming embarrassed. "The immediate family can go in and view Mr. Sternadel. If you will accompany me, I will take you to the viewing room."

The floors of the funeral home were carpeted, and the walls were hung with paintings of reproductions. Bowls of colorful scented potpourri sat on Victorian end tables along with boxes of tissues. The furniture was upholstered with thick plush velvet.

My daughter and I followed the gentleman down the hallway to Room 1. A book with a ballpoint pen sat on a wooden pedestal just outside the door. Only a few names were written in the log. I picked up the pen and signed my name. Handing the pen to my daughter, I waited until she had signed before I proceeded to walk through the doorway of Room 1.

The man stood in front of me, blocking the way. "I'm sorry, ma'am, but I can't allow you to go inside."

"This is my *mother!*" Becky thundered with immense authority.

"Oh, I'm so sorry. I didn't realize. I sincerely apologize. Both of you can view Mr. Sternadel. Please spend as much time as you need. I will make sure nobody disturbs you."

Becky peeked inside the room. "Mother, I can't do it. I can't go in there."

"I'll go first," I said, walking through the door and over to the coffin.

Jerry was laid out in a dark gray casket lined with white satin and white velvet. His eyes were closed. There was no smile on his face. The blue suit he was dressed in looked very familiar. I was almost positive Jerry was going to enter into the hereafter in the same blue suit I had bought him years earlier. My daughter was standing just outside the door.

"It's okay, sweetheart. Come on in. This may be your last chance to be with your dad."

Becky slowly ambled through the door. Her cheeks were red, and tears streamed down her face. She dabbed at her eyes with a crumpled tissue.

"Honey, it's okay," I whispered softly, reaching out and drawing her close.

She looked down at her dad and then glanced up at me. She closed her eyes. "I can't believe Daddy is dead. I don't know what I'm going to do without Daddy."

"I know, sweetheart, I know," was all I could utter. My own urge to cry over the cruelty and anguish I knew she was feeling was about to overwhelm me. Plus, the sight of my ex-husband was a disturbing and shocking image. He had always been so healthy and strong. Now he lay lifeless in a coffin. I might have felt differently if he had been terminally ill for a long time. But for Jerry to have been poisoned to death in the prime of his life was an idea I found hard to fathom.

I watched as my daughter gradually edged closer and closer to the coffin. She reached down and took her dad's hand in hers and then turned and looked at me. "Mother, his hand is cold and hard." She ran her fingers through his hair. She stroked his face. Then she slowly backed away and walked toward the foot of the casket. She raised the lid and looked at her dad's feet. "Body bag! Mother, he's in a body bag."

Walking over and peering into the casket, I saw Jerry's feet were encased in ivory muslin. "I guess his feet were so swollen they couldn't put his shoes on."

She promptly closed the lid and walked back to the head of the coffin. She bent down and started examining her dad's face, pushing his head from side to side, "Mother, look at all the scratches and bruises on Daddy's neck. Daddy, I'm so sorry. I didn't know what was happening to you. Daddy, forgive me. Please, forgive me."

"I don't think anybody knew your dad was being poisoned until it was too late."

"Daddy looks so awful. Mother, he suffered so much in the hospital. Look at where all the tubes were in his hands. Look how swollen his face is. When Daddy was in the hospital, the nurse put IVs in Daddy's feet and toes because all the veins in his hands and arms had collapsed."

"Becky, please don't do this to yourself. You did everything you could to help your dad."

Tears streamed down her cheeks. "Did Daddy know I loved him? Do you think Daddy loved me?"

Reaching over and tenderly wiping away my daughter's tears, I said, "Yes, darling, your dad knew you loved him. And he loved you too. He may not have shown it at times. But I guarantee you, Daddy loved you and Sandy very, very much."

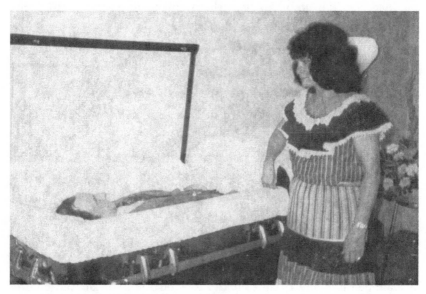

Jeannie Walker at funeral home viewing Jerry Sternadel

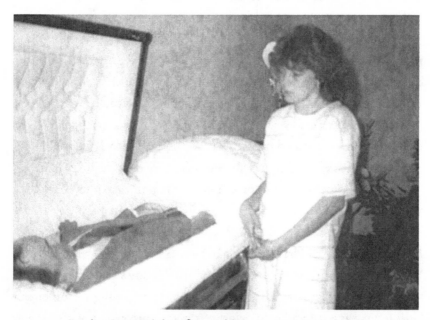

Becky Sternadel at funeral home viewing her dad

"Mother, I'm going to help them catch whoever did this," my daughter said as she sauntered across the room to a nearby bouquet. She clipped off a red carnation, smelling its sweet aroma. She walked back to the casket and gently placed the red flower into the lapel of her dad's suit. She looked at me. "Yellow was Daddy's favorite color, but I couldn't find a yellow one. I know he liked red too."

My daughter was grieving intensely over her dad's demise. I wanted to do something to lighten the emotional difficulty she was experiencing. "Honey, why don't you check the cards on the flower arrangements?"

"Okay," she said as she wiped tears from her eyes and walked over to an arrangement, picked up a card, and read it.

While my daughter was occupied looking at cards of condolences, I moved closer to the coffin and closely studied the corpse of my ex-husband. His hair was thin on the top, but he still had those curly red sideburns. His face was badly swollen, but I could still see the twenty-two-year-old I had married back in 1963. I thought about the good times we had shared together. I wished things could have been different.

I wanted a good look at Jerry. Taking my eyeglasses out of my pocketbook and putting them on, I immediately noticed Jerry's right ear seemed to have a pinkish tone to it. I reached down and touched it. His ear felt soft and warm. I turned his head and looked at his other ear. The left one was a dull ash color. I reached down and touched it. It was cold and hard. I touched his face. It was cold and hard. I felt his right ear again. It was definitely warm and soft. I felt this must be a sign.

"Becky, come over here for just a minute and take another look at your dad. Tell me if you see anything out of the ordinary."

My daughter walked over to the coffin. She stared for a moment at her dad's body. "I didn't notice it before. But Daddy's right ear looks pink." She reached down and touched it. "Daddy's ear is soft. It feels warm." She turned her dad's head to the side, touching his other ear. "His left ear is hard and cold. Mother, do you think Daddy is trying to tell us something?"

"Yes, I think it means everyone is going to hear about your dad being poisoned to death."

"Do you really think Daddy is telling us that? I sure hope you're right. 'Cause Lou Ann is trying to keep everything hush-hush. She swore there would not be an investigation."

"Honey, the police know Daddy was murdered. And I'll do everything I can to make sure whoever poisoned him is caught and punished. You have my word. I won't stop until his killers are brought to justice."

Becky leaned down and kissed her dad on the cheek. "Daddy, you can count on us. We know who gave you the arsenic. They're going to pay for it."

"Sweetheart, I don't want you to think I'm being morbid. But I would like to take some pictures of your dad."

"That's why you brought the camera, isn't it? I'm just glad you remembered."

"Well, you know how much I like taking pictures," I replied, unzipping my bag and taking out my 35mm camera.

"I wish I had a camera as nice as yours."

"When I become a millionaire, I'll buy you one," I said, as I snapped a picture of Becky standing by her dad's coffin.

"Mother, you're funny," Becky said as she straightened her dad's tie.

I continued snapping photos as my daughter spruced up her dad's clothes.

"Okay, now let me take some pictures of you," Becky said as she took the camera and began snapping away.

"I am thankful we were able to see your dad alone, just the two of us. Getting to spend time with him by ourselves is the icing on the cake ... if there *is* a cake." I glanced at my watch. "Would you believe we've been here for over two hours?"

"Wow, the time flew by," Becky said. "I'm surprised they didn't come in and run us out."

"Honey, we better go. We don't know when Lou Ann might show up. I don't want to tangle with her—not today anyway."

"Okay, I'm ready to go. Bye, Daddy."

I glanced over my shoulder for one more look at the father of my children before my daughter and I left the viewing room. I whispered, "I love you, Jerry."

After leaving the funeral home, I drove directly to the local newspaper office. As fate would have it, there was an article about the murder in the *Times Record News*. That evening, when I drove over to the funeral home, I noticed my son's truck in the parking lot.

"I'll go inside the funeral home and tell Sandy to come out here," Becky said.

"Okay," I replied. "But don't start any trouble with Lou Ann."

"What? Me cause trouble?" Becky responded.

It wasn't very long before both Becky and Sandy came out of the funeral home and walked toward me.

Sandy gave me a long hug. "Mother, it's so good to see you. But I have bad news. Lou Ann is inside the funeral home sitting at the front door watching for you. She is planning on keeping you out of the funeral home. She told everybody it would only be over her dead body that Jeannie Walker gets to view Jerry Sternadel in his coffin. She is so afraid you might come inside the funeral home that she won't even go into Daddy's room. She just keeps sitting at the front door watching for you."

"Well, Lou Ann is a little too late in trying to keep me from seeing your dad. Becky and I were at the funeral home this afternoon and stayed for over two hours with him."

Sandy said, "Wait till Lou Ann hears that! She is going to be pissed."

Becky quickly said. "It's our dad. We're his only children. We have a right to be with him and so does Mother. She was married to him too."

"Well, I'm just saying that Lou Ann is going to be pissed. She'll probably find out that Mother got to see Daddy."

"Well, Mother didn't murder Daddy. Lou Ann and Debbie Baker did!" Becky exclaimed. "Mother hasn't done anything wrong!"

"I never said Mother did anything wrong," Sandy replied.

"Listen, you two, this is not the place or the time to get upset with each other or to have this kind of discussion. After your dad is buried, we will do whatever is needed to bring Lou Ann and Debbie Baker to justice, if they poisoned your dad. Lou Ann would love to tear us apart, but that is *not* going to happen. Not now, not ever!"

I told my son and daughter to go back inside the funeral home. "I am counting on you to be sociable and nice to everyone. While you are doing that, I'll go get a motel room. From there, we will figure out what we need to do."

The next morning, I woke up very early and quietly dressed while my daughter was still fast asleep. I drove directly to Sheriff Bogard's office in Henrietta.

"Mighty good to see you today," he said, greeting me warmly. "I've got some news for you. Sternadel's widow had his will probated this morning. She couldn't even wait until the poor guy was in the ground. I'd sure like to see what that last will and testament says. Do you think you'd want to go over to the courthouse and get a copy of the will so we can take a look at it?"

"I sure would, Sheriff, if you think I could get a copy."

"Well, I don't know why they would deny you. After all, you're the mother of his two kids. I'll call over there and tell them you're on the way. When you get the copy, come on back over here. Then you and I can take a gander at that will."

The Clay County courthouse was right across the street. I walked over and got copies of the will. Quickly glancing at it, I was surprised to see Lou Ann was the sole beneficiary. Now I knew why she had filed the probate so fast. She knew she would inherit everything. Holding the copies next to my chest, I walked briskly back to the sheriff's office. He was waiting for me by the front door.

Taking the copy of the will that I handed him, he walked back to his office, motioning for me to follow. He sat down at his desk and immediately began scanning the document. I sat down in a chair and started scrutinizing my copy. It didn't take long before I noticed the initials on the bottoms of the pages did not look like Jerry's handwriting. I was wondering what I could do to challenge the handwriting.

"If I were you," Bogard said, looking over the top edge of his glasses at me. "I would get your kids to bring a wrongful death suit against the widow. I'd also have them contest this will."

"If I have anything to do with it, they will do just that," I replied.

"I believe the funeral is tomorrow. Just so you know, I'm going to have uniformed and plainclothes officers at the church and out at the cemetery. I know you're Sternadel's ex-wife, but maybe you could stay a few days after the funeral and help us fill in some blank spaces. You might know something that other people don't. Any information you could give us would be helpful. Think about it. I'll talk to you after the funeral."

Jerry Sternadel as a youngster

Jerry Sternadel in his twenties

Jerry Sternadel playing table tennis in high school

Jerry Sternadel with his church softball team

Love Gone Awry

Jerry Eli Sternadel was born in Wichita Falls, Texas, on February 18, 1941, to Marchlene Mazell Wilbanks and Eli Will Sternadel. Eli was a farmer and Marchlene a housewife.

Jerry was a good-looking, freckle-faced kid with short, curly brown hair. He grew up in Petrolia, a small town fifteen miles outside of Wichita Falls. He participated in every sport the school offered and became the star basketball player for Petrolia. After high school, he enrolled at the local university in Wichita Falls. He was gregarious and full of ambition. He was also gutsy and strong-minded. He attended Midwestern University full-time while working part-time at the local dairy in Wichita Falls. His job was loading crates of milk onto delivery trucks.

I was born in Terrell, Oklahoma, in 1942 to Woodrow and Alta Maxwell. My dad was of Cherokee Indian ancestry. He was a struggling farmer, and my mother was a housewife.

Most people said my Indian lineage showed in my high cheekbones, black hair, and dark brown eyes. I grew up and went to school in the rural town of Lone Wolf, Oklahoma. We lived out in the country on a dirt road with the nearest neighbor a mile away. My sisters and I rode the school bus to and from school. I was a conscientious straight-A student. I loved singing. By the time I was a sophomore, my father could not eke out a living farming in the Oklahoma plains, so we packed up our belongings and moved to Wichita Falls, Texas. I graduated from Wichita Falls High School. In 1963, I began working as a bookkeeper at Gobles Dairyland in Wichita Falls.

Every day, as if it were a ritual, a guy with curly brown hair and red sideburns would walk by my office and peck on the window. "Go to lunch with me?" In spite of the fact that I always ignored him, Jerry Sternadel continued tapping on the windowpane, asking me to go to lunch. I kept working and wouldn't even look up.

Jerry was very determined. He had made up his mind to tap on that window till hell froze over, if that's what it took to get my attention. He had also decided that I was the girl he was going to marry.

One day I surprised both of us when I looked up and said. "Okay, just this once, I'll go to lunch with you!"

Jerry was on cloud nine as we walked to the corner café at Eighth and Indiana. He was a gentleman, politely opening the door and escorting me inside the restaurant to a corner table. The song "Crazy" by Patsy Cline was playing on the radio. He looked at me and said, "That's what I am. I'm crazy about you. The first time I laid eyes on you, I knew you were the girl for me. There's no doubt about it. You're going to be my wife."

I started going out with Jerry on informal dates. He played for a church softball team. I loved watching him pitch. On more than one occasion, he pitched a no-hitter. I gladly attended the games to cheer for him and his team.

At one particular game, a guy walked up to the car in which I was sitting and watching the game.

"I heard that guy pitching is your boyfriend."

"Maybe, he is," I replied.

"Well, I guess you know he's a rinky-dink!"

I responded, "I'll have you know, Jerry Sternadel is an excellent pitcher."

"I don't think you'd know a good pitcher if you saw one. He should be more like me. I'm the pitcher for the other team. If that guy was good enough, he'd be on my team."

I was beginning to get irritated with this cocky softball player. I was glad when I noticed Jerry walking toward us.

"I see you've met my friend, Dwight Ledford. Has he been saying bad things about me?"

"All I told your girlfriend is that you are a rinky-dink."

"Did she believe you?"

"No, she didn't believe one word. Looks like you've got a winner in this one. Not only is she bright, but she's also beautiful."

I didn't know it at the time, but Jerry and Dwight had been good friends for a very long time. As time passed, I learned why they were so close.

Dwight was a genuine gentleman who was married to a lovely woman and had three adorable sons. He was totally honest and forthright. He and Jerry helped each other improve their pitching skills. The softball championships almost always came down to two teams, Jerry's team, First Presbyterian, and Dwight's team, Downtown Baptist. Even though they were competitors, they had great respect for each other.

When there weren't any games, I had plenty of time to get acquainted with Dwight when we all went golfing together. I grew to be very fond of Dwight and his family.

I married Jerry Sternadel before the summer ended in 1963. Soon I became pregnant.

Jerry quit college and took a full-time job working for a company delivering linens and uniforms to businesses. After just a few months, he was promoted to a managerial position and no longer drove the delivery truck.

When our daughter was six months old, I became pregnant again. It was about this time when Dwight began having very painful backaches. Dwight still played golf and softball, but the pain caused him to miss games. One doctor put Dwight in constraints at the hospital, saying a strain caused the back pain. But when he went to another doctor, he was diagnosed with something much more severe than back strain. He had a malignant progressive disease in which the bone marrow and other blood-forming organs produce increased numbers of immature or abnormal leukocytes. He had leukemia. There was no treatment or cure. The disease had a poor prognosis. The doctors gave Dwight six months to a year to live. They told him to put his life in order.

Dwight's wife, Marlene, was devastated. Jerry and I were heartbroken and distraught by the horrible news. We did not want to believe our good friend had a disease that would take him away from us.

Dwight started taking medications and doing everything the doctors suggested. Soon he began feeling tired all the time and became anemic. The least little thing would make him ill, and he would wind up sick in bed. One day, he came over to our upstairs apartment around noon. Jerry was at work. Dwight said that he felt as if he was coming down with the flu and didn't want to jeopardize my health and the health of the baby I was carrying. So he stayed downstairs while he and I conversed with each other. He told me that he was planning a baby shower for Jerry. The shower was going to be for men only—no women would be allowed, not even me. We worked out the details of the surprise shower while Dwight held onto the railing downstairs and I stood at the top of the stairs. It was just like Dwight. Instead of dwelling on his life-threatening illness and imminent death, he was thinking of his friend.

Jerry was surprised beyond imagination to be given the kind of party that typically a woman gets when she is having a baby. He was also humbled and moved by the unselfish mindset of Dwight, who was suffering horribly from the disease that was swiftly killing him.

At work, rumblings began about laborers wanting to join a union. The owner told the managers to discourage the unskilled workers from joining and warned the managers of what would happen if they didn't heed his advice. Of course, Jerry did not heed the owner's warning and started befriending and encouraging the workers to stand their ground to get a union started.

Each day, I would drive to the office to pick up Jerry after work. One morning, Jerry called and told me he was going to fill in for a sick employee and drive a delivery truck on a route to Oklahoma. I was sitting in the car out in the parking lot at the precise time he had told me to come pick him up that afternoon. I waited and waited. The sun had set and it was starting to get dark, but Jerry still had not arrived. I saw a light on in the office and went inside. I told Jerry's boss I was getting worried about my husband and asked if he had heard from him.

The boss told me Jerry had had engine trouble with the truck. Jerry was going to stay in Oklahoma and drive back the next day after the truck was repaired. He said that Jerry had just called, asking him to tell me what had happened so I wouldn't worry. Jerry's boss suggested I go home and get some rest. "Your husband will be back tomorrow. You have my word on that."

At ten o'clock the next morning, my father-in-law, Eli Sternadel, called. "Jeannie, I just got a telephone call from Jerry. He said he's locked up in jail."

"What! Jerry can't be in jail. He stayed overnight in Oklahoma for his boss. There must be some kind of mix-up."

"All I know is that Jerry just called. He asked me to come to the Wichita County jail. He said he was arrested in Oklahoma yesterday and extradited back to Wichita Falls this morning. He said something about his boss having had him arrested. I'm on my way to the jailhouse right now."

"Eli, I want to go with you. Could you come pick me up? Will you ask Marcy if she will watch Becky for me?"

"I don't think you're in any shape to be doing that. That baby is due any time now, isn't it?" Eli responded.

"I'll be okay. Please let me go with you."

"Okay, we'll be there in about thirty minutes."

When Eli and I got to the Wichita County jail, I saw Jerry's boss coming out of the jailhouse. I said, "That's Jerry's boss. I need to talk to him. Go on ahead, Eli, I'll catch up with you."

"Okay, if you're sure! I'll go inside and see what I have to do to get my son out of jail."

I caught up with Jerry's boss as he was walking down the sidewalk.

"Did you have my husband arrested?"

"Yes, I did!" he answered.

"Why? What did he do to be arrested? I thought you were Jerry's friend as well as his boss. At least, that's what you led us to believe."

"I told all my managers to stop the union shit. But Jerry wouldn't listen. He went and sided with the idiots who wanted to bring a union into my workplace. I'm going to use him as an example. Besides, as far as I am concerned, he stole money and linens from my company. That's why he was arrested. Look, I'm sorry you're pregnant and all, but Jerry should have stayed clear of the union, like I asked him to."

"I can't believe you would do this to Jerry. He was a loyal employee. He never stole anything from you. Your business grew because of Jerry. He worked his head off for you."

"Yeah, well ... he should have listened."

"Please drop the charges against my husband."

"I can't do that! I'm not having a union in my place of business. If Jerry would've just kept his mouth shut ... But no, he couldn't do that! He encouraged those goons to get a union started. This union business would have already been over if he would have just stayed out of it. But now that union shit is going strong because those guys liked Jerry and listened to him. Now he is going to pay. You better find your husband a good lawyer. He's going to need one!"

"Please! You know what you are doing is wrong. I pray God will forgive you."

"I don't believe in God. I'm an atheist! Always have been. Always will be! As far as I'm concerned there is no God, no afterlife, no nothing. It's just what a man can do for himself. Whoever has the gold makes the rules! That's all there is! Go get a lawyer. That's the only way your no-good husband is getting out of jail!"

I saw Eli coming out of the doorway of the jail and started walking toward him.

"Jeannie, you can't go in there. Jerry said he didn't want you to see him like that. He's pretty torn up. My son is not a weak man, but he's sitting in that jail cell crying like a baby. I guess that's why he told me to keep you out of there. What we need to do right now is go get an attorney to get him out of that damn place. I know a good lawyer. We'll have him out of jail before the day is out."

Eli and I went straight from the jail to a lawyer's office. Eli wrote a check to the lawyer for $1,000 and slapped it down on his desk.

"Get my son out of jail!"

He turned and looked at me. "You and Jerry can pay me back whenever you're able to. If you don't ever get the money to pay me back, so be it! Don't worry about it. We need to get Jerry back home where he belongs."

The lawyer took the check, and Jerry was released from jail that very afternoon.

A month later, the boss formally dropped all charges against Jerry. But he swore Jerry would never work for anyone in Wichita Falls again. And he did a good job of keeping his word. Jerry was unable to find any kind of permanent employment anywhere in Wichita Falls. Jerry filled out lots of applications and went on job interviews. But his former boss had passed the word around, so nobody would hire him. He was forced to take low-paying part-time work and odd jobs to support us.

After the birth of our son, I quickly began looking for work. I took a secretarial job at White's Stores Incorporated in Wichita Falls. White's was the corporate headquarters for White's Auto Stores. Dwight Ledford had worked at the corporate office before he became ill.

Dwight was now hospitalized in serious condition with pneumonia. He was dying. Jerry and I went to visit him on his deathbed. Dwight's wife, Marlene, met us in the hallway of the hospital. She told us not to expect Dwight to recognize us. "Dwight didn't even recognize me. He is struggling so hard to live. But the doctor says it's only a matter of minutes. Dwight was asking for you. I know he wants to see you."

Jerry and I walked, hand in hand, down the hospital hallway. We quietly stepped into the room and stood by the side of the bed. Dwight slowly opened his eyes and looked up at us. He reached out, taking our hands in his and said, "Here's my two rinky-dinks."

Those were the last words Dwight spoke. He took his last breath as the nurse was escorting us out of his hospital room.

It seemed the entire community of Wichita Falls turned out for Dwight Ledford's funeral. Everyone who had ever met Dwight loved him. The loss of such a good man left an empty hole in a lot of hearts.

Dwight's death seemed to cause Jerry to spiral downward into depression. He took his friend's death hard and was also worried about finding employment.

In an effort to encourage and cheer up my husband, I began taking short breaks from my job and going with him on interviews. After one particular job interview, Jerry walked very slowly back to the car where I was sitting and waiting. His extremely slow pace, coupled with the dejected look on his face, told me that he had not gotten the job. He opened the car door and climbed into the driver's seat where he slumped over the steering wheel clutching it tightly.

He turned his head to look at me. "No matter how hard I try, I can't find a damn job. I can't put food on the table. I don't know how we're going to pay the hospital bill. I'm no good for you or anybody else. I'm going to take you home. Then I'm going out for a while."

I didn't like the tone of his voice. "Where are you going? What are you planning to do? Everything will work out. We'll manage. It's just a matter of time before you find the job just for you."

He looked me right in the eye. "You want to know what I'm going to do? I'll tell you. But get it through your head right now. You can't go with me! And you can't stop me! I've gotta do what I've gotta do! There's no other way!"

I replied, "I don't know what you're planning to do, but, I *am* going with you!"

"No, you can't go with me! Don't you understand! I'm no good for you or anybody else! I'm going out to a pasture and blowing my brains out!"

My initial reaction to what I heard Jerry say was shock and disbelief. I had never seen him in such dark despair and anguish. I prayed silently, asking God for his wisdom to help my husband get through this hopelessness. A thought came into my mind about my childhood and how my wishes and others had come true. I had to get my husband's mind off of killing himself.

"Jerry, do you remember me telling you about people getting their wishes when they told me what their wishes were? Do you remember me telling you that?"

"Yeah, I remember. What's that got to do with me?"

"I'm going to give you a wish. You can wish for anything you want. But you get only one wish. So make it a good one!"

He turned and looked at me. He tightened his grip on the steering wheel and banged his hand against it a few times. Then he sat motionless for a couple of minutes. All at once, he blurted out, "Okay, here's my wish! And I made it a good one. I want to be a millionaire by the time I'm thirty-three!"

"Gosh, Jerry! Did you have to put a time limit on the wish?"

"That's my wish. I want to be a millionaire by the time I'm thirty-three."

"How old are you now?"

"Let me see." He thought for a second. "I'm twenty-six."

"Gee whiz, that's only seven years away. Okay, the first thing we need to do is find you a job. You'll need to enjoy your work, if you're going to be a millionaire. What kind of work would you really like to do?"

"Huh, I never really thought about it. I like working with my hands and being outside."

For some reason beyond comprehension, the words seemed to flow from me. "Okay, you have three choices. You can be an electrician, do construction, or be a plumber."

Jerry looked at me and shook his head. "Forget about me being an electrician. I'd probably get electrocuted. Forget about construction. I don't like my back hurting, and I don't want to dig ditches. But a plumber, umm … I might like being a plumber."

"Okay, plumbing it is," I quickly said.

"But I don't want to be cleaning out dirty toilets or crawling under houses. I only want to work on new jobs."

"New jobs it is," I replied.

"Okay, I'm ready to go now," he said calmly. "I just remembered my cousin is a plumber. Maybe he needs a helper."

Jerry did get a job that day in the plumbing trade as an apprentice plumber. He was a fast learner. Within six months, he took the journeyman plumber's exam in Austin and passed with flying colors. Since he was then officially a licensed plumber, he felt he should look for employment at a bigger company that paid more. A year later, he went to work for Jerry Gamble Plumbing in Wichita Falls.

Things were starting to get better in every way for our family. Most of all, Jerry liked being a journeyman plumber, and I liked my secretarial job.

One of my coworkers at White's didn't have many friends, so I befriended her. Carolyn and I often went to lunch and talked about our relationship with God. Although Jerry and I were members of St. Paul Lutheran Church, that didn't keep Carolyn from repeatedly asking me to go with her to First Baptist Church, where she was a member.

One day, Carolyn told me her church was having a revival and begged me to go to with her. She said a professional football player for the Dallas Cowboys was going to give a testimonial. She kept at me until she persuaded me to go with her. I asked Jerry to go with me to the revival. He said he didn't want to but that it was okay for me to go. He said he would watch our two babies.

Family portrait of Jeannie and Jerry Sternadel with their two children, Becky and Sandy

Carolyn and I met up at First Baptist and sat in a pew in the back row. It was a nice service, but I was looking forward to going home. I knew Jerry would let the children stay up later than usual and they would be cranky the next day.

When the football player finished his testimonial, he began asking people to come forward and be saved. All of a sudden, I rose from my seat and turned to Carolyn. "I've got to get saved!" Walking down the aisle to the front of the church and getting saved made me feel as if my heart was overflowing. I was crying tears of joy. I wanted to shout out to the world how great God was.

After the service, I thanked Carolyn for inviting me. "It was an experience I will always remember and cherish. I feel so close to God. I hope I always feel this way."

I hurried home to share the exhilarating experience with Jerry. It was almost ten o'clock that night when I excitedly drove into the driveway. To my surprise, I found the front door locked. I didn't have the key and was about to knock on the door when Jerry opened it. I started telling him about the wonderful experience as I began walking through the door.

He blocked me from entering. "You're not coming in this house. You can sleep out in the car tonight, bitch. You didn't go to church. Church services don't last this long. You were out whoring around. You were lying about going to church. I know you were out screwing around with who the hell knows who. You're not walking through this door, slut! We don't want you here!" He slapped me in the face, pushed me backward, and slammed the door shut.

Standing outside in the dark, I was stunned and dumbfounded. I could not believe Jerry had locked me out of my own home. What was I going to do? I had to go to work the next morning. Where was I going to sleep? I thought maybe if I left and drove around for a little while, he would calm down and let me in. I got back into the car and started driving. Where I was going, I didn't know. I was driving down Archer City Highway in a stupor with no destination in mind. I thought about the wonderful experience of being saved by the grace of God. I felt heavenly love had filled my heart and soul.

Soon I noticed there was a full moon shining brightly and lighting up the night sky. I began enjoying the drive in the beautiful moonlit night. I solemnly prayed for God to touch Jerry's heart. The highway was deserted due to the late hour. I thought watching the moonlight bounce off the water at Arrowhead Lake would be enjoyable, so I took that turnoff. I had gone only two miles down the paved road when the headlights of my car illuminated a large bird standing in the middle of the road. Upon closer inspection, I recognized the bird as a large owl. I thought the wise old owl would fly away as my car got closer, but it remained standing in the middle of the road. I had to drive around it to avoid running it over.

I didn't think too much about the bird of prey being on the highway at night, except that it seemed bizarre that it did not fly off when my car approached. I thought maybe the owl hadn't taken flight because my headlights momentarily blinded it. That was a rational explanation, and I dismissed it. But a little farther down the highway, I came upon two owls standing in the middle of the roadway. I slowed the car down almost to a stop, expecting the birds to fly away, but they stood their ground. Once again, I thought the reason was that the headlights had blinded them. But the owls' huge eyes seemed to stare directly at me as I drove slowly around them.

Although the sight of the huge birds on the road was strange and unsettling, I dismissed it again. I drove only a little farther when I came upon *three* owls standing in the middle of the road. I slowed the car to a full stop so the birds could fly away to safety. The three nocturnal birds of prey with large forward-facing eyes and hooked beaks just stood their ground and glared. I thought maybe the owls had come upon something dead in the highway. But when I scoured the highway for signs of a roadkill, I did not see a dead animal or anything that would attract the birds.

I looked at the huge owls standing their ground in the road just ahead of my car. All three seemed to have a scary look about them and were glaring straight at me. I honked the car horn, but they remained standing in the road as if in a trance. I edged the car off to the side of the road to keep from hitting them. As I passed, all three turned their heads and followed my every movement with their gaze. The moon was shining so bright that when I looked into the rearview mirror, I could clearly see the owls. It seemed they were warning me to stop going in the direction I was traveling.

Again I dismissed the owls and turned onto the service road leading to the lake. I traveled only a short distance when I noticed the night sky had suddenly become pitch black. At that very instant, my vehicle suddenly began accelerating. Nothing happened when I took my foot off the gas pedal. The accelerator was stuck. My car was speeding faster and faster down the very narrow and winding dirt road. I gripped the steering wheel and began stomping on the brake pedal. Nothing happened. My car was out of control. The brakes were like jelly, but I continued pumping them in an effort to slow down. It was as if all the brake fluid had been drained from the master cylinder.

I tried turning the steering wheel but could not move it. The car was completely out of control and heading straight for the dam. I knew if I didn't stop the car soon, I would be crashing over the spillway into the raging, icy water below. I felt something breathing down my neck from behind the driver's seat. A cold chill shot through me. My reaction of looking into the rearview mirror was almost instantaneous. What I saw made my blood curdle. In my mirror I saw two eyes that looked like fiery red-hot coals. I knew immediately the Devil was in control of my car. The Prince of Darkness wanted to kill me and take my soul to hell if he could.

I glanced at the speedometer: ninety miles per hour and climbing. Lake Arrowhead Dam was just up ahead. The car was going too fast to negotiate the curve. I was going to die in an awful way. I looked up at the pitch-black sky that had been so beautiful a short time earlier. I screamed, "God Almighty, please help me!"

A mighty turbulence welled up inside my car from the Devil's rage and fury at hearing God's name.

If this was going to be my last day on earth, I was going to die praying to God, who granted me salvation.

"The Lord is my Shepherd. I shall not want. He maketh me to lie down in green pastures. He leadeth me beside the still waters. He restoreth my soul. He leadeth me in the paths of righteousness for His name's sake. Yea, though I walk through the valley of the shadow of death, I will fear no evil, for thou art with me. Thy rod and thy staff, they comfort me."

The evil beast transformed itself into a gigantic serpent, hissing and coiling itself around my neck and squeezing.

"Thou preparest a table before me in the presence of mine enemies."

The hellish monster's head started shaking back and forth.

"My cup runneth over."

Finally, the serpent from hell began relaxing its stranglehold on me.

"Surely, goodness and mercy will follow me all the days of my life, and I will dwell in the house of the Lord forever. Amen."

My car should have crashed into the dam, but instead it came to a full stop in a gentle way without throwing my body forward into the steering wheel or through the windshield. Instantaneously, a full moon lit up the night sky.

Satan had been shackled and brought to his knees by God. I looked into the rearview mirror. The evil, fire-red, brimstone eyes were gone. I realized the demon was gone, but I began to tremble and shiver uncontrollably. I started weeping. Through my tears, I saw that my car was sitting at the very edge of the spillway. I realized just how close it had come to plunging over the edge. As I sat motionless, looking down at the dam and the rushing water below, I gave many thanks to God for saving me from Lucifer.

Driving away from the dam, there were no more incidents, and I arrived safely at my home on Cynthia Lane. I pulled into the driveway and parked. Emotionally drained and physically exhausted, I lay down on the front seat, prayed, and gave thanks to the Almighty.

Before dawn, I woke up to a noise. Jerry was standing outside the car, tapping on the window. "I'm sorry! Jeannie, I'm sorry. The Devil got into me last night. I promise you that will never happen again."

A bouquet of flowers was delivered to me at work the next morning. It was from Jerry.

The card read, "I love you. Please forgive me. You are my life."

I did not know it at the time, but sleeping in the car that night had been just the beginning of the seemingly endless mental and physical abuse I would suffer and endure in the days and years ahead.

In the late sixties, financial hardship was finally behind us. Jerry Gamble Plumbing was securing a lot of commercial plumbing jobs due to the quality workmanship and fine reputation that Jerry Gamble and Jerry Sternadel had established in the business community.

Jerry and I became good friends with Jerry Gamble and his wife, Nancy. We often dined and went different places together. Soon a lot of businesses were calling our home wanting to speak with Jerry. My husband was highly regarded within the plumbing industry. When I suggested we start our own business, Jerry told me that he had to have a master plumber's license. I said, "I'll help you get it."

Jerry thought about my idea for a short time and decided that he would apply for the license. He failed the exam on the first try, but I was certain it was only because the babies and I had gone with him to Austin for the test. I told him so. "I know you could not concentrate on that exam. You were too busy worrying about us sitting outside in the hot car. Every time I looked up, there you were coming back to check on us. I don't believe there was any way you could have passed that test. You were too worried about us. But I know the next time you take it, you'll pass with flying colors."

"Maybe, but there were a lot of things on the exam I was not sure of—like how to rough in and top out the plumbing on a multistory building, plus calculating the correct amount of material. I just wasn't able to do it! Anyway, we don't have the money for me to try again."

I was determined that Jerry get his master's license. I knew he was capable. All he needed to do was to study. I was going to do everything possible to make sure he passed that exam so that we could start up our own business. I called Austin and requested a new application. I mailed it back with the deposit, using money I had saved. I felt the six-month waiting period gave me plenty of time to tell Jerry what I had done and then for him to study for the exam.

When the notification of the date of the exam came in the mail, Jerry acted like he was mad. But I could tell he was happy I had sent in the application. He began studying, and I helped him. At the end of every workday, he and I would study. On the weekends, we studied.

Everything was going smoothly until the wee morning hours of April 25, 1969.

The loud ringing of the phone awakened me. I quickly switched on the light and reached for the telephone. Still half asleep, I muttered, "Hello."

The voice on the other end of the line asked, "Is this the home of Jerry Sternadel?"

"Yes," I tentatively replied.

"Is Jerry the brother of Bobby Sternadel?"

"Yes."

"I need to talk to Jerry. We have an emergency situation!"

Jerry stirred awake, sat up in the bed, and asked. "Who is it?"

Bobby Sternadel (right) with his mother and brother, Marcy and Jim Sternadel

I looked over at Jerry. "I don't know who it is, but he wanted to know if you are Bobby's brother. He said it was an emergency."

Jerry grabbed the phone. After a brief silence, he said, "My mother and dad are in Fort Worth." Following a short pause, he turned a pale ash color and gasped. "Oh, no!" His face took on a look of horror.

He hung up the phone and said, "They need me to come to Waurika. Bobby has been involved in a bad car accident."

The medical examiner had told Jerry he had been unable to reach his parents. Jerry's dad had recently taken a job as a foreman on a construction job in Fort Worth. He and his mom were living in Forth Worth during the week and coming home to Petrolia on the weekends.

Jerry and I quickly got dressed and bundled up our two youngsters in blankets. It was still dark when we started driving across the state line to Waurika, Oklahoma. I thought it was peculiar that the medical examiner had asked Jerry to come to a funeral home instead of the hospital. But it all became perfectly clear when we arrived. Jerry's younger brother, Bobby, had been killed in a one-car accident a few hours earlier. The body had been transported from the Waurika hospital to the funeral home. Jerry had the sad task of identifying his twenty-year-old brother.

Jerry told me to take the babies back to the car and wait for him there. I watched as he walked with a man dressed in a dark suit to a back room. They closed the door behind them. I took my children back to the car and sang lullabies as they snuggled close. When they went to sleep, I covered them with a blanket. As I sat in the car waiting for my husband to come out of the funeral home, I thought of Jerry's brother.

Bobby had been a nice-looking young man with deep dimples and a sweet personality. I had seen Bobby that very afternoon. He had driven over to our home right after he got out of his college classes for the day. I thought he had come over to take his young niece and nephew to the ice cream parlor. (Both of Jerry's younger brothers, Bobby and Jimmy, had a habit of dropping by and taking Becky and Sandy out for ice cream. When they brought them home, the children always wore chocolate, strawberry, and vanilla ice cream all over their faces and clothes.) Bobby walked up to the door. I could tell from the look on his face that he hadn't come over to take the kids out for ice cream. He walked into the house and sat down on the couch.

"Jeannie, I'm sorry to disappoint the kids, but I need to talk to you. Right after I got out of my classes today, I went to Kay's Jewelry Store.

I picked out an engagement ring for Beverly. I was going to ask her to marry me. But when I drove home, I had this in the mail."

I took the official-looking envelope from Bobby and glanced at the document inside. It was a letter from the draft board.

"Jeannie, I don't want to go to Vietnam. I don't want to die fighting a war overseas."

I tried to find words to comfort him. "Bobby, you don't need to be talking like that. I just know you are not going to Vietnam. And you are not going to die fighting a war." As I was saying this to my young brother-in-law, a premonition came over me that Bobby would soon be dead but wouldn't die overseas.

"I was going to ask Beverly to marry me. I think she knows I love her with all my heart. Bev and I could get married when she finishes high school. She'll be a senior next year—that's right around the corner. But now I'm being drafted to go fight a war. I'm going to die."

"Bobby, you are not going to die fighting a war."

"Are you sure?" he asked.

"Yes, I'm sure. That's what I feel. You are not going to die fighting a war overseas."

Bobby stood up and looked at me, "Yeah, Jeannie, you're right! I'm not going to die overseas. I'm going to die right here in the United States. I'm going to die in a car crash. But there's only going to be one car involved. My car! I'm going to die in a one-car accident."

"Bobby, please don't talk like that! You have a full life ahead of you. You're going to be okay."

"That's the way it's going to be. I know it. I just now felt it! I'm going to die in a one-car accident. I gotta go! Thanks for talking to me. You're the best! I always feel better when I talk to you. I'll come by tomorrow and let you know what Bev says."

"That's the way to be. Stay positive, honey. Things have a way of working out! I know Beverly's answer will be yes. You're a great catch for any young lady. Please come by and see me tomorrow."

"Bye, Jeannie. I love you."

"I love you too, sweetheart."

As Bobby was driving away, an ominous feeling hung over me like a dark cloud. I could not shake the feeling that I would never get to see him again.

The car door opening and closing brought me back to the horrible reality that I was sitting outside a funeral home and Bobby was dead.

Jerry said, "I can't believe that sorry S-O-B couldn't clean my brother up. I'm glad I didn't let you go in there. It looked like Bobby's head was cut off in the accident. It was horrible! I almost threw up seeing my brother like that. And now I've got to call Mom and Dad. I guess I'll wait till daylight, and then I'll call. I don't know how I'm going to tell them."

Jerry called his parents in Fort Worth. They were barely able to speak. The funeral home had already contacted them. They were packing a few things and leaving immediately.

I asked the next-door neighbor to babysit for our kids because Jerry was dead set on finding out how the fatal accident had occurred. On the long drive to Waurika, Jerry and I discussed how precious Bobby was and how life turns on a dime.

Jerry went inside the funeral home while I sat outside in the car. It wasn't long before I saw an Oklahoma state trooper pull up to the funeral home and go inside.

A little while later, Jerry came back outside. He sat down beside me in the car. "I know how Bobby was killed. I talked to the trooper who investigated the accident. The coroner called and asked him to come speak with me. On the way here, we drove right by the crash site where Bobby was killed."

We left the funeral home, driving down Highway 70. Right after we passed the Waurika Cemetery, Jerry slowed down and pulled the car off to the side of the highway. On the rural thoroughfare just ahead of where we stopped was a sharp curve and an intersection to a dirt road with a stop sign. Jerry pointed to the bend in the road.

"That's where it happened. Right there on that curve. The trooper said it was a one-car accident. No other cars were involved, and Bobby didn't have any passengers with him. It was last night at about 11:35. Bobby apparently lost control of his automobile. It skidded, struck a road sign, and rolled over five times. Bobby suffered a fractured skull when he was thrown from the vehicle. He was pronounced dead on arrival at the Waurika hospital.

"The trooper said that, from the look of the accident scene, Bobby must have been driving at high speed and couldn't safely make the curve. He didn't know if Bobby had fallen asleep or just didn't realize how fast he was going. From the skid marks, it appeared Bobby tried to negotiate the curve. But the back end of the car hit the stop sign for the intersecting road, which put the car into a dangerous skid. The car rolled up and down into the ditch and then flipped over several times. Bobby wasn't wearing a seat belt. The driver's-side door flew open when the car flipped. The car door cut the top of Bobby's head off when he was thrown from the vehicle. He was killed instantly. Maybe knowing Bobby died instantly and didn't suffer will give Mom and Dad some comfort."

Looking into Jerry's eyes, I could tell he was trying to put up a good front, while all the time he was suffering deeply. Jerry liked to act as though he was macho and strong. He worked hard to keep his feelings well hidden. But I was aware of how he hid his tenderness so that people would not think he was weak. I knew he was hurting and in a lot of pain from the loss of his youngest brother. I wished I could help him understand that at times even strong men cry.

Beverly and the entire Sternadel family were in a state of overwhelming sorrow and shock. Marcy and Eli kept saying their kids should be burying them and they should not be burying one of their kids.

The funeral service was held at 2:30 on Sunday, April 27, at St. Paul Lutheran Church in Wichita Falls. Bobby was buried in Petrolia Cemetery.

After the burial, all of Bobby's family and friends congregated at Marcy and Eli's home in Petrolia.

Beverly felt guilty that she hadn't been with Bobby that night. She walked over and sat down close to me.

"I am so torn up! Bobby wanted me to go with him for a drive the night he was killed. But I had a lot of homework and tests to study for. I told him I couldn't go. He begged me to take a ride with me. He was so lonely with his mom and dad being in Fort Worth. I feel like if I had gone with him, he would still be alive.

"He asked me to marry him. Look, here's the engagement ring he put on my finger just a few hours before he died. He called me just before he went driving around. He told me he had cleaned up the house so it would be spic and span when his mom and dad came home this weekend. I loved Bobby so much. He was an angel. I don't know how I'm going to make it through this."

I looked over at Beverly. "Bobby was an angel. Maybe that's why God took him at such a young age. He was the best kid I've ever known. He would do anything for anybody. I loved him to pieces. He was always coming over to our house and picking up the kids and taking them to the ice cream parlor. He came over that afternoon. I guess you and I are the last people to see him alive. Bobby told me how much he loved you."

"Jeannie, that means a lot to me. I know Bobby would have been a good husband and a good father. He loved your kids. I'm going to miss him. I loved him so much! It hurts so bad. Will the hurt ever go away?"

"As time passes, the hurt will fade. I honestly don't know when the hurt will go away. But you have a lot of good memories that will last you a lifetime. Think about all the good times you had with Bobby. Remembering those good times will help you get over the hurt. Cherish those memories! I'll pray for you. Come see me or call me anytime you need someone to talk to. I'll be there."

A few days after Bobby's funeral, I had the strangest feeling that his spirit had not left this world. I felt his "presence." When I cleaned the house, Bobby's ghost was walking beside me. I kept telling myself that what I was thinking and feeling was improbable and impossible. I tried dismissing the "presence" I felt as being a figment of my imagination.

One night, when I was preparing to go to bed, the "presence" was very strong in the bedroom. I saw an apparition of Bobby standing by the side of the bed.

Suddenly, Jerry sat straight up in the bed. "Who's there? Bobby, is that you? Jeannie, did you see Bobby standing at the side of the bed? I saw him when you came into the room. I wasn't dreaming. Bobby was there. Did you see him? He's not there now! But did you see him?"

I didn't know what to say because I knew Bobby's spirit was there. "No, Jerry I didn't see anything. It's only been a few weeks since Bobby died. I know how much you loved him and how bad you miss him. Maybe you were dreaming."

"I sure hope I was dreaming! I don't want a ghost hanging around our house, not even if it's my brother's ghost," Jerry said as he lay back down and pulled up the covers.

I lay awake all night. The next morning, I felt Bobby's presence following me. Every step I took, Bobby was there. He didn't say anything at first, but I could feel his "presence." After another couple of weeks, I was becoming ill at ease with Bobby's spirit being with me every waking moment. I could hear him asking me to help him. But I didn't know how Bobby needed help and I didn't know how to help. I began praying for God to give me the answer on how Bobby needed help and the wisdom to help him.

A couple of months after Bobby's tragic accident, Nancy Gamble quite unexpectedly dropped over. "I'm sorry I didn't call you. But I was in the neighborhood. I've been meaning to bring this book over for you to read."

"That's sweet of you, Nancy. I read in my spare time between taking care of Becky and Sandy. What's the book about?"

"It's about a race-car driver and his wife."

I thought, *Why would Nancy think I would be interested in a book about a race-car driver and his wife?* Jerry and I went to a lot of places with Nancy and Jerry Gamble, but we had never gone to a car race or even a car show with them.

"Jeannie, I'm honestly not sure why I brought you the book. But I just kept having the feeling that I needed to give it to you. I enjoyed reading it. You might enjoy it too. But it kind of gave me the creeps with the guy dying and his wife saying his spirit was hanging around her. Anyway, something compelled me to bring it over to you. I hope you read it."

The next day, I started skimming through the book. I felt as if Bobby was looking over my shoulder and scanning the book with me. The book was about a NASCAR driver who crashed into the rail at a racetrack and died instantly on the scene. After his death, his wife confided to close friends that she believed her husband's spirit was with her and had not passed over to the other side. The wife said her husband's spirit was asking her for help. But she didn't know how he needed help or how to help him. She began praying for divine intervention and an answer on how to help her husband.

One day, an idea popped into her head that her husband needed help passing over to the other side. The widow said somehow she knew her husband needed to let go and walk toward the light. In the book, the NASCAR driver's wife confronted her dead husband's spirit. She told him that he was dead and he needed to let go of the living and go toward the light. After she told her dead husband this, she felt his spirit let go, and then he passed over to the other side. She knew he was at peace after he walked toward the light. She said she never felt his spirit again.

I believed the book was the answer to my prayers and the way to help Bobby. When I finished reading the book, I knew exactly what I had to do.

The next time Bobby's spirit asked me for help, I said. "Bobby, you know how much I love you. But you need to let go. You need to pass over to the other side. That's the only way you will be at peace."

I heard his spirit say, "I want to stay with you. I don't want to go anywhere else. I want to stay with you. Jeannie, I'm scared. It's dark where I am. Please help me."

"Bobby, sweetheart, I'm trying to help you. But you can't stay here. You need to go to the other side. You need to go toward the light."

"Why can't I stay with you?"

"Bobby, you can't stay here with me. This place is for the living. You're not alive. Honey, you are dead."

"I'm not dead! I'm here with you. I can't be dead."

"Yes, honey, you are dead. You died in a one-car accident."

"I'm dead?"

"Yes, Bobby, you died in the car accident. I love you, sweetheart. But you need to go to the other side. Go toward the light! You'll be happy there. I love you and wish you were alive, but you have to go toward the light."

"I see the light!"

"Sweetheart, go toward the light."

I heard his spirit faintly say, "I love you, Jeannie."

Then there was silence.

After that, I didn't feel Bobby's presence. I knew he went toward the light and to the other side. Although I knew he was in a better place, I was going to sorely miss him.

The days seemed to go slowly and solemnly after Bobby's passing.

It was time for Jerry to go to Austin and take the test for his master's plumbing license. Jerry and I got up very early that morning. He questioned why I wasn't ready to leave with him.

"I can't go with you today. I don't want to disappoint you, but the kids and I are staying home. That test is too important to have you worrying about us sitting outside in the car. I know in my heart you won't pass if we go. I'd love to go with you, but you have to go by yourself."

I gave him a quick kiss, "Better get going. I'll be praying for you. You won't be alone—God will be with you."

Jerry drove to Austin for his second try at the license. When he returned later that day, he said he felt sure he did well on the exam.

The results came in the mail a few weeks later. Jerry had passed the test with flying colors. He continued working full-time for Jerry

Gamble Plumbing while we started bidding on residential and small commercial jobs that Gamble wasn't interested in. All we owned to start our plumbing business was Jerry's master plumber's license, a pickup truck, some plumbing tools, and an intense desire to succeed. We named the business Jerry Sternadel Plumbing.

I helped figure out the cost estimates and personally delivered the bids to customers. At first, we could barely afford the necessary supplies for the successful bids we secured. There wasn't enough money left over to pay a plumber's helper, so I became Jerry's apprentice helper on the plumbing jobs. We didn't have the money to pay for a babysitter, so we took our small children to the job sites with us. I would find a safe, clean spot inside the building where I could keep an eye on them, and then Jerry and I proceeded to do the work.

Before long, we were securing larger commercial jobs. We ran Jerry Sternadel Plumbing on high morals, quality work, and guaranteed on-time completion. We didn't turn down any jobs, big or small. And we were always honest and fair to our customers. We began winning bids on large commercial jobs in the surrounding areas. I finally talked Jerry into quitting his job with Jerry Gamble Plumbing.

Profits from the various jobs we did went to purchase additional tools and supplies. We saved every penny we could. Our business grew bigger and bigger. In 1970, we hired two full-time employees and purchased two good used pickups. For a while, we were able to operate from our home by storing plumbing supplies in a shed and the garage. But the business outgrew the little buildings. We bought a nice piece of land just outside of Wichita Falls and built a large workshop for our thriving business, along with a new brick home.

In 1971, we threw our first summer barbecue party. Jerry bought a whole pig for the feast. He started roasting it early in the morning. Later that afternoon, we charcoaled steaks and hamburgers and set up kegs of beer and soft drinks. Over a hundred people showed up. Jerry was the perfect host and I the perfect hostess.

Life was good, until Jerry started accusing me of cheating on him. Talking on the phone with a supplier or customer brought accusations that I was making dates. It got to the point that Jerry would either telephone or drop by the plumbing office every fifteen or thirty minutes.

One day, he came into the office hollering, "Well, I caught you today, bitch. I knew I'd catch you sooner or later!"

"What on earth are you talking about?"

"I saw you at the Country Club Golf Course. Did you think I wouldn't recognize the car? You and some guy were making out right there in broad daylight!"

"Jerry, I don't have any idea what you are talking about. I haven't left the office all day. I have been billing invoices."

"Yeah, yeah! Well, next time, slut, I'll walk up to the car and knock on the window. After I beat the shit out of the guy, I'll take care of you!"

No matter what I said, Jerry did not believe I was not out at the country club that day making out with some guy. He didn't believe me until one afternoon when we went to check on a job site close to the country club. I saw the car first.

"Look, that car on the side road is exactly like mine."

Jerry glanced at the automobile. "Let's go have a closer look," he muttered while driving over to the car parked on a side road alongside the Country Club Golf Course.

It was identical to mine. A male and a female were inside the car kissing.

"Well, I guess that's me sitting in the car with that guy," I said sarcastically. "And I guess that's my car, even though you're driving my car."

"Okay, it wasn't you I saw that day. I apologize. I'm sorry. I'm just too damn jealous about you. Maybe if I was happy I wouldn't be like that."

"What do you mean if you were happy? Why aren't you happy?" I questioned. "I thought you had everything you ever wanted. You have a wife who loves you. Your two kids love you to pieces. And you have a thriving business that will make you a millionaire some day."

"Yeah, but it's not my dream!"

"Well, then, what *is* your dream?"

"Owning a horse ranch! I know I should be happy with what we have. Truth is I've always wanted to own horses and race them. But it will never happen!"

"Do you remember Dwight Ledford telling us the secret to happiness was giving thanks to God?"

"Yeah, I remember. I do give thanks to God."

"Do you remember that day when we were sitting in front of the supermarket? The time you were turned down for that job after the interview? Do you remember that day and what happened afterward?"

"Yeah, I remember. I won't ever forget it. But I'm not a millionaire either!"

"You said you wanted to be a millionaire by the time you were thirty-three. You do remember saying that, don't you? You are not thirty-three, are you? We have some money saved up. We can spend it on anything we want. If you want to own horses and race them, why don't we start looking for horses to buy and land to build a horse barn and corral?"

"We don't have enough money to do all that!"

"You didn't have a job that day either, and look at us now!"

Jerry and I purchased a parcel of land that wasn't far from our home and workshop and contracted for a horse barn and corral to be built on the property.

One day, Jerry came into the office with a grin on his face. "I've been keeping my eye on this old gray mare. But every time I go by the place, the owner tells me the horse is not for sale, even though there's a HORSE FOR SALE sign on his fence. If *you* talked to the guy, he'd sell it to you. It's an older horse, but it looks like a good breeding mare. C'mon, take a ride with me."

We drove over to where Jerry had seen the sign. At first, the man said no, he decided he wasn't going to sell the mare. But I wasn't ready to give up. I kept talking to him. Finally, he said he would take $50 for the mare, with one condition. We had to take a donkey too.

A couple of days later, we picked up the mare and the donkey.

Jerry began speaking with horse trainers, who suggested a place to have the mare studded with a good stallion. We talked to the owner of the stud stallion. He was willing for a price to let his stallion attempt to impregnate the mare.

With $2,000 cash in our pockets for the stud fee, Jerry and I loaded up the mare and took her over to meet the stallion. The stallion did the rest. When we brought the mare back to the ranch, everyone was certain she was pregnant.

A few weeks later, the man who sold us the old gray mare drove up to the plumbing office. "I'll give you $500 right now for the old girl."

I asked Jerry. "Do you want to sell the mare back to this gentleman?"

Jerry replied, "No! The mare is not for sale."

The man threw his hands up in the air and left in a huff.

A couple weeks later the man was back. This time he offered us $5,000 for the mare. Jerry wasted no time in telling him she wasn't for sale at any price.

The next day, I took a ride over to the man's house. "I don't believe $50 was enough to pay you for the mare. I don't want you thinking we played you for a fool."

"Well, I was thinking I was pretty foolish to let you have that mare. But you did some fine talking that day or else I wouldn't even have sold her to you."

"Why are you wanting to buy her back?"

"After I sold her, I heard that damn old mare is a descendant of the King stallion."

"I wish you had come over earlier. We would have given her back then. But we took the mare and had her mated with a stud stallion. She's pregnant with a colt. But I'll give you back the donkey and $1,000."

The man walked around his yard for a bit and then came back and said, "I wouldn't feel right taking your money. Basically, I just lost out. A deal is a deal! You can keep the mare and the donkey."

"I believe that when someone does a good deed, then that person deserves a good deed in return. I would consider it a favor if you would take the money. Consider it a gift."

"Well, if you put it that way. I could use a little extra spending money. Thank you. I wish you and your husband good luck. Maybe you'll get a winning colt out of that old gray mare."

The mare's colt was born healthy, strong, and full of vim and vigor. One look was all a person needed to see that little colt was a surefire winner. As a two-year-old, he proved he was a descendant of the great King. He won every race Jerry entered him in. The prize money provided the resources to buy more mares to breed and more colts to race.

That first colt was Jerry's dream come true.

But no matter how many horse races he won, he wasn't satisfied. No matter how much money the plumbing business made, he wasn't happy. He became exceedingly jealous and even became furious when I spent extra time with our two children. He told his friends he thought he was ugly and felt I was too pretty for him to keep. He began abusing me on a regular basis and constantly accused me of having affairs. He stopped me from having contact with anyone.

He started worshipping money. He said, "Money talks and gives power to those who possess it."

It was my belief that love of money was the root of evil, which gave rise to selfish and wicked actions. I wanted to bring Jerry back into the fold of believing in Christ and having a personal relationship with the Lord. In desperation to save our marriage, I made arrangements to see a marriage counselor. I begged Jerry to go with me.

Jerry said he didn't need to go to a marriage counselor because there wasn't anything wrong with our marriage. He said he didn't need a counselor and wasn't going to let anybody tell him what he should or should not do. "I'm not wasting my money on a quack."

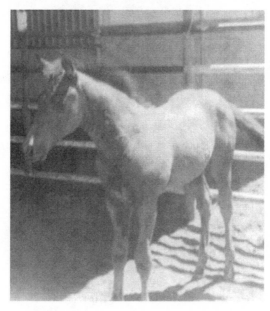

Jerry and Jeannie Sternadel's first colt

The Sternadel horse barn and corral on the outskirts of Wichita Falls

Jerry Sternadel at home on the ranch

Jeannie Sternadel with quarter horse

Jerry's wildly insane behavior was beginning to cause me anxiety and depression. In secret, I began going to group therapy meetings to learn how to cope and keep my head above water. After a month, I told Jerry about the group therapy sessions.

He said he wanted to go with me. "I want to check out the crazies who attend these sessions."

One session turned into several. Jerry enjoyed the therapy sessions. He talked openly about how he felt and what he thought. At one meeting, the psychologist asked Jerry to describe his relationship with me. "I think we have a good relationship as long as she does what I tell her to do. If I had to describe Jeannie, I would say she is like a beautiful rose."

The psychologist said, "If you put a rose in your hand and keep holding it, that flower is going to wilt and die. Did you know your wife feels as though you are smothering her?"

"Why would she feel that way?"

"It seems that you want to keep that beautiful rose in the palm of your hand. And that's suffocating your wife. Jeannie, why don't you tell your husband how you feel?"

Having the freedom to speak, I said, "Jerry, I love you and love doing things with you. I love going golfing with you. I love watching you pitch in softball games and strike the players out. I love going to basketball games with you. I love everything we do together. But I can't go anywhere by myself without being berated or accused of cheating. I can't talk to anyone without you giving me the third degree about what was said. I feel as though I am under a microscope. I don't have any personal freedom. I don't know what I have done to make you feel that you can't trust me, but I can't take it much longer. No matter how I try, I can't win your trust or respect."

"I trust you about as far as I can throw you," Jerry responded with a chuckle.

"Does Jeannie keep you from doing things?"

"No, she lets me do whatever I want to. But I don't want to go anywhere without her, except maybe to work. I like doing things with my wife. I have more fun when she is with me. She makes positive things happen. Like when I go golfing, I know I am going to have a good score if she is with me. She's my good luck charm."

"Your wife needs freedom, just like you do."

After that therapy session, things began getting better between us.

Jerry thought I had a beautiful singing voice, so he suggested I take voice lessons at Midwestern University. He actually signed me up at the university with the voice instructor. With his encouragement, I began singing solos at church and other engagements. Jerry loved hearing compliments about my singing voice and talent. It gave him bragging rights of sorts. He also loved golf, and so did I. He bought a set of women's golf clubs for me, and we started entering husband-and-wife golf tournaments.

Happy times in 1969 for Jeannie and Jerry Sternadel

Jeannie on her 175cc Bultaco motorcycle

Our family started having a lot of fun together. We even went to a motorcycle dealership and bought a 250cc Yamaha motorcycle for Jerry, a 175cc Bultaco for me, and Yamaha minibikes for Becky and Sandy. We had fun riding our bikes up and down gullies and through the pastures around the perimeter of our ranch.

The fun on the dirt bikes ended when our young daughter lost control of her minibike and bounced off a fence. Becky's right arm was cut wide open on barbed wire. Jerry drove like a madman to the emergency room in Wichita Falls. It took twelve stitches to sew up the wound.

Not too long after that unfortunate incident, our two children were outside playing in the backyard. They were pretending they were golfing. Becky swung the club and hit her brother in the face. An inch closer and the club would have knocked Sandy's eye out of the socket. Jerry was working on a job site. I rushed the children to the emergency room. Once there, one of the nurses took Becky into another room and played games with her while I stayed in the room with Sandy, who was rightfully screaming and kicking. I was instructed to hold my young son still on the gurney so the doctor could tend to the deep cut. Sandy screamed and kicked the entire time the doctor was stitching up the wound above his eye. I breathed a sigh of relief when the doctor finally finished and Sandy stopped screaming and kicking.

Suddenly, I felt dizzy and lightheaded. Just before I fainted, I saw Jerry walking into the emergency room. He was just in time to catch me and keep me from falling to the floor. Smelling salts brought me back to consciousness.

When we returned home from the hospital, Jerry was madder than a hornet. He blamed me for the accident, saying if I was a better mother the incident would not have happened.

Jerry quit going to the group therapy sessions. He went back to constantly berating me for anything and everything. He ordered me to stop singing because it didn't give me time to be the kind of mother I should be. He made me quit the therapy sessions. The mental and physical abuse he inflicted upon me was escalating.

Jerry was suffering from some kind of disorder or illness of the mind. He would not seek professional help. He thought getting help to deal with problems only made him appear weak.

As time went on, his behavior became even more erratic. He constantly accused me of cheating on him. I held out hope for happiness, but I knew the time would come when I had to leave Jerry. The final straw was when he started verbally abusing the children. I packed up a few belongings and left with the children to a safe haven. I loved Jerry, but I realized we just weren't capable of living together. Through the years, we had become incompatible.

Jerry begged and pleaded with me to come back to him so we could start over. He promised things would be different. But I had heard him say those words too many times before, and then when I would go back, it was always the same: a short honeymoon period and then the abuse would begin all over. I knew in my heart, things were not going to change.

I managed to get a secretarial job to support my two children and myself. After the waiting period of a six-month separation, I filed for divorce.

Jerry was enraged when he received the divorce papers. He threatened to kill me if I didn't come back to him. He said if he couldn't have me, then nobody else could either. He began following me everywhere I went. He warned me that if I went through with the divorce, he would kill me before he let me take any of the business, money, or horses away from him.

Jerry approached and threatened my boss. I was fired the next day.

When I applied for my next job, I told the interviewer right off the bat about my estranged husband. Mr. Brown, the president of the savings and loan, told me that if I was a good worker and reliable, my estranged husband's behavior would have no bearing on whether I kept the job.

Feeling secure in my employment, I leased a mobile home in a trailer park. It was all I could afford. Often, I would see Jerry slowly driving by the mobile home.

One morning, on my way to work, I pulled into a gas station to fill up for the week. As I sat in my car, I noticed the attendant putting the gas nozzle back into the gas pump without putting gas into my car. I thought that particular gas pump was out of order and I would have to move my car to the next pump.

The attendant walked over to me. He said, "Can I rub you for luck? You are one of the luckiest people I have ever come across. I don't know how in the world you ever got your car to the gas station."

"What are you talking about?" I asked.

"Lady, there's sugar all over the gas cap and down inside the filler neck. It looks like somebody put sugar in your gas tank. I'm surprised the car made it this far. You're lucky the car didn't seize up. If I were you, I wouldn't even start it back up. If it was my car, I'd have it towed to the car dealer and have them check it out. You'll really be lucky if the sugar didn't get sucked into the engine. It's going to cost you a bundle if it did. Somebody sure has it in for you to put sugar in your gas tank."

I was in shock. After thanking the attendant, I went inside the gas station. Using the pay phone, I called for a truck to tow my car.

Later that day, I learned just how lucky and blessed I was. The mechanic from the Ford dealership said, "Someone did put sugar in your gas tank. But somehow it wasn't sucked up into the engine. I don't know how, since you drove it at least a couple of miles. We couldn't find any sugar in the gas lines or anywhere inside the engine. We took the gas tank off, cleaned it, and completely checked out the car from top to bottom. You're either very lucky or it was divine intervention. Maybe you ought to get a locking gas cap."

As I was preparing supper for the children and myself that evening, my next-door neighbor came over. "I thought you might need to know that I saw a man snooping around the rear of your car last night. Don't know what he was up to, but when I walked outside and hollered, the guy jumped into a pickup and took off. I walked over and took a look at your car but didn't see any body damage."

I asked my neighbor to describe the man and the pickup. I knew then it was Jerry who had put the sugar in my gas tank.

Later that evening, I contacted Jerry. I knew it wouldn't do any good to say anything about the sugar, because he would just deny it. I asked, "What will make you happy?"

"If you won't come home, then sign everything over to me. I want the ranch, the business, the horses, and all the bank accounts signed over to me. If you do that, I give you my word that I'll leave you alone and won't try to get custody of the kids."

I was fully aware of how unhappy Jerry would be without money. In order to get my half of the community property, we would have to liquidate all our assets. I didn't feel in my heart that Jerry could start all over if I made him sell everything. How could I deprive him of his wealth when it was his wish to become a millionaire? With the belief that Jerry would keep his promise, I signed the papers giving him the ranch, the horses, the money, and everything else we owned together.

In the 1972 divorce agreement, I was awarded custody of the minor children and all the property in my possession, including the 1969 Ford LTD that Jerry had tried to ruin by putting sugar in the gas tank. Jerry was awarded everything else and was ordered to pay child support of $100 a month for each child.

A permanent injunction was issued ordering Jerry not to go to my place of residence and my place of employment. He also was prohibited from communicating with me in any manner or means, except to exercise his visitation privileges with the children, and he was prohibited from threatening, molesting, assaulting, injuring or in any way attempting to harm me.

Right after the court proceedings, Jerry walked over to me. He shot me a hateful look as he handed me a piece of paper. "Somebody is going to have to bury you in one of these."

The paperwork was the deed to two cemetery plots in the Garden of Faith at Crestview Cemetery in Wichita Falls.

Even though Jerry had a restraining order against him, he continued to stalk and harass me. I started attending group therapy sessions. I needed the mental and emotional help the group offered. At one meeting, I openly discussed the tactics and behavior of my estranged husband. I told the group that Jerry was following me and constantly threatening my life with a deer rifle that he carried with him at all times. I asked the group for advice.

Members of the group told me they would gather to discuss my situation and try to come up with a viable solution. A couple of sessions later, the group said, "Call his bluff! We all think he will back off if you do that. He needs to see that you are a strong woman who will stand up for your convictions."

After a lot of prayers, I decided I would do what the group suggested.

A few days later, I had to go to the pharmacy to get a prescription for one of my children. As usual, Jerry was following me. He pulled up to the drugstore and parked his pickup beside my car. I came out of the pharmacy and was walking toward my car when I saw Jerry get out of his truck. He pointed a rifle straight at me. "Are you coming back to me? Do I have to shoot you right now?"

I was frightened, but I looked directly at him and said, "Go ahead and shoot me! I don't have anything to lose but my life. Go ahead and shoot me!"

Jerry appeared shocked and dumbfounded. This was a side of me that he had never seen before. His mouth twisted into a grimace. He quickly walked back to his truck and placed the rifle on a rack over the seat. He jumped into the pickup and sped away.

Over the next months, Jerry continued to stalk me. When I stopped at a traffic light, he would pull up beside me. After getting my attention, he raised his rifle and pointed it directly at me. When the light turned green, he put the gun down and sped away.

On January 17, 1973, Jerry came over to my house on the pretense of picking up the children. Becky and Sandy were over at a friend's house playing. Once inside the trailer home, he tried hugging and kissing on me. Then he forcefully shoved me toward the back of the trailer into a bedroom. He threw me down onto the bed. "What you need is a little loving."

"Stop it, Jerry! You'll have to kill me before I let you rape me again."

He immediately stopped and walked to the door of the bedroom. "I want to know once and for all if you've come to your senses. Are you coming back home where you belong? I love you! You need a nice house to live in, not a run-down trailer home."

"This is my home, Jerry. I'm sorry, but I'm not coming back to you. I love you, but we can't live together. We're not compatible. I can't make you happy. We need to go our separate ways. For the sake of our children, we need to be friends."

"This is your last chance. If you don't come back right now, I'm getting married. I want an answer right now!"

"I already gave you my answer."

"Oh, yeah! Well, you're going to be sorry."

"Are you getting married because you love this woman?" I asked.

"Hell no!" he quickly responded.

"Then why on earth are you going to get married?'

"It's none of your damn business, but I paid for her divorce from the S-O-B she was married to. Her divorce was final yesterday. I want somebody to cook for me, wash my clothes. She will do whatever I tell her to do. Lou Ann may be ugly as sin, but I don't have to worry about her leaving me like you did. I'm never going to marry a looker again."

"Does she have children?

"What's it to you?"

"I just want to know because you're getting married for the wrong reason and you know it. If you don't love this woman and she has children, you need to think about them. You will be making a big mistake if you don't love her."

On January 27, 1973, Jerry Sternadel married Lou Ann Maag (née Ford) in Wichita Falls. Jerry was almost thirty-two and Lou Ann was twenty-five.

Lou Ann Ford was born on November 2, 1946, to Barbara Ratliff and John H. Ford. It was alleged that Lou Ann had had a twin sister (Betty Sue Ford) who'd died at birth. When Lou Ann married Alva Paschal Maag on July 18, 1969, in Dallas County, she already had an eighteen-month-old daughter. By the time her divorce from Alva Maag was finalized on January 16, 1973, she had another daughter, four-month-old Holly.

Although Jerry was now married, he kept showing up at my house, begging me to come back to him. He said he realized his marriage to Lou Ann was a big mistake, but he was going to stay married to her so he would have somebody to do the cooking and cleaning.

Jerry warned me not to remarry or else he would take away what I loved most, the kids. However, a year and a half later, I married a fellow I was introduced to by a mutual friend. Donald Walker was a slim, handsome man with dark brown hair and brown eyes. He was studying to become a psychologist. Donald loved my children as much as I did.

When Jerry read of my marriage in the local newspaper, he became furious. He sent Lou Ann to pick up Becky and Sandy from elementary school. This was the event that led to the fistfight between Lou Ann and me at her house.

After that, I had a worrisome and sleepless weekend. Very early on Monday morning, someone rang my doorbell. A man in a dark suit was standing at the door. He thrust a manila envelope into my hands, saying, "You've been served."

The package contained court papers from Jerry's attorney, Bill Browning. Jerry had filed for sole custody of the children, claiming I was an unfit mother. I contacted a lawyer immediately and countersued for custody.

Jerry went off on a tangent about the lowlife I had married and how he was going to get even. He began threatening the lives of the children. "If you don't let me have the kids, you won't get them back alive. You hurt me! Now I'm going to hurt you, bitch. I'll kill the little brats before I let you and that scumbag have them. I warned you not to marry!"

"Jerry, you can't mean what you're saying."

"Oh, no! Well, bitch, just try me!"

"You know you love those kids as much as I do. Please don't say things like that!"

"I hate the little brats. I don't care if I go to prison. I don't have a life. I died when you left me!"

"Jerry, I gave you the business, money, horses, everything, because you gave me your word. I trusted you enough to think you would keep your promise. I have never stopped you from seeing Becky and Sandy. They love you. They're your own flesh and blood."

"I'm not so sure of that! Everybody in this town has probably fucked you!"

"How can you say that? You know that is not true!"

"I've seen men looking at you. You think I didn't notice! I'm through talking. Let me know what you want to do. If the little brats wind up dead, it'll be your doing, not mine."

I was devastated. Donald suggested I get the pastor at the Lutheran church involved. He also suggested talking to Jerry's best friend. I took my husband's advice and confided in the pastor and Jerry's good friend. They said they would try talking sense into Jerry.

Jerry's friend talked to Jerry and then got back to me. He said I should be prepared for the possibility that Jerry might carry out his threat. He said Jerry would regret it later, but he might kill the children out of spite.

The pastor recited the Bible story in which King Solomon was going to cut a baby in half because two women both claimed to be the mother. To save the baby's life, the real mother told the king that the child belonged to the other woman.

Giving Jerry sole custody of my children was the only way of keeping them safe.

But Jerry still wasn't satisfied. He started calling and harassing my husband. When Donald answered the phone, Jerry would tell him nasty lies. Every day, Jerry would call. Every day, Donald would hang up on him.

Although I was granted visitation rights, Jerry would not let me visit the children. I filed contempt charges against Jerry again and again. Each time Jerry received the contempt charges, he and his lawyer would get the judge to dismiss the charges as being unfounded and without grounds.

Out of desperation, I confronted Jerry and begged him to stop harassing us. I also begged him to let me see the children.

Jerry was relentless in his cruelty to me. The daily harassment continued and so did his refusal to let me exercise my visitation rights with the children. He told me if I didn't stop hounding him, he would have his lawyer file for child-support payments. "I did you a favor when I didn't ask for child support. I was ordered to pay you two hundred bucks a month, so why shouldn't you have to pay me two hundred or more? Besides, the couple of times I let you take the little brats, they came back all messed up. I'm warning you, bitch, back off or get ready to stuff my pockets!"

Being full of angst and anxiety, I was so nervous and overwrought I couldn't eat or sleep. The least little thing made me burst into tears.

Fourteen months of constant harassing phone calls and my crying all the time made Donald fed up with the situation. He told me he loved me, but he couldn't take the harassment. "Jerry won't ever stop hounding you. His hate is consuming him. My hands are tied. I'm not knocking it, but you love your kids so much that you won't ever be happy without them. And there's nothing wrong with that. I would give anything if I could help you get custody of your kids back. But there is nothing I can do. Maybe if I am out of the picture, Jerry will have a change of heart toward you. You deserve to be happy. I'll pray Jerry has a change of heart." Before Donald Walker walked out of my life, he said, "I love you, Jeannie. But I want a divorce."

Jerry did not have a change of heart toward me. His heart only grew colder. He said I was a loser who couldn't even keep a scumbag husband. He tortured me by bringing my children over to my house, pretending he was going to let me have visitation and then driving off with the kids crying.

Jerry's friend told me the best thing I could do was to move away from Wichita Falls. "Maybe you should consider going to another state. One of you has to turn those kids loose. I know Jerry won't do it. Your kids are being torn apart. As their mother, you have to think about their mental and physical health. It's a tough decision for you to make. But I know you will do the right thing for the sake of your children."

The judge said, "Contempt charges don't mean anything to your ex-husband. I have imposed fines and even jail time. This doesn't keep him from violating the court order. I'm sure all this is having an impact on your kids. One of you needs to stop this craziness. That would be the best thing for everyone, especially the kids."

After a lot of soul-searching, I reluctantly packed up my belongings and rented a U-Haul. I wasn't sure about my destination, but I planned to go as far away as I could from Wichita Falls, Texas. All I took with me on the long, one-way trip were my memories.

I ended up on Long Island, New York. I rented an apartment and secured a job as an executive secretary. Once a year, on my two-week vacation, I flew back to Texas. I always had high hopes of executing my summer visitation rights with my children. I would notify Jerry of the date I would be arriving in Wichita Falls. He would pack up the children and take them to Ruidoso, New Mexico, returning to Wichita Falls after I had left. The same scenario happened year after year.

My friends in Wichita Falls were secretly watching over my children. They assured me they had given my telephone number and address in New York to my children. I thought of having them rent a post office box in Petrolia for Becky. But, I knew my two children rode the school bus, so Becky wouldn't be able to go pick up the mail.

From time to time, Becky would call me collect from the pay phone at school. She told me Lou Ann watched her like a hawk.

My daughter asked her schoolmates if she could use their address to receive letters from me. The girlfriends agreed and told their parents that Jeannie Walker was a friend.

Lou Ann regularly searched Becky's room. Inevitably, she would find letters from me that Becky had hidden. After Becky got a beating, Lou Ann would go to the parents of Becky's friends and threaten to take civil action if they did not stop the letter writing to Jeannie Walker.

Becky would then seek out another friend.

Jeannie with happy memories of her children

In 1976, I received a very distressing letter from my daughter. She wrote that her stepmother had beaten her. She had black and blue bruises from the beating. I immediately contacted the Wichita Falls child welfare agency and made a formal complaint about my daughter being physically abused. The agency said they would investigate my complaint and inform me of their findings.

I received notification from the agency saying they had found no indication of physical abuse in the Sternadel home. The child welfare official said they did observe bruises on Becky's back and upper torso, but that the bruises could have been caused by anyone. Since there weren't any witnesses to corroborate the child abuse claim, they would have to dismiss the complaint as unfounded. However, because there were bruises on the child, they would ask Becky's teachers to keep an eye on her, and a child welfare official would check on Becky periodically.

On January 31, 1977, I received a letter from one of my daughter's school friends.

Dear Jeannie,

I'm so sorry I haven't written sooner. I hope you haven't been worried about Becky and me. We're doing fine at school. Becky wanted me to tell you that a man and a lady came to see her at school. Becky has been having a lot of trouble at home. She thinks that everybody hates her. She has been getting into trouble and grounded for such small things. She is down and depressed. She doesn't feel like she's been loved as the other kids have. I don't have much to write about, but I thought it was time to write because you might get worried. And I haven't been able to get some stamps because I didn't have a good enough reason. Becky wants to see you. She wants to live with you. I guess this is all. You can still write us, we haven't got in trouble over this yet, so just keep writing. I hope you had a wonderful Christmas and a Happy New Year. It's getting dull around here so write me soon.

Love,

Anne Taylor*

I promptly wrote back to Anne thanking her and enclosed a letter for my daughter.

Another of my daughter's friends wrote and told me that a woman kept coming to their school and talking to Becky. The friend said that she heard one of her teacher's say that the lady was from social services and was checking on Becky and Sandy to see how they were being treated at home.

In January 1979, I received a letter from the Texas Department of Human Resources.

Dear Mrs. Walker.

I talked with your daughter, Becky Sternadel, on 11-15-78. She is a very attractive girl, fashionably dressed and neat in appearance. She told me that her father forbade her to correspond with you because you and she made a complaint about her stepmother to the Wichita Falls Child Welfare. She said that she would like to live with you. Since Becky is fourteen years old and under Texas law has the legal right to say with whom she wants to live, you could perhaps engage an attorney and attempt to regain conservatorship of her.

I talked with Mr. Sternadel on January 23, 1979. He was very difficult to reach for an appointment. He was not informed that I had spoken with Becky. I asked him what your visitation rights were. He said that he thought that it was in the summer at his house. He said that he does forbid Becky to see you and correspond with you because it is his opinion that Becky has problems after being in touch with you.

If you wish to pursue a more liberal visitation with Becky, I would suggest that you review your visitation rights and if they are being denied, you could possibly file contempt of court charges against Mr. Sternadel with the aid of an attorney or ask for a change of guardianship.

Sincerely,

Jolene Waggoner*

After receiving the letter from the Texas Department of Human Resources, I engaged an attorney on Long Island as was suggested by Ms. Waggoner. When Jerry received the court papers, he didn't waste any time threatening to kill the children before he would let me see them or let them live with me.

My lawyer suggested the next time I went to Texas that I should bring the children back with me. He informed me that if I could get the children to New York, Jerry would have to fight me for custody in the state of New York instead of in Texas. The lawyer made the suggestion (off the record) for me to kidnap my children. He said he would stand at the ready to file the necessary court papers to protect my children and me when I returned from Texas.

There was one person in Wichita Falls I thought I could trust enough to confide in about getting my children to New York. But this woman contacted Jerry and informed him of my intentions.

Jerry wasted no time in calling me. He bragged that my friend had called and tipped him off about the ruse I was going to try to pull. He warned me that if I did try to take the kids from Texas, he would have me arrested for kidnapping as soon as I reached Dallas–Fort Worth Airport.

I called my once-trusted friend, who said, "Yeah, I called Jerry and told him what you were planning to do. He would have known that I was the one who helped you. I have to live in Wichita Falls, not you. I'd be the one facing the music from Jerry Sternadel, not you. He would probably kill me for helping you take his kids away."

All I could do was pray to the good Lord to watch out over my children and keep them out of harm's way.

In the early eighties, my two children were old enough to speak up to their dad. They stood their ground and started spending summers with me in New York.

In 1985, out of the blue, Jerry called. He said he had a small problem. He had bought a home in Archer City, had completely furnished it, and had signed it over to one of his girlfriends. And now his girlfriend had jilted him. He was thinking about having one of his friends go there to steal the furniture and then trash the place. He asked me what I thought he should do.

I didn't know if Jerry was joking or what. I told him what he planned on doing was against the law. I asked, "Does Lou Ann know about your girlfriend?"

"Hell, yes! Lou Ann knows about all my girlfriends. Hey, just forget I even called. I'm going to make that bitch sign a promissory note or else I'll have Browning sue her. She is going to be sorry she turned her back on me."

Jerry began calling me on a regular basis after that. The last time I talked to him was the beginning of May in 1990. He said he had found out that Lou Ann and his bookkeeper were stealing money from him.

"I discovered $35,000 missing from one of my bank accounts. I haven't checked the other accounts yet. But I told those two bitches I want my money back. And when I get the damn money back, I'm divorcing Lou Ann and firing Debbie."

I replied, "I hope you didn't tell Lou Ann you plan on divorcing her after you get the money back."

"Hell, yes, I told her. I told both of them that if I don't get my money back, somebody is going to be arrested for embezzlement. They both know that I damn well mean it. That fat bitch can threaten me all she wants to now. The time limit is up, and she can't do a damn thing to me."

I didn't know what Jerry was talking about when he said the time limit was up. But I did know that I left Jerry with everything when we divorced. "Jerry, I did not leave you with everything just so Lou Ann could wind up with it. That is supposed to be our kids' inheritance."

"Hey, I know what I'm doing! Those two fat bitches are giving me my money back or else I'm going to the cops. Lou Ann knows all she gets is the $100,000 I already gave her."

"I don't think you should have told Lou Ann about divorcing her. I hope you know what you're doing."

"I'm not stupid like some people I know. I put things in writing. Lou Ann signed a prenuptial agreement before I married her. I don't believe people's promises like you do. I know what I'm doing."

"I sure hope so."

"Hey, are you coming to Texas this year?"

"Yes, I am."

"When do you think you'll be here?"

"Sometime in either June or July."

"Give me a call when you get to Wichita Falls. We'll go have coffee. Hey, I've been meaning to say something about the birthday cards you send me every year. You can leave out those Bible verses. What did you mean by put my savings in heaven where it counts?"

"I meant you should try to help people because you have the means to do so. A person can't worship money and God at the same time. It's one or the other. God can do things for you that money can't."

"That's what I thought you meant. Hey, I know I've hurt you, and I've been meaning to say I'm sorry. I'm trying to change, but it's not easy. I never heard anybody say you were bad-mouthing me. I have a lot of regrets and a lot of things to make up for. When you get to Texas this year, maybe we can start over."

"Everybody does things they regret. I did a lot of things that I regret. I wish it could have been different between us. But we had two healthy, wonderful kids together. Jerry, I've prayed a long time for us to be friends."

"Hey, call me when you get into town. We'll have coffee and talk about the good times. Don't worry your pretty little head. I'm getting the money back! It's our kids' inheritance."

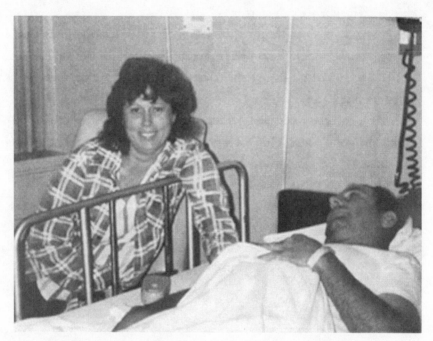

Jerry Sternadel in the hospital with second wife, Lou Ann

Hospital Emergency

*Behold a pale horse, and his name who sat upon him was
Death, and Hell followed with him.*
—Revelation 6:8

At noon on Tuesday, May 22, 1990, Jerry Sternadel joined his wife
and bookkeeper for lunch. They all ate taco salads. Shortly after
eating his, Jerry developed severe abdominal cramps accompanied by
nausea, severe vomiting, and diarrhea. He suddenly felt extremely weak
with shortness of breath. Around four o'clock that afternoon, he took
suppositories and felt better. He went to bed and slept all night.

The next morning, he felt weak but cooked himself an egg and toast
for breakfast. Then he drove out to the horse barn where he talked to
two good friends, Ken and Kathleen Harney.

"Yesterday, I was sick as a horse. I know Lou Ann and Debbie Baker
have been stealing from me. Now I think they're feeding me shit to
make me sick."

The friends were not sure whether Jerry was saying this in jest or
whether he really meant it, so they just shrugged it off.

Ken said, "Maybe you got food poisoning from something you
ate."

Jerry answered, "I know I was poisoned from something I ate, but I don't think it was food poisoning. They went to Taco Bell and brought back food and we all ate together and I'm the only one that got sick. I've been sicker than a dog since I ate that salad they gave me."

Ken said, "I sure hope you get to feeling better. Be careful what you eat from now on."

Jerry needed to check on a couple of plumbing jobs that morning, but he felt too weak to drive. He had his bookkeeper drive him to town. At one job site, he ran into his old friend and former boss Jerry Gamble, who was now the state plumbing inspector. He told him he wasn't feeling good and had been real sick the day before.

Gamble said, "Don't shake hands with me. I'm fixing to go on vacation, and you're gonna give me that twenty-four-hour virus. You look bad. Maybe you better go home and lie down."

Jerry went straight home, got some leftovers out of the refrigerator, took a bite, and washed it down with 7UP. Within thirty minutes he was nauseated and vomiting and had diarrhea with a mid-abdominal pain shooting through to his back. His vomiting was extremely violent. The diarrhea was severe, and he fainted three or four times trying to get to the bathroom.

One of Jerry's employees came into the house to check on plumbing instructions for a job and found his boss very sick. Jerry was immediately loaded into the car by his workers and taken to the hospital emergency room.

At 4:15 in the afternoon on May 23, 1990, Jerry was admitted to the hospital. He was put into the intensive care unit and given intravenous fluids. In the hospital, the nurse checked on him every fifteen to thirty minutes. Lou Ann was in the room with him.

The doctor's diagnosis was acute gastroenteritis and/or possible food poisoning. Jerry stated his abdomen hurt and his rib cage was tender from nausea and vomiting.

Dr. Humphrey wrote in his report of May 23, 1990, that Jerry Sternadel was a "well-developed, well-nourished forty-nine-year-old white male, who appeared acutely ill. Patient was in good health until 5-22-90. Patient does not smoke and denies use of alcohol. He denies ingestion of any toxins. He is a plumber by trade and also raises and races horses. He has two children and two stepchildren. He gives no history of eating anything in the past five days that some of the family did not also eat. There is no history of accidental poisoning."

At 12:01 AM, the nurse checked Jerry and noted her patient was resting comfortably with no nausea or vomiting. During this time, Lou Ann and Debbie Baker were in the room with Jerry. Lou Ann gave her husband a drink of 7UP that Debbie had brought to the hospital. When the nurse returned at 1:10, she found Jerry vomiting violently. She immediately gave him a Phenergan suppository and called Dr. Humphrey to notify him of her patient's vomiting, kidney failure, and drop in blood pressure.

At 5:50 AM, Jerry was awake and alert with no more vomiting or nausea throughout the rest of the night.

On Thursday, May 24, at 8:00 AM, Lou Ann and Debbie Baker visited Jerry in his room. Jerry distrusted his bookkeeper, but continued to trust his wife. He took the *Coca-Cola* Lou Ann had brought and drank some of it. Even though he was of the opinion they might have put something in his food a couple days before to make him sick, he believed the soft drink was safe to drink.

At 8:30 AM, the nurse returned to Jerry's room. She found him vomiting, and his blood pressure had dropped again. Two hours later, he had passed 300 cc of liquid yellow diarrhea. He rested comfortably the rest of the day and had diarrhea one time but no nausea or vomiting.

At 10:00 PM, Lou Ann and Debbie Baker visited Jerry again. They were alone with him in his hospital room and stayed for over two hours.

At 12:45 AM, the nurse returned to find Jerry nauseated and vomiting. He was given medication for nausea. Fifteen minutes later, he had diarrhea.

At 2:00 AM, Jerry started requesting water but was told he could have only ice. He told the nurse that the ice tasted funny and felt like it had needles in it. He said he was going to call his wife and have her bring him some ice from home. He complained of his throat feeling sore.

The nurse started checking Jerry continuously every fifteen to thirty minutes until he finally improved. He was moved to a private room in stable condition.

On Friday, May 25, at 10:40 PM, Becky arrived from Arlington, Texas, to visit her dad. She stayed at the hospital with him in his room. Jerry continued to improve with each passing day while his daughter was at his bedside. He was sitting up in the bed and reading the paper. He even told his workers to come to the hospital so he could give them orders on different plumbing jobs that he needed finished.

On Monday, May 28, Jerry continued to improve. He was released from the hospital at 1:15 PM. At her dad's insistence that he would be fine, Becky drove back to her home in Arlington.

Sometime during the day on Tuesday, May 29, once again, Jerry became nauseated, started vomiting, and had diarrhea five times. Although he had taken medicine twice during the day, he was only able to dribble urine. He was readmitted to the hospital at 10:30 PM. On his first hospital visit, he had weighed 195 pounds. Now his weight was up to 225, and his stomach was swollen and distended.

Dr. Humphrey wrote in his report that he had initially thought Jerry Sternadel had acute gastroenteritis and/or food poisoning. However, the lab tests and findings had not tallied with this diagnosis, and his patient's symptoms were too severe, prolonged, and varied to fit into this simple category. Dr. Humphrey's plan was to rehydrate his patient. The doctor also stated in his report that he was beginning to suspect the possibility of some other toxin. The doctor informed Jerry's wife that trace amounts of arsenic had shown up in toxicology tests.

On Wednesday, May 30, Jerry's hands and legs were badly swollen. He was moved to an enteric isolation room. He started getting concerned over medications and requested test results. He was informed the test results were not yet back. The next day, his gait was steady and he was able to slowly walk around his hospital room. He took a shower and then went back to bed.

On Friday, June 1, Jerry was sleeping when the nurse came into his room. But Lou Ann informed the nurse that her husband was urinating frequently. Jerry woke up and said he felt better. He got up to use the bathroom and took a shower. He watched television and read the paper. His skin was warm and dry. His breathing was even and unlabored. His wife remained in the hospital room with him. He had no noted distress.

On Saturday, June 2, Jerry was discharged from the hospital at 2:00 PM. At 3:15 PM, Lou Ann drove him home from the hospital.

When they arrived at the ranch, Jerry's son went outside to help his dad get into the house. He walked over to the driver's side of the car and spoke with Lou Ann.

"Lou Ann, I want you to know that Holly had a boy over last night. This morning he drank some Cran-Apple juice that was in the icebox. The kid got real sick right after he drank it. He was vomiting and had diarrhea real bad all day. The kid was so sick Holly had to take him to the clinic."

Lou Ann quickly responded, "Help me get your dad into the house. I've got to go to the clinic where the boy is and check on him."

(After Jerry's death from arsenic poison, the authorities asked Lou Ann about the boy. She denied knowing him and denied knowing he had gotten sick at her home after drinking juice from her refrigerator. She told the sheriff the boy was a stranger whom she saw looking sick in the parking lot of a drugstore where she had gone for her husband's medicine. She said she felt sorry for the boy when she saw he was so sick. She stated that she paid for the boy's care only because he said he didn't have any money.

However, when the sheriff talked to the sick boy's mother, she said Lou Ann paid her son's bill and then left the clinic right after that. She stated that Lou Ann did not even have the decency to stay with her son while he was deathly ill. She said her son looked really sick, and she could tell something was very wrong with him. "He looked more dead than alive. His face was really pale, and he looked acutely ill. I asked him what happened. He told me he drank some Cran-Apple juice from the refrigerator at the Sternadel house. His throat started burning right after he drank the juice, and he got sick immediately after that. He had stomach cramps, vomiting, and diarrhea. He told me he thought he was going to die. I stayed with him at the clinic until the doctor released him, which was only a few hours later. Then I picked up the medicine the doctor prescribed and took him home with me. He was still real sick two weeks later."

The boy's mother was in shock when the sheriff told her about Jerry Sternadel dying from arsenic poison. She made sure that tests were done on her son's hair and blood samples. The toxicology tests came back positive for arsenic and showed her son had 278 mcg of arsenic in his system almost three weeks after he drank the poisoned juice. "My son drank juice that Lou Ann Sternadel had in the refrigerator to give to her husband.")

Around five o'clock, that Saturday afternoon, Jerry's mother, Marcy, came out to the ranch to check on her son. She made some homemade potato soup and brought it with her. Jerry told his mother he felt a little better but was still weak. Marcy saw to it that her son ate a small portion of the potato soup. She also made sure he drank some water because he said he had not drunk any fluids all day. She could tell her son was very sick. She wanted to stay all night at the ranch, but she needed to go to work early the next morning. She stayed at the ranch until ten o'clock that night and then went home.

The next day, Sandy walked into his dad's bedroom to see how he was feeling. He spotted Lou Ann and Debbie Baker standing over him. He noticed the women were spoon-feeding something to him. "What are you giving Dad?"

Lou Ann answered, "We're trying to get your dad to sip some Cran-Apple juice. The doctor said he needs some liquids. He's too weak to drink from a glass, so we put some juice in a tablespoon. He is only taking small sips, but at least he's getting some liquid."

Sandy questioned, "That's not the same Cran-Apple juice the boy drank, is it?"

Lou Ann replied emphatically, "No! No! We poured that juice out."

"Well, Daddy doesn't need to drink anything that might have gone bad. Are you sure you poured that juice out?"

"Yes, Sandy, I poured that juice down the sink myself! This is from a different bottle."

"Do you think Daddy is going to be all right? I wish I could stay here with Daddy, but I've got to go to work. As soon as I get back tomorrow night, I'll check on Daddy and stay with him."

On Monday evening, June 4, Sandy returned to the ranch. He walked into the bedroom to check on his dad. He was shocked when he saw Jerry's face and body were badly swollen. He immediately noticed he was having difficulty breathing. He knew he needed to be in the hospital. He walked through the house and found Lou Ann sitting in the living room watching television. "Daddy is real sick. How come you didn't take him to the hospital? Daddy should be in the hospital!"

"Oh, your dad is just fine. Anyway, the doctors can't help him."

"I'm taking Daddy to the hospital right now!"

Lou Ann protested. "Jerry don't need to be in the hospital. We are not taking him there."

Sandy exclaimed, "Oh, yes, we are! Even if I have to get the neighbors to help me carry Daddy to the car, he's going to the hospital."

Lou Ann walked to the master bedroom and stood in the middle of the doorway. She glared at Sandy. "I already told you, Jerry is not going to the hospital. They can't help him. Besides, Jerry told me he doesn't want to go back to the hospital."

"Get out of my way!" He pushed Lou Ann out of the doorway and looked inside the bedroom. He saw his dad lying on the bed, gasping for air. Sandy could not understand why Lou Ann did not want his dad taken to the hospital, because anyone could look and see how grave his condition was. He thought about calling an ambulance. But knew being out in the country he could get his dad to the hospital quicker if he drove him there. He immediately raced next door, woke up the neighbors, and asked for their help. The neighbors came over in their pajamas and helped Sandy carry his dad to the car. Then Sandy rushed him to the hospital.

In the wee hours on Tuesday morning, June 5, I received a call from my son.

"Mother, I just got back from taking Daddy to the hospital. Daddy is real sick. Do you know where Becky is? She needs to get to the hospital if she wants to see Daddy alive. The doctor told me that if I hadn't gotten Daddy to the hospital when I did, he probably would have been dead by morning. Mother, when I got home from work, I looked in on Daddy. I could tell he was real sick and having difficulty breathing. I told Lou Ann we needed to get Daddy to the hospital. She told me Daddy was doing just fine. I told her I was going next door to get the neighbors to help me carry Daddy to the car. Lou Ann kept standing in the door. I had to push her out of the way. She followed us to the car saying it was ridiculous to take Jerry to the hospital. She said I was being a fool. Mother, I just don't understand why Lou Ann didn't want Daddy taken to the hospital!"

I was just as dumbfounded as my son about Lou Ann's actions. "I don't know why Lou Ann didn't want Jerry in the hospital. But you did the right thing by getting your dad to the hospital. I'll call Becky. I'll let her know her dad is back in the hospital and she needs to get there as soon as possible."

That morning, I was on the phone with my daughter in Arlington, Texas. "Becky, your dad is back in the hospital. Sandy called me. He said your dad is real sick and almost died last night. You need to get to the hospital as soon as you can."

"Mother, I've been sick myself. I've missed a lot of work, plus I have a lot of files to catch up on. You know how Sandy exaggerates things. But as soon as we hang up, I'll call and check on Daddy."

"I honestly don't know how sick your dad is, but I do know how upset your brother was. This is your dad we're talking about. I'm sure your employer will understand. I want you to get to the hospital as soon as you can. And please call me and let me know how your dad is."

The Grim Reaper Strikes

At 10:54 PM, June 4, Jerry was back in the emergency room. He was cyanotic on arrival. His skin was mottled and cool to the touch. His abdomen was very distended and soft to the touch. An IV was started in his right wrist. His blood pressure was very low, 77/37, and he had a rapid pulse. He was having irregular heartbeats, indicative of sinus tach, and his respiration was labored. He told the nurses he'd had episodes of fainting with severe nausea, vomiting, and diarrhea just two hours prior to his arrival.

Jerry was immediately treated and then admitted to the intensive care unit at 1:30 AM.

At 1:45 AM, June 5, the nurse on the ICU floor noted the following: "Received patient on cardiac monitor and foley catheter. Blood pressure 58/32 and intravenous line intact. Patient looks drawn, unshaven, with dry scaly skin, sallow in color. Patient has generalized raised, red rash on abdomen, ankle and peripheral edema noted. Lomotil was given for diarrhea. Patient stated, 'When I tried to walk prior to coming to hospital, my legs gave out on me.'" The nurse also noted Jerry's right foot had a big scrape on it and was bluish in color.

At 8:00 AM, Jerry's wife and bookkeeper came to visit him in his room. The doctor came in to check on Jerry. The physician talked to Lou Ann and gave the nurse medication orders.

Around 10:00, Lou Ann gave Jerry some soft drink she had brought to the hospital. After seeing to it that her husband drank most of the 7UP, she and Debbie left the hospital.

At 10:45, Jerry had a seizure-like episode in which his hands and feet flailed up in the air with jerking motions; this lasted approximately thirty seconds. He then vomited around the NG tube, which had been inserted earlier that morning.

At 11:20, the hospital phoned Lou Ann at home and asked for permission to insert a central line and a spinal tap.

By noon, Jerry appeared to be hallucinating and seeing objects not visible in the room.

At 1:00, a doctor inserted a right internal jugular for intravenous infusion. An hour later, a nurse notified the doctor of bloody output coming from Jerry's mouth.

That evening at 7:35, Jerry's wife, mother, and bookkeeper were in the hospital room with him. Dr. Humphrey was also at the hospital and spoke with Jerry and his family. Jerry was alert but did not have any gross motor coordination in his arms and hands. He could not hold his water glass without spilling the water. He had a generalized raised rash to his body with peripheral and ankle edema.

Jerry's mother glanced over at Lou Ann and the doctor. Marcy said, "Get some specialists in here. He's got the money. Get some doctors who have some sense. Dr. Humphrey is only a diet doctor and can't get Jerry well. Jerry's not getting any better, he's getting worse."

Jerry looked at his wife and said, "Yeah, Lou Ann, get me some different doctors. Some good doctors, who know what they're doing."

Dr. Humphrey stood listening to the patient and his family discussing him and said nothing. The doctor shrugged his shoulders and walked out of the room after glaring straight at Lou Ann.

"And another thing," Jerry's mother continued. "Why is Debbie Baker at the hospital all the time? She's not family. So why is she here in Jerry's room all the time?"

Lou Ann walked away from Marcy without answering.

On Wednesday, June 6, at 1:00 AM, Jerry's blood pressure was 82/46. He was unable to hold his water cup.

By 7:30 AM, Jerry was occasionally hallucinating with intermittent confusion.

The nurse wrote in her report: "Patient awake, alert, oriented to person and place but has periods of hallucinations thinking he has some keys and dirt on his bed. Patient is able to follow requests and answer questions appropriately. Has a right IV and catheter. No redness or edema at site. Lung sounds clear in upper and lower lobes bilaterally. Abdomen slightly distended. Has a foley patent and draining amber-colored urine. Patient is able to move arms and hands well at request. States he feels a little sick at his stomach."

At 8:00 AM on June 6, Lou Ann and Debbie were in his hospital room. Dr. Konappa Murthy came into the room and examined Jerry. The doctor said Jerry needed to be put in protective/reverse isolation and explained the reason.

Dr. Konappa Murthy wrote in his report the following: "Morning of 6-06-90, patient had improved his urine output only to a small degree. His total intake was about 9,000cc and output was about 6,000cc, mainly in the form of vomiting and diarrhea. His urine output was only 880cc. He continues to have large amounts of output from the nasogastric tube and also continues to have frequent diarrhea. Neurologist, Dr. Danny R. Bartel, saw him on 6-06-90 and he felt the patient had progressive pancytopenia along with increasing abnormalities of liver function tests. Dr. Bartel felt this was probably from a toxic state. The exact toxin could not be identified at that time. This patient, prior to coming to the hospital, had seen Dr. Humphrey in his office and had urine toxicology screening done that revealed arsenic in the urine. Quantitative tests had not been done, as there was not enough urine sample left. At this point, another arsenic level was ordered immediately. Patient was well until May 22, at which time he was admitted to the hospital for what appeared to be food poisoning, and then was readmitted for what appeared to be relapsing course of similar complaints. Overall symptoms and lab picture resemble a toxic shock picture. Patient is able to follow requests and answer questions appropriately, skin color ruddy red. Patient is able to move arms and hands well at request. Hand grips equal and strong. Patient states he has occasional tingling of hands. Patient states he feels stronger. At this point, it was felt that patient needed to be in reverse isolation, and he was placed in reverse isolation."

At 10:00 on the night of June 6, 1990, Jerry told the nurse he wanted to get his clothes so he could leave the hospital. "I'm leaving this hospital. I've got to get out of here. They're trying to kill me. I'm going to Dallas where some good doctors are so I can get well. I need my clothes!"

The nurse told Jerry she could not allow him to leave the hospital. Jerry started yelling at her. "Give me my clothes! I need my clothes so I can get out of this hospital!"

The nurse left Jerry's room and went to the nurse's station. She immediately called Jerry's wife to inform her about the situation. Lou Ann told the nurse to strap Jerry down to the bed if necessary to keep him in the hospital.

"Give him a sedative. I'll be there as soon as I can get dressed."

At 11:00, Lou Ann and Debbie Baker arrived at the hospital. They stayed all night in the room with Jerry. Nurses came into the room and checked on Jerry every fifteen minutes.

On the morning of June 7, between 5:30 and 5:59, the nurse left the room for a short period of time. Lou Ann and Debbie were left alone in the room with him.

Jerry started calling for the nurse and screaming out for help. Lou Ann ran to the nurse's station and told the nurse to give her husband something to settle him down. "He's getting wild. He needs something to help him rest, the poor baby."

The nurse responded to Lou Ann's request that her husband needed a sedative and gave Jerry 10 mg of Haldol intravenously.

Jerry woke up groggy from the medication he was given. He was agitated. He slowly sat up and tried to get out of bed. He was too weak to stand. But he said he wanted his clothes so he could get out of the hospital.

Lou Ann and Debbie Baker were in his room. Lou Ann raced to the nurse's station. She told the nurse Jerry was trying to get out of bed and was becoming combative and out of control. The nurse promptly responded and raced into Jerry's room. She advised her patient to lie back down in bed.

Jerry told the nurse he wanted his clothes so he could get out the hospital. "I've got to get out of here. They're trying to kill me."

The nurse told Jerry she could not let him leave the hospital.

Jerry became increasingly agitated. "You're helping them kill me!" he screamed as he pushed the nurse away.

The nurse called for hospital security. The security team rushed into Jerry's room.

Jerry struggled with them but was quickly overpowered. The security team held Jerry down while orderlies applied restraints to his wrists and tied his hands down to the hospital bed. Jerry kicked at the security team. He screamed and hollered out, "You're all in it together. You're all trying to kill me!"

The security detail responded by grabbing Jerry's legs and using leather restraints to strap his feet to the bed. By 6:35 AM on June 7, Jerry was completely strapped down to the hospital bed with restraints on both his wrists and feet.

The nurse wrote in her report the following: "7:00 AM: Patient extremely confused and hallucinating with paranoid thoughts that everyone out to kill him. Wife and sister (Lou Ann and Debbie Baker) are with patient at his bedside. 8:45 AM: Patient remains extremely confused with delusions of persecutions, 10 mg Haldol to be given slowly in right and left IV. 9:35 AM: Dr. Bartel here. Patient remains combative and loud with delusions of persecutions, 4-point restraints applied to patient."

At 8:00 AM, on June 7, Jerry Gamble came to the hospital to visit with Jerry. During the investigation after Jerry Sternadel's death, Jerry Gamble gave the following statement:

I went down there [to the hospital] and saw Jerry's wife and his secretary sitting out in the hall. They were wearing little paper gowns and had a mask on their faces. Debbie Baker recognized me, but Lou Ann didn't. Of course, I don't know if I had ever been around Lou Ann that much. I never have been out to their house or their shop because it's outside the city limits of Wichita Falls. I told Lou Ann that I was sorry Jerry was sick.

Lou Ann said, "Well, he had a turn for the worse during the night and they called me about ten o'clock last night and said they were having all kinds of trouble with him and ... uh ... he was talking out of his head."

Debbie Baker said, "So would you like to go in and see him? Why don't you go in and see him and calm him down. He has been real upset."

I said, "Sure." So I had to put a gown and mask on. Lou Ann and Debbie helped me do that and I walked in and I saw Jerry had some tubes, one running up his nose and I believe he had a little ... uh ... a hospital gown on. His hands and feet were tied to each side of the bed with some sort of restraint. Jerry raised his head up and looked at me when I walked in.

He said, "Gamble!"

I said, "Yeah, Jerry! What in the world are you doing up here?"

He said, "Oh, I'm sick. They've been doing all kinds of tests on me."

I said, "Well, you're gonna have to get well so that you can get out. You gotta get a lot of things going, you know."

He said, "Gamble, you gotta help me get out of here! They're trying to kill me. I'm gonna die! I've got $35,000 missing. They took it. Those two women took it. They're trying to kill me. They fed me shit. Lou Ann and Debbie, they're trying to kill me. You gotta help me get out of here! You gotta help me! Cut me loose! Gamble, cut me loose!"

'Well, Jerry, you know … uh … I can't let you out of here. I mean … I can't help … I can't untie your … cut you loose."

He said, "I've got $35,000 missing …"

I said, "Are you sure, Jerry?"

He said, "Yeah, I'm sure."

I said, "Well, what happened to it?"

"They took it!" Jerry said, raising his finger and pointing at the door. I assumed "they" meaning Lou Ann and Debbie. They were the only ones there besides me. They were standing right outside the door. They could hear what Jerry was saying.

"Cut me loose! Gamble, cut me loose!"

I said, "Jerry, I can't. You're up here in the hospital. You know you have your wife here. You know you got doctors. You're in the intensive care unit. How much safer could you be?"

He said, "Look, they're not taking … they're not … get me some real doctors. These doctors don't know what they're doing. They don't know what's wrong with me. I'm dying! Those two women are trying to kill me!"

I said, "Well, Jerry, I'll tell you what …"

He said, "Cut me loose, Gamble! My car's downstairs. Go down there and get in that car and you can take me to some real doctors."

I said, "Jerry, you know I can't just cut you loose. I'll tell you what I'll do. I gotta go to work, but I'll come back this afternoon and if you're not better, then we'll see about … I'll see what I can do."

He said, "It'll be too late, Gamble. I'll be dead by then. Cut me loose, Gamble! Please, cut me loose!" Tears welled up in Jerry's eyes. "You just gotta help me. Gamble, you just gotta help me."

I went out into the hall where Jerry's wife and secretary were. I said, "You know, he's in there saying some pretty rough things. He's pretty upset."

Lou Ann said, "Well, he's been out of his head. They had to restrain him 'cause he's been trying to hit people."

I said, "Have the doctors come in. Do they know what's the matter with him?"

Lou Ann replied, "No, they're still running tests. They also did a bone marrow test. They don't have the results back." She walked into the hospital room and said, "Honey, uh, are you … are you feeling better?"

Jerry kinda raised his head up and said, "I can't believe you'd do this to me, not you!"

Lou Ann said, "Honey, I haven't done anything. We're just trying to find out what's the matter with you and get you well."

Jerry said, "Uh-huh! Well, I'll tell you what. You're gone! When I get out of here, I'm divorcing you. You're gone! You understand, bitch? You're gone!"

Lou Ann came out of the room and said, "I just can't stand him talking to me this way. He's never talked to me like this before. I just can't stand it. Debbie, you go in there and see if you can calm him down."

Jerry was hollering loudly, "Untie me! Untie me!"

Debbie Baker looked at Lou Ann and said, "Look, I'm just his secretary. I don't … this is going a little bit beyond my job." Then she walked into Jerry's room.

I couldn't hear what Debbie and Jerry were saying 'cause Lou Ann was talking to me saying, "He's talking out of his head. They are gonna have to do something to make him rest so he'll stop talking out of his head like that. Jerry talking out of his head like that makes me feel so bad. I just can't take it anymore. I've been up here since one o'clock. They've gotta give him some medicine so he can rest, the poor baby."

I said, "Well, have the doctors been in?"

She said, "No, we're waiting for the doctor now."

At about that time, Debbie Baker came walking back out of Jerry's room and exclaimed, "I can't do anything with him!"

Lou Ann said, "Debbie, go get the nurse. Get the nurse. They gotta give him something to ease the pain. Settle him down."

So the nurse came up, and then the doctor came up, and Lou Ann said, "Have you come here to ... to fix ... get my baby well?"

The doctor said, "Well, that's what I'm here for."

Lou Ann said, "What have ... you got to get ... you gotta find out what's wrong with my baby and get him well."

The doctor said, "I already know what's wrong with him." [The doctor knew the toxicology test revealed his patient had arsenic poisoning. The doctor also knew that Jerry did not have a chance of survival, although he kept doing all he could.]

Lou Ann says, "Oh no! It's not that."

I asked Debbie Baker, "What does the doctor think is wrong with Jerry?"

Debbie said, "It's Guillain-Barré Syndrome."

Debbie Baker also told my inspector that Jerry had Guillain-Barré Syndrome when she called my office to turn in an inspection. There wasn't any mention of poisoning. After I left the hospital, I went and told my boss and a couple of other people what Jerry was saying. It was kinda upsetting. Jerry's wife and bookkeeper both said he was out of his head, but he was pretty clear in the things he said. I mean, he was really asking for help. He started crying right there at the hospital. Before I left, he said, "Gamble, you gotta help me. You just gotta help me."

When I asked him about the money, he said, "They got it. They're in it together."

I didn't hear anything about any poison until the day after Jerry died. My wife heard it on the news or read it in the paper that Jerry had died and that it had been arsenic poisoning. Then I felt really bad.

The investigator said to Jerry Gamble, "The day that you called and talked to Lou Ann, I believe you said it was the fifth of June. You called the ranch, and she said Jerry was in the hospital. Was he doing all right then?"

Jerry Gamble replied, "Lou Ann said he was in the hospital, but he was doing better, is what she said. When I went to visit Jerry, Lou Ann said the hospital called her at home at ten o'clock that night. The nurse said Jerry got violent and had a turn for the worse. Lou Ann said the nurses had to restrain Jerry and they had her there trying to … she said, trying to calm him down. I assume Debbie Baker was trying to help Lou Ann. I don't know. Jerry wasn't violent when I was there. Lou Ann was telling the nurse, 'You gotta give him something to calm him down,' but he wasn't violent or anything when I was there. Then the nurse went in and Jerry said, 'What are you doing?' The nurse said, 'Oh, I'm gonna give you something to help you.' And Jerry said, 'You're a scumbag just like the rest of them.' I feel real bad 'cause Jerry kept begging me to cut him loose. I planned on going back to the hospital the next day, but I got called away on some jobs. I feel real bad about what happened to Jerry. He was my friend."

On June 7, Jerry's symptoms changed from ones consistent with ingesting arsenic to ones consistent with inhaling arsenic. The suspicion is that when Jerry Gamble left the hospital that morning, one of the women may have stood at the doorway of the hospital room while the other woman put something over Jerry's mouth and nose causing him to breathe in arsenic dust. To avoid suspicion, both women promptly left the hospital afterward. Lou Ann and Debbie Baker were seen leaving the hospital.

On June 7, 1990, Dr. Bartel wrote in his report the following: "Patient now agitated, confused, paranoid, violent at times—in restraints. BP 80/60, chest clear. Arsenic? On the morning of 6/07/90, the patient became confused, agitated, and was constantly trying to pull the IV lines out. He was also very paranoid and violent at times. He had to be restrained and even with the restraints, he could not be controlled completely. It was not clear as to what exactly caused the acute psychosis. At this point, the family was contacted, and they were explained in detail about patient's multiple organ failures. They were told that the exact cause of this was not clear at present. They were told that the etiological factor may be a virus. The family seemed to understand this. At 2:10 PM, the patient's condition and assessment remained unchanged."

Fighting for Life

I am the resurrection, and the life: He that believeth in me,
though he were dead, yet shall he live
—John 11:25

A t 3:00 PM on June 7, Jerry was lying in the hospital bed. He was
strapped down to the bed by wrist and leg restraints. He would rest
at intervals and then scream out, thrash around in bed, and pull at the
restraints. He was fighting for his life.

On Friday, June 8, 1990, the secretions draining from Jerry's
nasogastric tube tested positive for blood. His wife and bookkeeper
were in the hospital room.

People who came to visit Jerry saw both Lou Ann and Debbie Baker
stick a cotton swab into Jerry's mouth and rub something onto his
tongue. (A security guard later said he believed the cotton swabs tested
positive for arsenic.) Soon after the two women stuck swabs into Jerry's
mouth, he began coughing and spitting up small amounts of thick tan
mucous. His tongue became extremely swollen. He had ulcerated areas
on his lower lip, which were oozing blood.

At 8:15 AM, Dr. Konappa Murthy came in to see Jerry. Lou Ann and
Debbie were in the room, and the doctor spoke with them.

Dr. Murthy wrote in his report the following: "On the morning of 6/08/90, the patient was still agitated, but he was not confused. He was answering questions appropriately. He had developed swelling of the tongue, it was felt the swelling may be from the use of Haldol and Thorazine. Patient had faint bowel sounds and his diarrhea had improved. Again, the family was visited. They were explained in detail that patient had developed multiple organ failure and that he was not responding to the treatment that we were giving. Wife told of high levels of arsenic."

At 11:20 AM, Dr. Ulrich wrote in his report, "Patient off Dopamine. Condition little improved—toxic insult could be developing. Awaiting arsenic results. Reviewed with family in detail."

At 12:30 PM, Lou Ann and Debbie were in the room with Jerry when the nurse came in to check on him. The nurse noted a tan-colored foamy excretion coming from Jerry's nose when he coughed. She glanced over at one of the women whose large eyes dominated her face. She thought the woman's bulging eyes resembled something wicked. "Yes, evil was what she felt she saw as the woman's pupils floated toward the top of her eyes, with an unusually wide expanse of white underneath." It seemed to the nurse that she was gazing into sunglasses that bounce back only the observer's own image, giving no clues as to the identity of the person behind the mirrored lenses. She quickly dragged her gaze away from the woman as she tried to organize her thoughts to tend and care for her seriously ill patient.

At 12:50, Jerry went into respiratory arrest. The nurse immediately called the emergency medical personnel on a Code 99 call.

Lou Ann insisted that her husband was okay and there was no need for all the emergency personnel or excitement. The nurse continued to respond to the urgency in her patient's suddenly deteriorating condition. Her patient was drifting away. His skin was cold and taking on the dreaded blue color of cyanosis. His heartbeat was faltering and sporadic on the monitor. All his vital signs were rapidly becoming incompatible with life.

At that point, Jerry had nothing going for him, except his unwavering will to live and the adamant refusal of his nurse to let him slip away. His heart stopped beating.

Dr. Harvey rushed into the hospital room and attempted to intubate with an endotracheal tube. A 7.5 ET tube was inserted instead through Jerry's mouth. The nurse "pushed" (rapid forceful injection) 30 mg of sodium bicarb to urge her patient's heart to beat.

And then, miraculously, life slowly pulsed back into Jerry's lifeless form. His heart began beating. Somewhere along the sure passage toward death, Jerry had turned around. He had returned from the world of the unknown. He was not alert, but he moved his arms and pulled against the restraints.

Jerry was now on a mechanical ventilator that would breathe for him.

Wordlessly, Lou Ann and Debbie stood just outside the doorway and watched as the doctors and nurses brought Jerry back to life. The women's faces were masked, except for what seemed like depraved smirks. Soon after the life-threatening episode, the two women left the hospital.

At 1:15 pm, Dr. Murthy wrote in his report, "Patient's condition suddenly deteriorated this PM. Patient developed respiratory distress, and this progressed to respiratory arrest. He was seen and intubated by Dr. Harvey. At this point, patient's condition has deteriorated further. This was discussed with Dr. Ulrich. He feels comfortable in transferring patient to Baylor. Attempts were made to locate his wife in the hospital and at home, but she could not be reached. Will apprise wife of guarded prognosis at this point."

Dr. Harvey wrote in his report, "Intubated patient in response to Code 99. Patient has large tongue and edematous laryngopharynx and regurgitated fluid. Air movement was maintained until intubation was successful. Could not ever visualize vocal cords. Trach tube in place with adequate ventilator clinically."

Throughout the rest of the afternoon, nurses constantly suctioned oral tannish foamy secretions that were coming from Jerry's nose and NG tube. He was agitated. His blood pressure was 104/58. A unit of plasma was hung per orders. Jerry did not have a strong cough reflex. He thrashed his arms around in the bed. By 4:45 PM, two units of fresh frozen plasma were hung. His blood pressure was 84/35.

At 5:00, Dr. Murthy spoke with Jerry's wife.

Dr. Murthy wrote in his report of June 8, 1990, the following: "Patient begun on parenteral nutrition, as he had not been eating since the day of admission. This afternoon, he developed respiratory distress, which progressed rapidly, resulting in respiratory arrest. At this point, Dr. Ulrich had contacted physicians in Dallas, mainly in Baylor Medical Center as well as in Southwestern Medical School, to see if any other diagnosis could be made. They also concurred with the diagnosis that we had. It was felt that the patient may be developing myocardial disease resulting in cardiomyopathy. The patient's family was again visited and they were apprised of the guarded prognosis."

At home on Long Island, I sat anxiously waiting for news about my ex-husband's condition. I had not heard anything from my daughter. At 9:30 PM, I decided to call the ranch. My son answered the phone.

Sandy informed me that his dad was in critical care and was getting worse by the day.

After I hung up, I called the hospital. The nurse in the ICU unit told me she could not give out any information on her patient, but she believed some relatives of Jerry's were in the waiting room. She promptly transferred the call to the telephone in the waiting room.

Renee Sternadel, Jerry's sister-in-law, answered the phone. She told me Jerry's condition was serious. The doctors seemed to be doing all they could. She said Lou Ann had told her and everyone else that Jerry had a virus and the doctors were treating him for it.

At 7:15 AM, on Saturday, June 9, Jerry had no urine output and no spontaneous movement or response to pinpricks in his feet or hands.

At eleven o'clock that morning, my daughter arrived at the hospital. After she went in to see her dad, she immediately called me in New York. "Daddy looks real bad. He has all kinds of tubes hooked up to him. He ... he ... Daddy looks like he is dying. Lou Ann walked over and asked me why I was at the hospital. She said Daddy was just fine and improving every day. Mother, he's doesn't look like he is just fine and improving. He's got tubes in his nose. He's got tubes in his mouth.

And he's got all kinds of IVs on both his arms and even on both his feet. They've got his hands and feet tied down to the bed … he can't even talk. I didn't know Daddy was this bad!"

"Becky, have you talked to any of your dad's doctors?"

"No, I just got here. I saw Daddy and then called you."

"Honey, you need to go and talk to the nurses. Tell them you want to know what's wrong with your dad. Tell them you want to talk to the doctors treating your dad. If they don't know what's wrong by now, then we better see about getting your dad to Dallas or some hospital where they can find out what is wrong with him. It doesn't sound like the doctors are helping your dad. It should not take this long to isolate a virus. If I have to fly to Wichita Falls, I will. But you know that will only make Lou Ann throw a fit or worse. But something has got to be done to help your dad. Find your brother and see if he knows what's going on. I'm depending on both of you to find out what's wrong with your dad and help him get better."

After hanging up from talking to me, Becky went directly into her dad's hospital room. Her stepmother and grandmother were in the room. Her dad looked up at her. He pulled against the restraints. She saw him raise one of his fingers and point to a cross on the wall.

"Daddy is trying to tell me something. I love you, Daddy. Don't worry I'm going to help you. Lou Ann, why is Daddy strapped down?"

Lou Ann glared at Becky. "He got violent with one of the nurses. They had to strap him down."

"There's something wrong with Daddy besides a virus. I don't care what you say, I'm going to talk to the doctors. Why don't they know what's wrong with Daddy? You can see how sick he is! He could die while the so-called doctors are trying to find out what's wrong with him! I'm going to tell the doctors a thing or two. We need to get Daddy to a different hospital where they can find out what is wrong with him."

"Becky, you just shut up! Who cares what you think! You're a troublemaker," Lou Ann said in a hateful tone as she grabbed Becky's arm and began trying to push her out of the hospital room.

"Leave her alone," Marcy said loudly to Lou Ann. "Becky doesn't have to shut up. She can speak her mind all she wants to. That's her dad! She has every right to talk to Jerry's doctors. Why *don't* the doctors know what is wrong with Jerry? We need to find out why. They sure don't seem to be helping him here. We need to get him to another hospital."

Lou Ann retorted, "The doctors are doing everything they can for Jerry!"

Just at that moment, Debbie walked into the room.

Lou Ann glared at her. "Where have you been? I needed you here. Becky is having a conniption. Maybe you can get the little troublemaker to shut up and calm down."

Becky said, "Debbie Baker doesn't have any business here in my daddy's room. She's not any kin!"

"Just what is Debbie doing here all the time anyway?" Marcy asked.

Lou Ann gave both her mother-in-law and stepdaughter an evil glare. "Debbie is here because I need her. She is helping me."

"Helping you do what? Making sure Daddy dies! I know you want Daddy to die. But you can't get rid of me," Becky retorted.

"Let's all calm down! Becky, this isn't helping your dad. I think you and I should go get something to drink. I'll personally make sure you talk to the doctor when he comes back," Marcy said as she led her granddaughter out of the hospital room and downstairs to the coffee shop.

At 2:00 PM, Jerry opened his eyes only slightly when the nurse loudly called out his name. He was given a second unit of blood. Lou Ann and Debbie Baker were at his bedside. He opened his eyes and saw the two women. He started thrashing about and pulling against the wrist and ankle restraints. He tried to move the breathing tube in his mouth with his tongue. He tried to scream for someone to help him get away from the two women. But the NG tube was keeping him from speaking.

He struggled and pulled against the wrist restraints with all the energy and might he could muster. But he didn't have enough strength to loosen the restraints that kept him tied to the bed. He started biting the thick tube that was in his mouth. He tossed his head from side to side and thrashed about in the bed.

Lou Ann ran out of the hospital room yelling, "Nurse! Nurse, he's getting wild. You need to sedate him! My poor baby needs something for the pain. He needs a sedative right now!

The nurse responded and went into Jerry's room. She saw her patient tossing his head from side to side and attempting to bite the oral airway. He was violently thrashing about in the bed. The nurse asked the women to leave.

After Lou Ann and Debbie left Jerry's room, he calmed down. The nurse gave him a third unit of blood in the IV in his left foot.

Becky and Sandy stood in the hospital corridor just outside their dad's hospital room talking to their grandmother about helping them move their dad to a better-equipped hospital. Lou Ann and Debbie walked up to the group and stood glaring at them.

Becky and Sandy said in unison, "Lou Ann, we're getting Daddy out of here and taking him to another hospital."

"I won't hear of it!" Lou Ann angrily exclaimed. "The doctors are doing everything they can to help Jerry. Another hospital could not do anything that they're not doing. We've already got eleven doctors looking after him."

Becky turned to her grandmother, "MoMo, don't we have any say in what happens to Daddy?"

Marcy replied tentatively, "Let's wait a couple more days. If your daddy is not any better by then, we'll get him to another hospital."

At 7:41 PM, I called the hospital and spoke to a nurse in the ICU. Once again, the nurse would not give me any information on how Jerry was doing. But she did say she thought Jerry's son and daughter were in the hospital waiting room and transferred the call to that telephone. I did not recognize the voice of the woman answering the phone. I asked if she knew Jerry Sternadel.

The woman said, "Yeah, I know him. I'm here with his family."

"Do you know how Jerry is doing?"

"Oh, he's doing just fine. It probably won't be much longer before Jerry is out of the hospital. He's making more progress every day."

I asked the woman what her name was.

"Debbie Baker," was the woman's response.

I asked, "Are you a friend of Jerry's?"

"I'm Jerry's bookkeeper. I'm a friend of Lou Ann."

I asked her if she knew whether Becky or Sandy were at the hospital.

"Oh, yeah! They're here! They're trying to raise hell, like they always do."

"Would you please ask them to call me?"

"Yeah, if I see them. Who should I tell them to call?"

"Tell them to call their mother. They have my phone number."

Sunday, June 10, sometime between 5:30 and 6:20 PM, Lou Ann and Debbie were alone with Jerry in the hospital room. Jerry began holding his breath, which triggered a high pressure on the ventilator. (Was Jerry holding his breath because the women had put something into the ventilator? During the murder investigation, three syringes were found in the plumbing office, and one contained liquid. The syringe containing liquid was discovered behind the butter door in the refrigerator.)

A nurse rushed into Jerry's hospital room. She asked the two women to leave. She gave Jerry 2.5 mg of Versed through the IV for restlessness and suctioned white thin mucous from the NG tube.

Throughout all of Sunday night, Jerry kept holding his breath, triggering high pressure on the ventilator. He thrashed about, pulling against the restraints and biting the endotracheal tube.

By 11:30 PM, he was unable to acknowledge commands. His feet, body, and scrotum were swollen badly.

By 1:00 AM, on June 11, the nurse was occasionally suctioning copious "white frothy" secretions from the endotracheal breathing tube. Jerry was still occasionally holding his breath, causing a high-pressure signal on the ventilator. He was no longer thrashing about and pulled on the restraints only occasionally.

By six o'clock that morning, the nurse was frequently suctioning "red frothy" secretions from Jerry's nose and mouth.

Jerry opened his eyes slightly and withdrew from painful stimuli. He did not move his legs. He had several abrasions on his face.

Several doctors came into Jerry's hospital room. The doctors were given lab results and were informed of his worsening condition and his tremendous weight gain.

On June 11, at 10:30 AM, Dr. Konappa Murthy wrote in his report, "Patient's condition about same. Arsenic levels in urine became available and the level is around 4,000 mcg. Accepted level of arsenic is around 100 mcg for human being. Will repeat level today."

Dr. Bartel wrote in his report, "Patient still agitated on IV Versed. Some volume overload: Patient needs dialysis. On steroid—will add Tetracycline. Arsenic toxicity still a possibility. Prefer viral explanations."

Dr. Ulrich's report said the following: "Arsenic level dramatically increased. Patient to be dialyzed today."

Throughout the day on Monday, June 11, the nurses continued to frequently suction large amounts of bloody oral and nasal secretions from Jerry. His weight had gone up to 257.4 pounds. His breathing was labored, and at times he gasped for breath. He had facial cyanosis. His abdomen was distended and firm. There were no bowel sounds present. He had no cough reflex. His urine output was very low and muddy brown.

Tuesday, June 12, there was a red rash over Jerry's entire body. Thick, bloody secretions oozed from his mouth and nose. He was gasping for air, even though he was on a ventilator. His blood pressure was very low. His condition was deteriorating. Dialysis was begun per Dr. Mankodi's order, and blood products were to be given while he was on dialysis.

Dr. Murthy came in to see his gravely ill patient. He gave orders to the nurse on medication and treatment.

At 12:10 PM, Dr. Harvey, Dr. Day, Dr. Bartel, and Dr. Mankodi discuss their critically ill patient's condition, prognosis, and therapy.

Dr. Bartel wrote in his notes, "Patient less arousable, pulmonary edema prominent, poor urine output, arsenic poisoning a possibility."

The report on the clipboard at the end of Jerry's bed read: "BP 50/46—Elevated arsenic level in urine discussed with patient's wife. Arsenic level in urine is being repeated."

Jerry did not tolerate dialysis well and was taken off of it. Code 99 was called. Jerry's chest was expanding very poorly even with the ventilator.

At 1:40, the Dopamine drip was increased, along with other medications, and CPR chest compression was begun in an effort to stabilize Jerry's deteriorating condition.

Later that afternoon, Dr. Murthy visited with Jerry's wife and family. The doctor explained in detail about his patient's guarded prognosis. Dr. Murthy said Jerry had been exposed to arsenic and had large amounts of it in his system. Dr. Harvey and Dr. Humphrey were also present.

After hearing the bad prognosis, Becky went straight to the pay phone in the hospital lobby and called me. "Mother, the doctors said daddy took a turn for the worse. Daddy is dying. I don't know what to do. Mother, tell me what to do!"

"I'm so sorry, sweetheart! Go to the chapel right now and pray. God listens to our prayers."

"What do I pray for?"

"Pray for God to forgive your dad his sins. Pray for God to help you and your brother. Just open up your heart and talk to God."

"Okay, Sandy and I are going to the chapel right now. We'll pray for Daddy."

Becky and Sandy went downstairs to the chapel in the hospital. They sat down on a pew in the back and prayed. Becky cried and cried until she could cry no more. Through her tears, she saw a vision of her dad rising up from the hospital bed and floating upward. A sudden peace came over her. She turned to her brother and said, "We've got to go back upstairs. Daddy is dead."

At 5:00 PM, the nurse could not find a pulse on her patient. She immediately called Code 99 and EMD compressions were begun. The doctors and nurses tried everything in their power to move heaven and earth and save their dying patient from the grip of death.

Jerry no longer had the will or the strength to continue his fight to stay alive. He could no longer breathe air to fill his lungs or coax his heart to beat. He gave up the battle he could not win against the Grim Reaper.

At 5:40 PM, he was pronounced dead by Dr. Konappa Murthy.

Becky and Sandy walked back into the critical care unit just in time to see the doctor come out of their dad's hospital room.

"I'm sorry, but we could not save him. He passed away a moment ago. I'm so sorry."

Becky used a crumpled-up tissue to wipe away her tears. She tenderly wrapped her arms around her brother.

Sandy was overwhelmed with shock and grief. He had just been given a tranquilizer ordered by one of the doctors.

Lou Ann acted as if she was overcome with emotion, while Debbie stood by the elevator and chewed nervously on her fake fingernails. A short time later, the two women were seen standing in the hospital corridor talking and laughing as if they had just heard a funny joke.

Suddenly, Becky screamed, "I'll tell you one thing. There's no way Daddy would poison himself." She pointed an accusing finger at her stepmother. "Look at the way she's laughing and carrying on. She is happy that Daddy is dead. I think she poisoned Daddy!"

Her comment was the first hint that the widow would become a murder suspect.

At 7:25 PM, on June 12, Jerry's lifeless body was transferred to the morgue.

Early the next morning, on June 13, his corpse was taken from the morgue to the Dallas Forensic Lab for an autopsy.

The Grave Site

On Wednesday, June 13, 1990, the same day her husband's body was being taken to Dallas for an autopsy, Lou Ann Sternadel was driving to the cemetery in Wichita Falls to make burial arrangements. Making the trip with Lou Ann were her mother-in-law, Marcy, and her good friend, Debbie Baker.

The widow asked Crestview officials if her dead husband had any burial plots. Diligently searching through their files, the personnel located two plots in the Garden of Faith section that had been purchased back in the 1960s under Jerry and Jeannie Sternadel's name. Lou Ann quickly said she wanted to use one of the plots.

"I'm sorry, Mrs. Sternadel, but our records specify those burial plots were awarded to Jeannie Sternadel in a divorce agreement between her and Jerry Sternadel. We would need her permission before you could use one of those plots to bury Mr. Sternadel."

The widow was left with no other choice but to purchase a burial plot. She quickly settled on two plots in the Garden of the Cross section of the cemetery.

The date of the funeral could not be determined until after the body was brought back to Wichita Falls from Dallas.

June 15, 1990, was a bright, sunny day. However, it was not a cheerful time. It was a tearful and sad occasion for people who had attended Jerry's funeral service and now were waiting for the grave site service. A green canopy tent had been set up in the Garden of the Cross section to provide shade from the scorching sun. The heavy cloth edges hanging over the sides of the tent were flapping relentlessly in the blowing wind.

I was standing close by the tent at the burial site, directing my attention to the black hearse and limousines that were pulling up and parking. I observed the pallbearers taking the coffin from the hearse and carefully carrying it to the grave site.

People were meandering around, but some stopped in their tracks to stare at Jerry's widow exiting from the chauffeur-driven limousine. They continued watching as Jerry's mother and grown children exited from another limo.

The tension in the air at the burial site was as thick as the bouquets that surrounded the coffin.

I walked over to the chair that had been set up for me just off to the side of the two rows of chairs arranged in front of the gray coffin for Jerry's widow and his immediate family. I was holding on to the back of the black velvet–covered chair. I watched my son and daughter walking toward the tent. I clutched the fabric back of the chair to steady myself. I looked at my grieving children. Their faces were etched with deep sorrow and anguish. They sat down between their stepmother and their paternal grandmother. It was apparent to me and everyone else that Becky and Sandy were experiencing tremendous agony over the sudden and tragic loss of their dad.

Jerry's widow was attired in a wrinkled gray-blue dress. She appeared happy and content as she sat in her chair. She turned around in her seat and started talking to Debbie, who was sitting right behind her. Lou Ann's clothing and entire behavior at the grave site seemed to be very distasteful, demeaning, and utterly dreadful.

I trained my eyes on the cheerful widow. I watched as she kicked off her scuffed-up shoes, stretching out her legs in front of her, as though she were on a leisurely and enjoyable picnic or outing. She showed no outward signs of heartbreak or grief. I soon noticed her hairy legs. It seemed obvious that Lou Ann did not care much for her husband. I tired of looking at the merry widow and glanced around the cemetery. I quickly spotted Sheriff Bogard and some other men nearby. The sight of the sheriff and other unidentified men proved the authorities were keeping a close eye on the widow and her friends.

When the grave site service ended, my son and daughter walked directly over to me. The three of us stood in a small circle hugging and comforting each other. Jerry's friends and acquaintances came over to our threesome, offering their condolences. Some said they knew how much I meant to my children. Many provided their addresses and telephone numbers. A few even offered an attorney's phone number. I noticed that most of the people who attended the grave site service were standing with me and my children, while only a handful were over by Jerry's widow and her family.

Sheriff Bogard walked over to us and offered his condolences. Then he asked Sandy and Becky to point out their dad's business associates.

As the sheriff was talking to my children, I observed Lou Ann get into the limousine she had ridden in earlier. Because of the soaring temperature, all the windows in the limo were rolled down. I moved to a position where I could watch her. The sun was shining in such a way that I could clearly see Lou Ann with a broad fixed grin on her face. She was totally unaware that I was watching her. I had the impression the grinning widow was enjoying the occasion. She started laughing, as if someone had told her a funny joke. It seemed her husband's funeral was a source of amusement for her. It was as if she knew she would be laughing all the way to the bank. I had always believed Lou Ann was deceitful. But now I felt she was depraved and wicked. She seemed to be enjoying the pain and anguish that my children were going through. A deep pain tore through me. I was suddenly sick to my stomach. I turned away from the unforgettable sight.

Lou Ann and her family left Crestview Cemetery in their limo. Sandy and Marcy left in another one. Becky remained behind at the grave site with me. She was standing under the canopy tent beside her dad's coffin. I kept a watchful eye on her as she began talking to her friend, Justin Garland*.

Sheriff Bogard walked over and stood beside me.

"That was quite a spectacle the widow put on. I can't believe that woman was sitting in the funeral car laughing. A person would think the woman could at least act like she was in mourning. After all, she was burying her husband, who just died a horrible death. I noticed your kids were crying their eyes out. If I wasn't sure before, I'm sure now that she poisoned Sternadel to death. I'm also fairly sure she had help killing him, and by God, I'm going to prove it, if it's the last thing I ever do. We'll see who has the last laugh."

I responded, "Seeing her carrying on like that made me sick to my stomach. I will help you every way I can in the investigation. I believe Lou Ann poisoned Jerry, and I also think she had help doing it. Lou Ann never made any bones about how much she hated me. But it looks like she hated Jerry too."

"Well, the first person I'd point a finger at who helped her would be the bookkeeper. If the autopsy confirms my suspicion that your ex-husband died from ingesting arsenic, then his death will be officially ruled a homicide. We already know he was poisoned. We're going to investigate the circumstances and go from there. We were just waiting for the funeral service to be over with. We don't know where the arsenic came from, but it's not difficult to obtain. It's found in rat poison and other pesticides. Come by my office when you get a chance. This is a rare investigation for the Clay County Sheriff's Department. We're going to need all the help we can get."

Bogard patted me on the back and went over to my daughter to say a few words to her. A little later he walked to his patrol car, got in it, and drove away.

I looked around the grave site and saw a man in a dark suit standing near the casket. I approached him and asked if he knew where I could find the grave tender. He said he was the grave tender. I explained to the gentleman that my daughter wanted to say her last goodbye to her dad and put a Father's Day card into his coffin. I asked if he would open the casket for her. The grave tender said he would be glad to open the coffin after everyone else had left.

I glanced around the burial site. I saw Debbie Baker and her husband, Tony Baker, standing by the side of a luxury car. Tony was talking on a phone. I instantly recognized the automobile. It was Jerry's Lincoln Town Car. I knew how protective and sentimental Jerry was about that car. It incensed me that the Bakers were driving Jerry's luxury car. But I was very curious as to why the Bakers were hanging around the cemetery, especially when everyone else had already left.

Instinctively, I reached inside my purse and retrieved my camera. I quickly pointed it at the Bakers and started snapping photos. I joked to myself that maybe the Bakers were scared Becky and I were going to steal the corpse. But my more serious thought was that perhaps the Bakers thought I was looking for evidence. I told the grave tender that everyone had left. He promptly opened the lid to the coffin, while I watched Debbie and Tony Baker out the corner of my eye.

Chair set up for Jeannie Walker at the grave site

**Debra and Tony Baker hanging around after
the grave site service for Jerry Sternadel**

When the Bakers saw Jerry's casket was being opened, Tony immediately hung up the car phone and trotted toward the grave site. I raised my camera, pointing it squarely at him. He abruptly stopped at a small tree just short of the burial site. I walked toward him, and he began slowly backing away. I kept snapping photos until he turned and raced back to the car where Debbie was waiting. When Tony reached the car, Debbie handed him the car phone. Just before I was directly upon the two nosy bodies, they jumped into the Lincoln Town Car and sped away.

I walked back to the grave site where my daughter was placing Father's Day cards and photos into her dad's coffin.

Becky Sternadel putting Father's Day card into her dad's coffin

Jeannie Walker was glad she was able to say her final
goodbye to her ex-husband, Jerry Sternadel

Sheriff Jake Bogard in his office at Henrietta, Texas

After the funeral, I decided to stay in Texas for a few weeks. I wanted to be with my children. Plus, I had a hankering to help in every way I could with the murder investigation. I drove to Henrietta to speak with the sheriff.

Jake Bogard had been sheriff for over sixteen years and had been in law enforcement for even longer than that. The rugged lawman was born on the RO Ranch near the Texas Panhandle. His dad worked in the oil field and bought a farm in Beulah. His grandfather was Dusty Rhodes from Sur, Texas. He had three sisters—Opal Roberts and Tommie Ann Gaston, both of Junction, Texas, and Barbara Kinnison of Seagraves, Texas—and a brother, Dusty, a cowboy.

In his younger days, Jake was a cowboy and worked on ranches in the panhandle. Jake was a well-built man with slightly graying brown hair, gray sideburns, and graying eyebrows. He looked like a lawman that a criminal wouldn't want to tangle with.

"Have a seat, young lady. I'm glad you came in today. Jeannie, I'll be brutally honest with you. A lot of fingers are pointing toward your son. Lou Ann and Debbie Baker are saying he hated his dad and wanted him dead. Some others are saying Sandy was the one who had the motive and opportunity to kill Sternadel. Right now, he is our prime suspect."

Wasting no time in replying, I said, "Sheriff, I can tell you for a fact, Sandy did not have anything to do with his dad's murder."

"Well, he's got a lawyer and won't talk to us. So that's kind of suspicious. Personally, I think Sandy is innocent. But we will find out one way or another."

I told the sheriff about Debbie and Tony Baker hanging around at the cemetery after everyone else had left. I said I had taken pictures of the Bakers.

"Could you make me copies of those photos?"

I said I would gladly make him copies. After leaving the sheriff's office, I immediately called Sandy and asked him to meet me. I loved my son to pieces, but I knew how hardheaded he could be. I was hoping he would listen to what I had to say.

Sandy met with me and we talked. He said he would try to abide by my wishes but was going to take his lawyer's advice above all else.

"Mother, you know I didn't have anything to do with Daddy's death. But those two women might try to frame me. I don't trust Lou Ann or Debbie or Tony Baker. I'm going to do whatever the lawyer tells me to do."

I replied, "I would feel a lot more comfortable if you were not living out at the ranch, especially while Lou Ann is out there. I'm glad you know you can't trust Lou Ann or Debbie or Tony. I believe they are all involved in the murder of your dad. Please be careful, son! I don't want to lose you too."

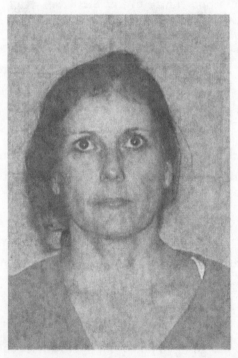

Mug shot of Debra Lynn Baker taken at the Clay County Jail

A Murder Suspect

Debra Lynn Newberry was born on August 5, 1956, in Hamlin, Texas, to Minnie Janice and Earl Wayne Newberry. Janice was twenty-two and Wayne was twenty-five. Their first child had been a boy who was stillborn. Janice and Wayne were obviously overjoyed at the birth of their second child, who was a healthy baby girl.

Wayne was a foreman with a construction company. Janice was a housewife. They lived in Stonewall County in the small town of Aspermont.

It seemed to relatives that as Wayne and Janice's daughter grew, she was becoming a very spoiled and difficult child. At five feet, eight inches, Debra was taller than most girls. She had dishwater-brown hair and piercing brown eyes. People who knew Debra said she had a peculiar personality along with a bad temper.

In 1963, when Debra was a teenager, her father took a job as assistant manager of White's Auto Store in Wichita Falls, Texas, and moved his family there. Wayne loved his job and had the respect and admiration of all his employees.

It was sometime in the seventies that Debra Newberry met Tony Baker.

Tony Lyn Baker was born on January 7, 1954, in Bonham, Texas, to Mr. and Mrs. Charles Baker.

On July 17, 1970, at the age of sixteen, Tony married Brenda Faye Walden. Minister Randall J. Johnson of Wichita Falls performed the marriage ceremony.

On April 21, 1971, Wayne Newberry's health suddenly began to deteriorate. Until then, Wayne had always been healthy and in good physical condition. His doctor, Dr. J. B. Hathorn, Jr., seemingly could find no reason for the unexpected decline in his middle-aged patient's health and could not determine the cause. Within a short period of time, Wayne's continuing bad health forced him to retire as assistant manager of White's Auto Store. Soon he went into a nursing home.

Within a few years after they wed, the Bakers' marriage was on the rocks. Brenda filed for divorce from Tony.

On April 7, 1975, a trial was held on the merits of a divorce between Brenda and Tony Baker in the 89th District Court of Wichita County.

On April 13, 1975, Debra's dad began having chest pains and difficulty breathing. The nurses at Woods Nursing Home in Wichita Falls immediately called Dr. Hathorn.

Wayne died in Woods Nursing Home at 1:33 PM on April 13. His body was taken to the Hampton Vaughn Funeral Home in Wichita Falls.

On April 15, 1975, Wayne Newberry rested in an open casket at Hampton Vaughn. People who visited the funeral home said Wayne's body was badly swollen.

Attending the funeral were Wayne's widow and daughter, Janice and Debra, and two of Janice's half-sisters. Wayne was buried in the Rochester Cemetery in Haskell, Texas.

A relative of Wayne later recalled that Wayne started getting sick with nausea, vomiting, and diarrhea in the early 1970s. The relative remembered that for some unknown reason, Wayne just couldn't seem to recover from what the doctors thought was a bout of influenza. Wayne gradually became sicker and sicker. He began having trouble keeping his balance and standing. Eventually, his poor health forced him to retire from the job he loved. His face, arms, legs, and entire body became very swollen. Soon Wayne became paralyzed and was unable to walk or move his extremities.

People who knew Wayne Newberry couldn't explain how he had suddenly become so sick and deteriorated so badly. Wayne's friends and employees knew him to be a man who was in good shape and full of vim and vigor.

It was believed that Wayne's teenage daughter, Debra, had persuaded her mother, Janice, to put Wayne into a nursing home in Wichita Falls. People believed Debra told her mother that taking care of Wayne's failing health was just too much for them to handle. They believed Debra kept saying that her dad would be better off in a nursing home.

Janice reluctantly put Wayne into the Woods Nursing Home located on Seventh Street in Wichita Falls. She visited her husband there every day.

Debra also made frequent visits to see her dad in the nursing home. She would push him around the nursing home in his wheelchair. On many occasions, Debra brought her dad his favorite foods that she personally cooked. She even baked her dad his best-loved cookies.

Wayne always perked up when his daughter walked into his room with a plate of goodies. Debra was the apple of his eye. Janice thought Debra was a good daughter for doing these things.

Debra's constant visits to the nursing home and the fact that she brought her father his favorite foods, along with his favorite drinks, impressed the employees of the nursing home. They thought Debra was the ideal daughter, one who doted on her dad and would do anything for him.

Janice Newberry was a dispatcher for the Wichita Falls Police Department and had lived in Wichita Falls for fourteen years. Not long after her husband's death, Janice started getting sick. She became nauseated, weak, and dizzy. Debra started telling everyone that her mother had diabetes and that the insulin injections were making her nauseous and weak.

Debra took over running the Newberry household. It seemed to people that it was easier for Janice to let her teenage daughter have her way than to quarrel with her.

Relatives said Janice did not think well of the twenty-one-year-old man Debra was dating. Janice did not care for the macho, five-foot-ten-inch chap who wore his hair in a butch haircut. She didn't like Tony Baker or his reputation.

Janice had learned Tony Baker was a married man and that his wife had filed for a divorce. Janice and Debra squabbled a lot over Debra's spending so much time with Tony.

On October 3, 1975, the divorce decree for Brenda and Tony Baker became official. There were no children born or adopted by this marriage, and none were expected.

Brenda was awarded a 1972 Buick Riviera, a Zenith TV-stereo combination, and all of the personal property and personal effects in her possession. Tony was awarded the auto in his possession, tape player, and all personal property and personal effects in his possession.

On November 24, 1975, seven months after her dad's death, Debra Newberry married Tony Baker. Justice of the Peace Eldon O. Morris of Burkburnett, Texas, performed the ceremony. Debra was nineteen and Tony was twenty-one.

On August 25, 1976, Debra Baker gave birth to a son, Charles Wayne Lee Baker. After the birth, people were of the opinion that Janice let her daughter order her around just so she could be around her grandson.

On November 26, 1977, the morning after Thanksgiving, Janice became very ill and collapsed. Debra called for an ambulance.

At 8:54 AM, Janice was a DOA at the Wichita General Hospital in Wichita Falls. Two days later, her body was transported to Hampton Vaughn Funeral Home. After the funeral service, she was buried next to her husband, Wayne, in the Rochester Cemetery in Haskell, Texas.

Relatives and friends were in shock over Janice's sudden death. It seemed that one day she was healthy and then, only a few months later, she was dead.

After the funeral service, Janice's relatives went over to the Newberry house to get a few things by which to remember their beloved Janice. Debra told them her mother had been throwing up all over the place and that she was too embarrassed to let them in the house because it was a big mess. She wouldn't even open the door wide enough for anyone to look inside the home.

The relatives told Debra they didn't care if the house was messy. They said they would even clean the house for her. Surely, Debra could understand why they wanted something as a remembrance of her dear mother. But Debra remained steadfast. She would not let anybody into the house.

Since Debra was an only child, there was nothing Janice's relatives could do but leave.

It seemed Debra wasn't sure how her mother had died. She told relatives it was from a stroke but told other people it was from diabetes.

As the sole beneficiary, Debra Baker inherited her mother's entire estate and life insurance policy.

Jerry Sternadel having a good laugh on his wife,
Lou Ann, at a family gathering

Search for Justice

In the early 1980s, Debra Baker ran into an old acquaintance named Lou Ann. She learned her friend was married to a wealthy Wichita Falls businessman. Debra told Lou Ann that she was unemployed and needed a job.

Lou Ann knew her husband was looking for a bookkeeper for his plumbing business. She told Debra she would try to get her the job. Lou Ann told her husband that an old friend of hers was a bookkeeper and desperately needed a job. Jerry hired her.

As the years passed, Debra and Lou Ann Sternadel became more than close friends. They became inseparable. They were so close that they kept no secrets from each other. It seemed to some people that Debra and Lou Ann might be lovers.

Meanwhile, Lou Ann and Jerry grew to hate each other. They went for weeks without exchanging a civil word to each other. For some time, they had lived very separate lives while residing in the same house. Lou Ann had been sleeping on the couch in the living room for over a year. Lou Ann and Jerry fought a lot about Lou Ann's unwavering and unusual friendship with Debra Baker.

The Sternadel household became charged with evil, as tension festered and tempers boiled over. It was only a matter of time before the fuse on the time bomb was lit in the Texas love triangle. After the bomb went off, Jerry Sternadel wound up dead.

After Jerry's funeral, I remained in Texas. My son was staying out at the ranch where Lou Ann and her daughter, Holly, were living and where Debra Baker stayed most of the time. I was worried about Sandy. But no matter how hard I tried, I could not talk my son into moving into town and getting an apartment.

Sandy said he was going to stay out at the ranch for as long as it took to protect his dad's property and personal belongings. He informed me that Lou Ann had hired Debbie's husband and that Tony Baker was taking inventory of everything his dad owned.

"Daddy would turn over in his grave if he knew Tony Baker was doing that. Daddy didn't allow Tony to set one foot on the ranch. He despised Tony. He wanted to fire Debbie, especially in the last few years. But Lou Ann always stood up for Debbie and helped her keep her job. I always thought something was going on between Debbie and Lou Ann. I know the only reason Lou Ann stayed with Daddy was for the money. But I don't know why Debbie kept working for Daddy. I know that checks were bouncing all over the place. Debbie and Lou Ann started telling Daddy that the post office was losing the checks they mailed out. I told Daddy what Debbie and Lou Ann were saying was bullshit, that the post office didn't lose my checks or anybody else's checks."

I advised my son to tell the sheriff everything he knew.

Sandy said, "I've retained a lawyer, and I will get his advice on what to do. But no matter what, I plan on living out at the ranch to keep an eye on things."

My son seemed to be handling his dad's death a lot better than my daughter, Becky, who was having a very difficult time and was under a doctor's care. I drove to Arlington to be with her and help her cope. At my request, Becky gave her doctor permission to discuss her treatment with me. The doctor told me, "Your daughter has a lot of mental issues. She told me that she and her dad argued a lot. She feels that somehow she is to blame for his death."

I asked the physician, "What would you do if Becky were your daughter?"

The doctor responded, "If I were you, I would stay with her as long as I could. I believe your daughter is suicidal. At this point in time, she needs to be treated with a lot of love and compassion. From what Becky has told me, she depends on you a lot more than you think. She needs you for mental support. She will do much better with you around. I'm afraid of what she might do if she doesn't have you to lean on."

After speaking to Becky's doctor, I called my employer on Long Island. I explained the situation I was in and said it was critical for me to remain in Texas a little while longer. My boss said he empathized with me, but he also had a business to run and needed me to get back right away. "I'll have to hire someone else if you decide to stay in Texas."

Once again, I had to choose between money and my children's welfare. It was not a hard decision to make. I stayed in Texas.

When my daughter started feeling better, both physically and mentally, I drove back to Wichita Falls to check with the sheriff on the investigation. Sheriff Bogard welcomed me into his office. In his slow Texas drawl, he said, "Well, I'll be honest with you: if you didn't live in New York, you would be a suspect. I'm finding out how shabbily Sternadel treated you in the past. For all intents and purposes, it seems Sternadel was a mean and ornery S-O-B. Matter of fact, I was wondering why you don't feel like some other people do. We've had more than one person say Jerry was a rat and was killed like a rat."

"Jerry did a lot of things to me that were very hurtful. I loved Jerry, but I didn't like the things he did to himself and to others. However, in the last few years, he honestly seemed to be changing. Anyway, I thought he was finally changing for the better. The last time I talked to Jerry was like talking to an old friend. We planned to sit down and have coffee together when I came to Texas over the summer. Through the years, I've been praying that Jerry and I could become friends. I truly believe the good Lord was finally making it happen. In one conversation that I had with Jerry, he apologized for the hurt he caused me. Down deep inside, Jerry was tenderhearted. But he kept that side of himself well hidden. One of the reasons I will do everything to help you put the people who poisoned Jerry behind bars is because I truly believe Jerry was changing into a God-fearing person. Let alone the fact he was my children's father."

"Well, I just wanted to clear the air. One by one, people who were acquainted with Sternadel are talking to us and giving statements. I received a call from Tambra Thornton. She said she was a partner with Sternadel on several horses. She believes Lou Ann and Debbie Baker murdered Sternadel. She said when she visited him at the hospital he told her that Lou Ann and Debbie were trying to kill him. He pointed at Lou Ann and Debbie and said, 'Those women are trying to kill me. They're feeding me a bunch of shit. And when I get out of the hospital, I'm going to get a divorce.'

"Tambra said she told the doctor what Sternadel was saying, but the doctor just said Sternadel was hallucinating. Tambra said after Sternadel died, she knew he wasn't hallucinating.

"She also said that one day before he died, she went out to the ranch to collect a bill that was owed her. Debbie Baker made out the check and Lou Ann signed it. Sternadel walked into the office at about that time and flew into a rage, saying, 'Nobody is to give a check without my permission.' Tambra said Sternadel called Lou Ann and Debbie everything in the book, and when she saw Debbie the next day, Debbie had bumps and bruises on her arm. But Debbie wouldn't tell Tambra how she got the bruises. Debbie said, 'Don't ask!' Tambra said in the past she had seen Sternadel beat Lou Ann."

I responded, "Jerry would not let anyone write a check without his knowledge. I know that for a fact. By the way, Sheriff, did you ever get permission to search the ranch?"

"Yep, the Texas Ranger, my deputy, and I met Lou Ann and Debbie at Sternadel's office, located right behind the ranch. Lou Ann gave me permission to remove anything I thought might be of use in the investigation. We took several items and sent them to the lab in Dallas to be tested for arsenic. Lou Ann told me that the day Sternadel died, she borrowed $25,000 from the bank and had Debbie Baker's name put on the bank account."

"Did Lou Ann tell you why she borrowed the $25,000?"

"Well, she said it was for funeral expenses. Funny thing, though ... Lou Ann borrowed the money on the morning of June 12, but Sternadel didn't die until that afternoon. Debbie Baker said she had never signed any checks in the past and that the check to the funeral home was the first one. She filled out the checks, and either Lou Ann or Jerry always signed them. Debbie said she worked for Sternadel Plumbing for seven or eight years. Excuse me, somebody's calling me on the squawk box."

After speaking to the sheriff, I drove back to Arlington to be with my daughter. There I received an unexpected phone call from a friend in Wichita Falls. The friend asked if I had heard anything about a teenager being poisoned out at Jerry's ranch. I had not. I thanked my friend for the information and immediately called the sheriff.

"You find out things fast, don't you? Well, I received a call from Mrs. Russell Bradley. She had heard about the investigation of a poisoning concerning Sternadel. Her grandson spent Friday night, the first of June, with Sternadel's stepdaughter, Holly. Mrs. Bradley said her grandson got very sick the next morning after drinking some Cran-Apple juice that was in the refrigerator at the Sternadel ranch. He was taken to the Wichita Falls Clinic and treated for what the doctors thought was a virus. She also said Holly's mother, Lou Ann Sternadel, came to the clinic. Mrs. Bradley's daughter and son-in law drove to pick up her grandson at the clinic, and when they went to pay the medical bill, they were told the bill was already paid."

I exclaimed, "You don't say! Well, that is very interesting."

"Well, I thought you'd think so. I talked to the grandson, Thomas Bradley. He said he had stayed the night with Holly Maag at the Sternadel ranch. Holly was just someone he had met at his stepsister's wedding and occasionally saw at the restaurant. He said the only reason he spent the night at Sternadel's place was because he didn't feel comfortable staying at one of his other friends' houses. When he got up the next morning, he poured himself a glass of Cran-Apple juice from the refrigerator. He said the two-liter bottle had about half of the contents remaining after he poured his glass full. His throat burned immediately after drinking the juice, and five or ten minutes later, he started throwing up and having diarrhea. He said Holly had a glass of milk and that nobody else was at the Sternadel home except Sandy, Holly's stepbrother.

"The kid said he drank the juice at about 10:40 AM, and was taken to the clinic that afternoon by Holly. He said he felt so sick he thought he might die. He told me Holly's mother came to the clinic for a few minutes while he was there and he thought Lou Ann paid the bill. He also said Holly's mother talked to his mother and stepfather before she left the clinic. I advised the boy to go have toxicology tests done. Funny thing, though … when I talked to Lou Ann, she never made any mention of Thomas Bradley or any boy getting sick in her home or going to the clinic and paying his bill."

After that conversation, I called the sheriff every day to find out if anything new had happened.

On June 26, 1990, Sheriff Bogard informed me that he had received the results from the arsenic test of Tommy Bradley. "That kid had 278 micrograms of arsenic in his system. We've still got to wait on the results of hair samples from Dallas."

"That poor boy was an innocent victim," I replied. "He just happened to be in the wrong place at the wrong time, and it will probably affect him the rest of his life."

"Well, I hope not! Did I tell you that Debbie Baker called us over the weekend? She said they found the Cran-Apple juice container. I think it's the one that the boy drank from. It was real nice of them to wash it out for us."

"What! They washed out the bottle?"

"Yep! They went and dug the juice bottle out of the trash pit behind Sternadel's barn. The outside of the bottle was all muddy, but the inside had soapsuds in it. Funny thing, though … me and my deputies and the

Texas Ranger had already searched that trash pit from top to bottom and didn't find any juice bottle. Then they go and pluck it out from the top of the trash pit."

"I sure hope it is the Cran-Apple juice bottle that had arsenic in it!" I quickly replied.

"Yeah, we're all hoping it is the original container. Lou Ann and Debbie may have done us a favor when they tried to wash it out. If there was any arsenic in that bottle, the water may have activated it. I'm sending it to the crime lab tomorrow. Jeannie, you do know that everything I tell you is strictly in confidence, don't you?"

"Yes, Sheriff. I know that. Anything you tell me stays with me. You have my word that I will keep everything you tell me confidential."

"Good," he said. "I'm going to tell you something else, in confidence. One of Sternadel's friends visited him in the hospital. He said it was around June 7. This friend said Sternadel told him that Lou Ann and Debbie Baker were killing him. Sternadel asked him for help to get out of the hospital and away from Lou Ann and Debbie Baker. Sternadel said he discovered $35,000 that Lou Ann and Debbie Baker had stolen from him. The friend said that Lou Ann and Debbie Baker were at the door of the hospital room and heard what Sternadel was saying. He said that he was embarrassed by what Sternadel had been telling him and told him he would be back that afternoon. Sternadel told him, 'It'll be too late then. They are out to kill me.' The friend said Lou Ann told him Sternadel was out of his mind and didn't know what he was saying. Lou Ann said, 'Why, only this morning Jerry told me he hated me.' Sternadel's friend said he left the hospital room right after that. Jeannie, you do understand this is not to be repeated to anyone, not even to your kids. You do understand this is strictly confidential?"

"Yes, sir, I do. Wild horses couldn't drag it out of me."

"Well, we still have a long way to go before we can make an arrest. I want to make sure we get everyone who was involved in the murder. That's all I've got right now. I have an idea I'll be talking to you in a few days. Don't worry, I'll keep you posted."

A week later, I spoke to Bogard again.

"Well, we had Lou Ann and her attorney in for a talk. We caught Lou Ann in a few lies, but we didn't contest it. We're just going to keep building the case."

"What did she say?" I questioned.

"She told us the boy who got sick was someone she didn't even know. She said she stopped at the pharmacy to pick up a prescription for Sternadel and saw the boy sick and vomiting in the parking lot and felt sorry for the kid."

"Oh, really," I said, as I pressed the telephone receiver closer to my ear. The sheriff had a tendency to talk more softly as he went along.

"Lou Ann also told us she poured the Cran-Apple juice out on June 14, because people were bringing food over and she needed the room in her refrigerator. She said there was only a little juice left in the bottle when she poured it down the sink. We also had a talk with Debbie Baker. Debbie admitted to giving some Cran-Apple juice to Sternadel just before he went into the hospital on his last visit. Debbie said she didn't know the juice had arsenic in it."

"So, Lou Ann is admitting she poured the Cran-Apple juice out and Debbie Baker is admitting giving Cran-Apple juice to Jerry."

"Well, that's what they are saying."

"That is very, very interesting!" I replied. "I'm sure this information will help you with the case. Sheriff, I've been getting anonymous calls telling me to stop causing trouble and to go back to New York. Do you think I am putting pressure on Lou Ann by staying in Texas?"

"Just the fact that you are still in Texas will aggravate her. Maybe you should stay here a little longer. You won't be in my way."

"I might just do that. Thank you, Sheriff, for everything you're doing."

After hanging up the phone, I thought how Bogard reminded me of the sheriffs in the Old West who would jump on their horses and ride until they caught the thieving, murderous culprits. I decided I was going to stay in Texas as long as it took for my daughter to get back some semblance of good health and to help the sheriff any way I could.

I called Sandy and asked if I could talk to his attorney. Sandy was reluctant at first but then gave me permission. The next day, I called the attorney.

He said, "I want you to know that the only reason I am talking with you is because Sandy gave me permission to do so."

I thanked him for speaking with me and told him the sheriff needed to talk to my son.

"I don't know what the sheriff wants to talk to Sandy about," he replied.

"The sheriff wants to talk to my son about the murder of his dad."

"Yes, I know that!" the attorney said with a disgusted abruptness.

"Did you know before Sandy's father died that a boy got sick after drinking juice out of the ranch?"

"Yes, I know that too."

"So are you going to let my son talk to the sheriff?"

"I don't know yet! By the way, where are you getting all your information? If it is from the sheriff, I'd be very careful what I told him if I were you. He can change things around."

I replied, "I am only interested in my son's welfare!"

"I hope you understand that my client is my main concern. I will discuss this case only with my client. I'm sorry, but that's the way it is. I'll tell Sandy you called and asked about him."

I found it hard to believe that my son needed to hire an attorney. I was very sure the sheriff didn't think Sandy had anything to do with his dad's murder. The sheriff had even made a point to tell me that Sandy was a potential witness, not a suspect. But I was glad I got to speak with my son's attorney, even though it didn't seem to have done much good.

A couple days later, I made the decision to find out the name of the friend who had spoken to Jerry in the hospital. I was in luck. The friend was Jerry Gamble. Through the years, I had kept in contact with Gamble. I didn't think he would mind my calling him.

We spoke for a few minutes before I got down to the main reason why I was calling.

"I heard you visited Jerry in the hospital before he died. I also heard that Jerry told you Lou Ann and Debbie were trying to kill him and Jerry told you they had stolen $35,000 from him? Can you tell me if this is true?"

There was a lingering silence before Gamble replied. "I believe I said something like that. I signed a written statement for the Texas Ranger and the sheriff. They told me not to discuss it with anyone. So I hope you understand why I can't talk to you about it. If it comes down to it, I'll stand up in court and tell the truth about what Jerry told me. I hate what happened to Jerry. I wish I could have done something to prevent his death. I know what happened is hard on you and the kids. The last time I saw Becky, she was in high school and working part-time at a drugstore in town. I hope your kids are doing fine. Be sure and tell them I'm very sorry about what happened to their dad."

"I understand. I'll give my kids your condolences. Thanks for talking with me. By the way, do you know Jim Sigafus? He said he was Jerry's foreman."

"Yeah, I know Jim. I thought he had been working for Jerry only a few months, but I can't be sure. Time passes so fast. I didn't know he was Jerry's foreman, though. Hey, it's been nice talking to you. I hope next time it is under better circumstances."

On the morning of June 27, I got up very early. I started scanning the newspaper to see if there was anything in it about the murder investigation. There was an article that mentioned new evidence. I finished reading it just as the phone rang. It was Bogard.

"Hi, Jeannie, I heard you called me yesterday. How are things going?"

"Hi, Sheriff. It's going fine! I just read an article in the newspaper about new evidence being discovered."

"Yeah, that was about the Cran-Apple juice bottle. It's at the lab. No results yet. Thought I'd let you know I've got Holly Maag coming in for a sit-down today. Debbie Baker is scheduled for a polygraph on July 17. Sandy and his lawyer are supposed to come in for a talk on July 3. Lou Ann and her lawyer say she won't take the polygraph. That's about it for now. Anything new with you?"

"I hope you don't mind, but I called Jerry Gamble. I told him the lawyer for the wrongful death suit wants to talk to him."

"Well, don't let Becky call him. She doesn't have any business calling Gamble or anyone else. You know how she is. She'll get too upset," Bogard said in a firm voice.

"I had an argument with my daughter about that very thing yesterday. I told her not to call Jerry Gamble. But she doesn't understand why she shouldn't call."

The sheriff replied, "I'll call and talk to Becky's lawyer and have him explain things to her. I'll call you later on today, after we have a talk with Holly."

"Sheriff, would you call Becky? She is understandably upset and wants to talk to you. She said you have the number where she works."

"Sure, I'll call Becky. I have her number. Talk to you later on."

At 4:30 PM, I received another call from the sheriff.

"Jeannie, I've got some good news. Sandy called and said he wanted to talk. He volunteered to come down to my office and answer some questions. He said he was doing this against his lawyer's advice."

"Oh, I am so glad. I was praying Sandy would talk to you. I know he doesn't have anything to hide. Did you get to talk to Holly?"

"Yeah, I talked to Holly. Her story has changed since the first time I talked to her. She sounds like she has been coached. The statement Holly gave us today is almost identical to Lou Ann's yarn. I wasn't surprised that Holly changed her story. The first time I talked to Holly was when I was out searching the Sternadel warehouse. Holly approached me. I didn't go up to her and ask questions. She volunteered the information about her friend getting sick and Lou

Ann going to the hospital and paying the boy's bills. Holly was telling the truth then. Now her story has completely changed around. But we'll get to the bottom of it.

"Holly said she would not take a polygraph. I'll have to wait for the test results from Dallas before we proceed. So I'm going to take Saturday and Sunday off. Before I hang up, next week is the July 4 holiday, and I'm going to go to a rodeo at Ardmore, Oklahoma. I'll talk to you sometime next week. Tell Becky that I could not get through to her at work.

"I almost forgot to tell you this interesting piece of information we just found out. Seems someone went to the public library in Wichita Falls around January or February and checked out two books on poisons and poisoning. Interesting little tidbit, wouldn't you say?" It sounded like the sheriff had a little glee in his voice.

I replied, "I'd sure like to know who checked out those books."

"So would we, but the library won't give us a name without a subpoena. That's our next step on the books. We've been interviewing more people and finding quite a few whom Jerry had talked to while he was in the hospital.

"Some of these people say they could kick themselves in the ass for not listening to him. They say Jerry was asking everyone for help. I talked to the doctor. Seems he is saying something different now than what he put in the medical report. I'll let you know more on that when I get all the details. Right now, we've got a lot more hard work ahead. Listen, it's late. I'm tired. I'm going home to take a long bath. It's been a scorching week. Talk to you when Sandy comes in."

Chief Deputy Paul Bevering on the phone discussing the case

Texas Ranger William Gerth, who helped investigate the murder

Jeannie Walker speaking with Sheriff Jake Bogard

On the Fourth of July, I drove my daughter to Wichita Falls. We went to Crestview Cemetery to place some fresh flowers on her dad's grave. On the way back to Arlington, we stopped off at the sheriff's office in Henrietta. The sheriff was in Oklahoma, but Chief Deputy Paul Bevering said they were working on putting a big crack in the case.

On July 6, the judge in Clay County granted a motion submitted by Bill Browning, Lou Ann's lawyer. The motion was asking the judge for permission to sell all the cattle and put the proceeds into the plumbing business. When the judge signed the motion, Lou Ann promptly sold everything she could for pennies on the dollar.

True to his word, the sheriff called me after my son came in to talk with him.

"I wanted you to know Sandy did come in to talk with us. He said he didn't know who killed his dad, but he wanted to help us catch whoever poisoned him. He said he had told Lou Ann about Holly's boyfriend getting sick after he drank Cran-Apple juice from the refrigerator. Right after he told her, she rushed to the clinic to see about the boy.

"I asked Sandy if he thought his sister had a right to contest the will. He said, 'She most certainly does, but I don't want to join her. I don't want the money. I only want to find out who killed our dad.' I asked Sandy if he thought his sister was throwing a monkey wrench into Lou Ann's business dealings by contesting the will. He said, 'It sure is, and I'm glad that she filed.'

"Sandy told me the same story about Thomas Bradley that Holly told me the first time I talked to her. I am sure Sandy is telling the truth that he doesn't know who killed his dad. Holly was telling the truth the first time, but now I am sure she is lying."

I said, "It's pretty obvious Holly is lying. You know, Sheriff, I'm kind of upset with Sandy that he wouldn't go in with his sister on the lawsuit. But I'm glad he came in and talked to you."

"Well, Jeannie, I guess Sandy has his reasons."

On July 16, a friend told me that Lou Ann agreed to take a polygraph test. I telephoned Bogard. "I heard something about Lou Ann taking the polygraph test. And I was wondering if the autopsy and forensic reports have come back."

"I can't really say much about the polygraph. But you can read between the lines. I'll be sending the polygraph results to Becky's attorney. I'll bet between you and your daughter that you can get the results. As far as the lab goes, those folks are sure taking a long time. They must be going over everything with a fine-tooth comb. I'll be glad when we get the results back. I'll keep you posted. Ten-four."

I did manage to get a copy of the polygraph test results, but not from the sheriff. Lou Ann's polygraph showed deception. Debra Baker's polygraph was inconclusive but showed deception on relevant questions.

The next day I called Bogard. "I heard something about diet pills."

"You do get information fast, don't you? Well, Ken and Kathleen Harney came in to see me. They said they were good friends of Jerry and Lou Ann Sternadel. On a trip to Denison, Texas, Lou Ann made some incriminating statements to Kathleen. A day before Sternadel got sick for the first time, Lou Ann gave Kathleen some diet pills.

"Funny thing, though … Lou Ann told Kathleen not to take the pills until after May 21. May 22 was when Sternadel got sick the first time. We heard Sternadel had been taking diet pills. Lou Ann might have opened up the capsules and replaced the medicine with arsenic. That's one way she could feed Sternadel arsenic and he wouldn't know about it. She may have wanted to get rid of Kathleen too, if she thought Kathleen knew too much. Kathleen brought the diet pills to us yesterday. It's a long shot, but we're checking every angle. We've already sent the pills to the forensic lab."

My curiosity was piqued. A few days later, I called Kathleen Harney.

"Did Lou Ann give you some diet pills?"

"Yeah, she did. They were pink capsules," Kathleen replied. "She gave the pills to me the day before Jerry got sick. When Jerry was in the hospital, she walked up to me and asked, 'Have you started taking the diet pills yet?' I thought she should be worried about her sick husband. Instead, she was worried about whether I had taken the diet pills and whether I had any to give back to her. I had gone to Denison with her to look for apartments for the men, 'cause Jerry was starting a job there. I think the trip to Denison was a week or so before Jerry started getting sick. On the way there, Lou Ann blurted out, 'I've never hurt anybody, but if I ever did, it's 'cause I've lost my mind. If anything ever happens to Jerry, I'm moving to Paris.' I asked, 'Paris, France?' She said, 'No! Paris, Texas. That's where my mother lives. If anything ever happens to Jerry, that's where I'm moving.' I thought that was strange. Ken and I went to see the sheriff and I gave him the pills. He said he was sending them off to be analyzed. I don't know if there was anything in those capsules. But, I witnessed Lou Ann and Debbie lying to Jerry and doing other things that are suspicious now. It's a scary thought, though. I almost took some of the pills.

"After Jerry died, Lou Ann ordered my husband to move some cattle so she could sell them. Ken told her that he worked for "Sterny," his nickname for Jerry, and wasn't moving any cattle or any of Jerry's property. She got spitting mad and started cussing, so Ken quit on the spot. We heard the guys who still work out at the ranch are scared to eat or drink anything. Most of Jerry's men have quit because they can't stand Lou Ann.

"The Monday before Jerry got sick, he came over to our house. He was happy and cheerful. He was bragging about the beets he had picked from his garden that day. He asked if we had any tomatoes growing. I told him I had only one tomato. He said, 'Well, you've got me beat on that, but tomorrow we'll be canning beets.' The next day was when he went into the hospital the first time. Ken and I both loved Jerry. He helped us out a lot of times. We feel really bad about Jerry's murder. We wish we could have done something more."

I responded, "You did all you could. Thank you for being good friends and for what you are doing now to help with the murder investigation."

Five weeks had passed since Jerry was murdered. I was physically and mentally exhausted. The pool at the Arlington apartment complex looked very relaxing. "Becky, it's such a nice day outside, let's put our swimsuits on. Lying by the pool will help both of us relax."

The next day, we went to have our hair done. The hairdresser was an attractive lady in her early thirties. She came over to me.

"Becky looks so thin. She has lost a lot of weight. Is she feeling okay?"

"She is having a hard time right now. We just buried her dad a little over a month ago. He was fed arsenic after he discovered his wife and bookkeeper were stealing from him. He was poisoned to death," I said softly, almost in a whisper.

"Oh, my God! That reminds me of a murder committed a few years back. Two men were in business together. One of the partners disappeared. Two years later, they found his body in the back of his pickup truck at the bottom of a lake. The silt from the lake had preserved his body. The police discovered the dead man had been severely beaten about the head. They thought the killer was the man's partner, but they couldn't prove it. About a year after they found the body, the dead man's wife accidentally slipped up and made some incriminating remarks. After her statements, the Texas Rangers started reinvestigating. The widow said she couldn't take the guilt anymore. She confessed that she and her husband's partner were having an affair and paid a couple of men to beat her husband to death. Then they put his body in the cab of his pickup truck and pushed it into the lake. The widow said her husband had found out about her affair and the fact that she and his partner had been stealing thousands of dollars from him. It's chilling to think of the ruthlessness of people who can take another person's life."

I replied, "The sad fact is that there are a lot of ruthless people in this world. But as far as my ex-husband's widow feeling guilty and confessing, I don't think she or the bookkeeper will ever confess. But we can always hope and pray."

On July 18, Sheriff Bogard called me. "Jeannie, would you tell Becky to quit calling the Dallas forensic lab? By law, they cannot tell her anything. The lab told me they have forty-three bodies they are processing from the Dallas area. This number doesn't even include bodies from other areas, including ours. We're doing everything here that is humanly possible to hurry this thing along and make an arrest. Becky is going to have to be patient. Tell her if she needs any information, she needs to contact her attorney."

"Yes, Sheriff, I will tell her. This murder is making her crazy. But I'll do everything I can to get her to stop making phone calls to the forensic lab."

A couple of days later, Bogard told me that he and Bill Gerth had interviewed Tony Baker. They asked Tony about a check that was made out to him for $1,250 from Jerry's checking account. "Tony Baker said it was a loan his wife had made to Lou Ann but later changed his story. We've been finding out Debbie Baker and Lou Ann have been lying quite a lot. We also talked to the nurses at the hospital and took statements and went to see Browning, Lou Ann's civil lawyer. He informed us Lou Ann had hired a criminal attorney. Tony Baker accidentally told us some information that can be used on the case. Another thing we learned was that just before Sternadel got sick, he sold one of his horses for $150,000 cash."

I said, "Jerry received cash anytime he could for anything he sold. He hid the cash from me, the government, and everybody else."

"That reminds me," Sheriff Bogard said. "Do you know a guy by the name of Jimmy Taylor?"

"Yes, I do! Jimmy Taylor and Jerry went to school together and were good friends. As a matter of fact, I found out in a roundabout way that Jerry asked Taylor to hold on to my gold coins so he could hide them from me. The coins were the only things I asked for in our divorce. Jerry agreed to let me have them. The gold coins were worth thousands of dollars. Jerry told me they were stolen, but a friend of Jerry's informed me Jerry took the gold coins over to Taylor to hide them from me. I never did get those gold coins."

"That's interesting," Bogard said. "I talked to Taylor the other day. He said he and Jerry were friends in school. Jerry was always giving him stuff for safekeeping. Maybe the next time I see Taylor, I'll ask him about the gold coins. But I wouldn't count on getting them back if I were you."

"Don't worry, Sheriff. I know I won't ever see those gold coins again."

"Well, Taylor said Jerry loved to put people down, especially those who worked for him. He said Jerry would steal jobs too. Taylor said he stole two jobs from him. He told me Jerry would pad tickets, steal from job sites, and basically do anything for a buck. He also said Jerry tried to put the make on every wife he ever did a plumbing job for. Taylor said back in 1985, Jerry had an affair with a woman who was his secretary years past and spent around $75,000 to buy his girlfriend a house. He said Jerry had $45,000 cash in a brown paper bag and $30,000 in checks and bought the house in Archer City for Janette Burger*. Jerry told Taylor and a couple of other friends he was leaving Lou Ann to go live with the girlfriend. Jerry even sent Lou Ann to live with her mother in Paris, Texas. But as soon as he put the house in the girlfriend's name, she up and shucked him. Jerry was furious and advised the secretary he would get even with her. He hired a private detective to trail and harass the woman. He asked Taylor to break into her house and rob the place. Taylor refused, so Jerry had one of his employees go steal jewelry and furniture that he gave the secretary to get part of his money back from the insurance policy he had on the stuff. A few days later, Jerry had Lou Ann come back home and they filed a civil suit against the secretary."

I said, "Sheriff, I remember Jerry telling me back in 1985 that one of his girlfriends jilted him. He also mentioned something about getting his lawyer to file a suit against her."

"Well, another thing. I don't know if this is true or not. But I was informed Lou Ann caught Jerry in bed with Stella*, her fifteen-year-old daughter. You can bet I'll be checking that out. Well, Jeannie, I hate to leave you on a sour note, but I've got prisoners coming in the door."

What Bogard said about Stella reminded me of a hot and humid day in July 1985, when I received a most unexpected phone call. My daughter had been visiting me on Long Island for a few weeks and had just left to drive back to Texas. When the phone rang that summer day, my first thought was that it was my daughter calling with some kind of car trouble. However, it was Lou Ann's daughter, Stella, on the phone.

Stella asked, "Is Becky there?"

I answered, "No, Becky left to go back to Texas yesterday."

"I really wanted to talk to you. I have to tell somebody. I can't stand it anymore. I'm sick of Jerry forcing me to have sex with him."

"Are you talking about Jerry Sternadel?" I promptly asked.

"Yeah, I'm talking about him. It makes me sick to my stomach every time he touches me. I can't stand him. He makes me sick. I can't stand it anymore."

"If this is true, you need to tell your mother. She needs to know."

"Are you kidding? She's the one making me do it. Every time I tell her I can't do it anymore, she says, 'Do you want us to get kicked out of the house? Jerry would kick us out with no money. It's not hurting you to do this little thing. He always gives you nice things afterwards, don't he?' That's what she tells me."

I was having a hard time fathoming what Jerry's stepdaughter was telling me. "Stella, how old are you? How long has this been happening?"

"I'm seventeen. He started coming into my bedroom at night when I was about twelve. At first, it was just kissing me good night, and then he started doing other things. Disgusting things, I can't say it ... it makes me sick to think about it."

"Will you tell the police what you just told me?"

"No! No, I won't. Mama would kill me if she knew I told you or anybody else. Jerry said he's going to divorce Mama and marry me. I don't want to marry him."

I was in a dilemma. I knew that Lou Ann despised me. In my imagination, I thought Lou Ann might have put her daughter up to calling and telling me this awful tale just to cause me distress. If Stella would not reiterate to the police what she had told me about being sexually molested, then Lou Ann would tell the cops that I was making a false report. She would say I was a jealous ex-wife and resentful of the loving home life she had with Jerry. However, I realized that if my ex-husband was molesting his stepdaughter, I had to do something about it. Stella needed to be in a safe place and away from Jerry Sternadel.

I said, "Stella, there must be someone in Texas you can trust enough to tell what is happening to you. You must get out of that house. Think hard! What about your grandmother?"

"There's my Aunt Jo Ann. I could tell her. She would believe me. She lives in Paris. If I went to live with her, she wouldn't let Mama and Jerry take me back."

"Call your Aunt Jo Ann right now! Tell her what you told me. If she doesn't come and get you, then I'll fly to Texas. I'll make sure you're in a safe haven."

"Okay, I'm going to call her right now."

"Please call me back. Let me know what your aunt says."

Although I waited for a telephone call, Stella did not call back. I learned from friends that Stella's aunt suddenly showed up at the ranch. Although Lou Ann objected, Jo Ann Flippen took Stella to Paris, Texas, to live with her.

It wasn't long after Stella moved to Paris that I learned about Jerry putting a certificate of deposit solely in Lou Ann's name for $100,000. It seemed Lou Ann had demanded $100,000 from Jerry in return for her not turning him in for sexually molesting her daughter. I believed Lou Ann had blackmailed Jerry. He had to give her the money or else he would have faced prison time. It seemed Lou Ann had allegedly prostituted her daughter for $100,000. I thought about telling Sheriff Bogard about Stella's phone call. But I figured he would find out on his own about the sexual molestation and the teenager's subsequent move to Paris.

In the course of trying to find out everything I could, I called Calvin Farr*. I was hoping he remembered me.

"Of course I recall who you are. I don't know how in the world Jerry wound up with that loser he took up with. I'm sure sorry about what happened to Jerry. At first, I couldn't believe it when I heard the gruesome way he died.

"I've been Jerry's official horse trainer for over fifteen years. He owned some real good horses. He spent a lot of money on them and raced the best. He had six horses at my place in Oklahoma and two in New Mexico. About a year ago, Jerry told me he was putting cash in different places here, there, and yonder. I told him he needed to let his wife, Lou Ann, know where the money was, just in case he got killed or something. He said, 'Fuck that bitch. I'm looking after number one.' I said, 'Well, let your kids know.' He said, 'Fuck them too. They don't give a damn about me.' Well, that conversation ended pretty quick. I usually talked to him four or five times a week. When Jerry was sick, his bookkeeper told me he had hepatitis but would recover. Then I heard at the track in Kansas City that he died from arsenic poisoning."

"Could arsenic be in the leg paint that Jerry used for his horses?"

"As far as I know the leg paint don't have arsenic in it. Jerry and Don Gatcher* were in business together making it. It's even got their label, Top Stride No. 1 by S&G Enterprise, that's Sternadel and Gatcher. You might try to find Gatcher in Fort Worth."

"Thanks, I'll do that. If I gave you the number, would you call and talk to the sheriff?"

"Sure, I'll help any way I can."

I gave him Bogard's phone number. Then I began trying to locate Don Gatcher. I was not having any luck. A few days later, I called Calvin.

"I've run into the same thing. It kind of disturbs me, 'cause he's got that one product I use a lot of. I'm out, and I have no way of getting hold of him."

"Did you get a hot check from Jerry?"

"Lou Ann signed the damn check. Jerry's name wasn't on it."

"Did it bounce or did the bank refuse to pay it because it was signed by Lou Ann?"

"It was insufficient. I had gotten it last year when I was going to Ruidosa, New Mexico. Jerry's colt was starting in the Kansas Futurity. I told Lou Ann I had a hot check that she wrote. Either Debbie or Lou Ann asked me to wait a week or so before I ran it back through the bank. I thought that was strange, 'cause Jerry never gave me a check that wasn't any good. He always signed the checks. But the last four or five years, I'd get a check every once in a while, that Lou Ann signed instead of Jerry."

"Do you know what happened to Jerry's horses?"

"There were two horses I had run that weren't going to make Jerry any money on the track again. One of them was named Texas Bandito. He was a pretty nice little horse. I forget what the name of the other horse was. I asked Lou Ann about those two horses when she was selling all that stuff. She said she was going to leave those two horses right where they were, 'cause she talked to Tambra Thornton and made some kind of deal with her.

"I thought I could get Gatcher's number. Hell, I told the sheriff I didn't think it was no problem at all. I had about a half inch of the leg paint that I actually needed and was using on a horse at the time. But, I told the sheriff I would package it up and send it to him so he could send it to the lab. He seems to think this particular leg paint has got some arsenic in it. As far as it having arsenic in it, I don't know!

"Like I told the sheriff, if there are other questions or anything, you just need to holler. Nobody deserves that. If you want to kill somebody, take a gun and blow their head off. Don't make them die slowly and suffer."

**Jeannie Walker meeting with Sheriff Jake Bogard and
Chief Deputy Paul Bevering in Henrietta, Texas**

I spent a lot of time flying back and forth between New York and Texas. But when I did fly to Texas, I always made a point to visit with Sheriff Bogard.

"Well, Jeannie, we learned the diet pills did not have any arsenic in them. So, that's not the way they were poisoning Sternadel. We've found out a lot of things about the suspects and the deceased. We talked to Jerry's number-one man, Jim Sigafus. He worked on plans and ran the business when Jerry was away. He said Jerry was a hard man to work for but did not lie. Sigafus knew Debbie Baker was stealing from Jerry through accounts payable to get money for herself. When Debbie became aware Sigafus knew of her scheme, she started telling Jerry lies about the foreman. Her lies caused a lot of friction between Sigafus and Jerry, so he quit. He said Debbie Baker and Lou Ann were very close. They ran together, ate together, watched TV together. The two women did everything together.

"He said when Jerry got sick, he was very bloated but didn't know what was wrong. Jerry said the doctors weren't doing anything for the bloating and couldn't give him any relief. He said, 'The doctors told me that bloating was part of "it," but they didn't tell me what "it" was.' Sigafus said this was on a Tuesday just prior to Jerry's last and final visit to the hospital. Then in July, Sigafus said he received a call from Ken Harney, who said he had quit working for Lou Ann. Sigafus said he was sure Harney could help us out a lot."

This is a statement Ken Harney gave to the sheriff.

"Lou Ann jumped me out, saying, 'The fucking sheriff doesn't know anything, and it is none of his damn business.' One day, I had taken a bunch of supplies to a job site. When I got back at about 4:15 PM, I saw Tony Baker and some unknown male helping him carry large cardboard boxes from the basement. They threw the stuff in the trash pit behind the ranch and set it on fire. I overheard Lou Ann tell Tony Baker to go to Kansas and pick up the horse trailer to move some horses. Lou Ann sold all the cattle and put the money in her maiden name of Ford. I was tired of her jumping all over me and cussing me out, so I quit."

Time seemed to be going so fast and yet so slow. The sheriff had prime suspects, but there was still no arrest or closure on Jerry's murder.

On Wednesday, December 12, 1990, I received a disturbing telephone call from Sheriff Bogard.

"I thought you should know that Jerry's accountant was found dead behind a store in Wichita Falls yesterday. Funny thing, though … Andrew Coker* called me yesterday. He said he had something important to tell me. I told him I couldn't meet and talk until the next morning. He said, 'Okay, I'll be at your office nine o'clock sharp, tomorrow morning.' And then the guy winds up dead the very afternoon he called me. The Wichita Falls police say Coker's death is a suicide. But I don't buy that. It just doesn't add up! I interviewed Coker on June 20, right after Sternadel died. He told me he prepared his taxes. He said when he did the books for Sternadel in 1989 that over $32,000 was not accounted for. He said Sternadel had a separate plumbing account with $87,200 in it. He also stated in the June 20 interview that Debbie Baker was a terrible bookkeeper. Coker is the one who told us about the big life insurance policy on Jerry Sternadel. I wish I would have just dropped everything and went to meet Coker when he called. Now we'll never know what he was going to tell us."

"This is terrible news, Sheriff. Was there anything in the newspaper about his death?"

"Yeah, I've got the newspaper article right here. I'll read it to you. It says, 'The blood-covered body of a Wichita Falls man was found behind the Cross Roads Flea Market on Tuesday afternoon by a woman driving through the parking lot. The man was identified as Andrew Coker, age 55. Detective John McClosky of the Wichita Falls Police Department said Virginia Neal of Wichita Falls was driving behind the flea market around five o'clock PM, when she noticed Coker's body in a seated position against the outside wall with his head slumped forward. Sgt. Drury of the Wichita Falls Police Department said he thought Coker had been there since about 3:00 PM but was not sure. Coker was dressed in a gray suit, with a white shirt and no tie. His gray hair was combed and parted on the side. A brown satchel was open next to him. Drury said Coker's glasses were inside. A bullet was found lodged in a metal rain gutter about three feet away from his body. Drury said, "Any death is treated as a homicide until we know otherwise. At this time it appears to be suicide. McClosky said a note was found on Coker's body at the hospital, but he had not seen the note and did not know what it said."' Well, that's what the article says. Jeannie, what do you think?"

"I think Jerry's accountant may have been murdered. And if he was, I have a pretty good idea who killed him!"

"Well, I plan on talking to Coker's widow the first chance I get. I'll see what she's got to say. I'll let you know when I talk to her. I could beat myself up for not talking to the guy."

A week later, the sheriff called to let me know he had spoken with the accountant's widow.

"Well, I just got back from talking to the widow. She said she didn't understand why her husband would kill himself. She said he wasn't depressed and they didn't have any money problems. She didn't even know Coker owned a gun. She said just the day before they went out and bought a bunch of Christmas presents for their kids and grandkids. She said she was expecting him to pick her up from her job as a teacher in the afternoon as he always did. But he never showed up. She had to get another ride home, and it wasn't like her husband not to pick her up after work. She said he always picked her up. She said they were planning a nice Christmas and looking forward to spending time with their family. She just couldn't believe her husband would do such a thing as kill himself."

"Why would he kill himself?" I questioned. "No money problems. Planning a nice Christmas with his family. It doesn't make sense."

"Well, the Wichita Falls Police said it was a self-inflicted gunshot wound to the head. I don't think it was self-inflicted. I think Coker was murdered. But it happened in Wichita County jurisdiction, and that's what they ruled it, a suicide. It's going to be a sad Christmas for Coker's wife and family. Jeannie, you were right when you said we're fighting the devil."

On January 21, 1991, the attorney for the wrongful death suit took a taped deposition from Lou Ann Sternadel, which later produced 376 pages. The following is some of Lou Ann's out-of-court testimony.

Lou Ann said she made no effort to find out who poisoned her husband.

She said Jerry was the only one who liked or drank Cran-Apple juice. She poured the Cran-Apple juice down the sink on June 14. She also said her mother, Barbara Ford, poured the Cran-Apple juice down the sink on June 14. She didn't remember talking on the phone with her mother about Cran-Apple juice mugs and her mother saying, "Don't worry, honey, we got rid of those bottles."

Her brother, Paul, was in prison in Huntsville.

Her teenaged daughter had gone to live with her aunt in Paris, Texas, in 1985.

Yes, Jerry had given her a $100,000 certificate of deposit.

She only learned the doctors had found a trace of arsenic the day before Jerry died.

She knew about the affair Jerry had had with Janette Burger.

She wasn't concerned about the Cran-Apple juice when the boy got sick and her husband had just gotten home from the hospital the second time.

She had no choice regarding the autopsy.

She filed the probate of Jerry's will on June 14.

Jerry had never said he was going to divorce her.

She did not know if Debbie had introduced herself as her sister. She did not remember telling Debbie on June 4 to give Jerry something to drink.

She knew of nobody who would want to kill Jerry.

When I got a copy of Lou Ann's deposition and read it, I knew she had lied in a lot of her answers. But why would she lie if she had nothing to hide?

On February 18, 1991, the attorneys for Lou Ann Sternadel made an offer to settle the wrongful death suit and contest of will out of court.

On March 4, the two lawsuits against Lou Ann Sternadel were settled out of court for an undisclosed amount.

On April 10, District Attorney Jack McGaughey called. He said he was very disappointed the civil suit had been settled out of court. He said a guilty verdict in the wrongful death suit could have been used in a criminal action against Lou Ann Sternadel.

A week later, I called Sheriff Bogard to tell him why the civil suits had been settled and to see if there was anything new with the murder investigation.

"Thanks, Jeannie, for giving me a heads-up. I was wondering what happened regarding the lawsuits. Well, on this front, the Bakers moved to San Antonio. There was a big moving van in front of their house this morning. Bill Gerth and I heard they sold their house. We believe Lou Ann paid for the moving van. Tony Baker moved to San Antonio a couple months ago and took a job as a truck salesman. They don't know it, but we're watching every move they make."

"What's going on with Lou Ann?" I asked.

"Well, we heard she is putting the ranch up for sale. Since your kids settled the suit against her, she has been selling all of Jerry's property. She recently sold the house in Ruidosa, New Mexico. I heard the people got it for around $150,000. I talked to the guy who was going to buy the horse barn, corral, and the land. He decided not to purchase anything from Lou Ann. I also heard that Lou Ann gave her lawyer a turkey for Christmas last year. It seemed the lawyer was scared to eat the turkey for fear it might be poisoned. Jerry Woods, one of Jerry's friends, made Lou Ann a really low offer on the ranch. I don't think she'll take it. But who knows? She is telling everybody Jerry is haunting the place and she's scared to stay there."

I said, "Jerry probably is haunting the house. Lou Ann knows who poisoned Jerry to death, that's why she's scared."

"Well, if I were her, I'd be scared too. The way they poisoned that poor guy to death, it wouldn't surprise me if he *was* haunting the place."

"Sheriff, did I tell you I finally got to talk to Jack McGaughey? I just kept calling until he finally called me back. He said he was really disappointed that the wrongful death suit was settled. He said if we had gotten a guilty verdict, he could have used it in the criminal action. I asked if he was going to do anything about the murder case. I said if Lou Ann Sternadel did not have anything to do with her husband's murder, then why wasn't she trying to find out who killed Jerry? He told me that my opinion did not help him with the case. That he still needed the arsenic poison or someone who saw Lou Ann, Debbie, or Tony put the arsenic in the Cran-Apple juice bottle."

Sheriff Bogard said, "DA McGaughey says a lot of things. But he's not going to do anything about the case in the way of presenting it to a grand jury or asking for an indictment."

"Sheriff, I was wondering if you got the results back from the bottle of leg paint?"

"Yeah, but it didn't have any arsenic in it. Well, I'm being paged. Gotta go! Jeannie, see what you can find out about the AG appointing a special prosecutor. Ten-four."

The AG's office suggested I contact the grand jury foreman and see if he would present the case at the next grand jury session. Another suggestion was to try contacting the governor's office to see if the governor could help. The AG also proposed filing a grievance against the DA and said the necessary paperwork would be mailed to me.

Later that week, I contacted the grand jury foreman. He said he would present the murder case at the next grand jury meeting. But he told me not to expect much, since the district attorney wasn't going ahead with the case.

I immediately called Sheriff Bogard and passed the information on to him.

"Well, I'm glad the grand jury will look at the case. At least we've got 'em to bring it up. They probably won't do anything, but Bill Gerth and I will show everything we've got."

The grand jury foreman was good to his word. He called a meeting of the grand jury to look at the murder case. Sheriff Bogard presented his evidence and talked to the grand jury for two hours. The sergeant of Texas Ranger Company C, William R. Gerth, presented his case and talked to the grand jury, backing up the sheriff. The grand jury decided to have a meeting with the district attorney, the sheriff, the Texas Ranger, and any others who investigated the murder case.

The most Bogard, Gerth, and I could do was to try to get DA McGaughey to call Tony Baker as a witness before the grand jury. I asked Bogard if he knew Baker's whereabouts.

"You bet we do. We keep track of all of 'em ... Tony Baker, Debbie Baker, and Lou Ann Sternadel. They committed a premeditated murder. I'm going to keep after 'em till I arrest 'em and get 'em convicted."

On May 20, Tony Baker was subpoenaed to appear before the grand jury. He was surprised to learn that anyone knew of his whereabouts in San Antonio.

Later in the day, Bogard called me. "What makes me sick is the way Tony Baker is bragging that he's going to take the Fifth Amendment on every question. But at least he won't have his lawyer standing beside him when he is asked the questions."

Tony Baker did take the Fifth Amendment on every question the grand jury asked.

The grand jury took no action because District Attorney Jack McGaughey did not ask for an indictment.

I called Texas Governor Ann Richards. She informed me that the only way a district attorney could be removed from office would be by an election, since he was an elected official. This meant we were stuck with DA Jack McGaughey for the duration, unless someone ran against him at the next election.

The next day, I received a call from Sheriff Bogard. "Jeannie, I could sure use your help. Do you think you could do some research on arsenic? We know Jerry was poisoned with arsenic, but we can't seem to find out what kind of arsenic was used. We're leaning toward the arsenic that was used for horses. But somehow that just don't seem right. Clay County doesn't have a big enough budget for us to do all the research we need done."

"Sure, Sheriff. I'll find out everything I can about arsenic."

That began my research to find out everything I could about arsenic poison. I got some phone numbers from a supplier in North Carolina and called every number. I contacted several companies that used arsenic acid in their production of wood preservatives, fungicides, and pressure-treated lumber. I contacted veterinarians and companies that were familiar with arsenic that might be used with regard to horses. I even talked to the doctors who worked on arsenic in cotton desiccant (a defoliant for cotton). For some reason, I kept thinking about rat poison. However, the strength of the arsenic in the rat poison I needed to locate had not been produced since the early 1980s. I contacted all the feed stores in Wichita County and nearby communities for products containing arsenic. I struck out, just as the sheriff and Texas Ranger had.

I bought a book about an arsenic murder case, *Poisoned Blood,* and read it. I decided to look into Cowley's Rat and Mouse Poison, the arsenic that was used to commit murder in that case. I located and called the author, Philip Ginsburg. I got as much information from him as he could recall.

From there, I contacted different chambers of commerce for information regarding stores that sold the rat poison manufactured by S. L. Cowley and Sons. I called several of the stores. Most of them stocked rat poison with arsenic but had not stocked the arsenic manufactured by S. L. Cowley and Sons for a number of years. However, one did recall Cowley's Rat and Mouse Poison. The business owner remembered it because it had a bitter taste and did not prove very useful or successful for killing mice and rats.

"The critters would not eat it," the proprietor said.

I thought, "If it had a bitter taste, Jerry would surely have known something was wrong if his food or drink was laced with Cowley's Rat and Mouse Poison."

On June 14, Sheriff Bogard called. "Jeannie, I need you to pick the brains of medical examiners and toxicologists. Somebody out there has got to know about arsenic and its effect on humans. We still think the poison they used might be some kind of arsenic used for horses. But we're no closer to finding it than we were on day one. Do you think you could help us?"

"I'll be glad to help. But people keep asking me what agency I am with." This was a question I kept getting as I called throughout the United States trying to get information that might help in the murder investigation. I told Sheriff Bogard that people were hesitant to tell me anything because I wasn't a member of a law-enforcement agency.

"Well, in the future, tell them you are a deputy with Clay County. Go get a Bible. I'm going to deputize you."

I put my hand on my Bible, raised my right hand, and repeated the oath of office.

"Okay, now you are official. By the way, I heard there's a book Debbie Baker and Jerry's widow may have gotten their idea from."

"Do you know the name of the book?"

"*Poisoned Blood*," the sheriff answered.

"Are you kidding? I bought that book just the other day."

"Well, maybe you should check out the arsenic poison that's in the book."

"I've already checked it out. I was told that arsenic has a real bitter taste."

"Well, we've got to start somewhere. Now, get busy, Deputy."

I started trying to locate toxicologists and medical examiners familiar with arsenic poisoning. I called the Alabama lab that had done the lab work on the Marie Hilley murder case. I called the poison center headquarters for information on arsenic poison.

I finally got in touch with the foremost expert in arsenic in Chicago, Illinois. The doctor/toxicologist was renowned for his expertise on arsenic. Dr. Jorg Pirl could analyze tissue samples (hair and nails) and fluid samples (urine or body fluids) and determine what kind of arsenic (arsenic trioxide) was used and when and what amounts were given with each consecutive poisoning.

Dr. Pirl questioned me, "How did you find out about me?"

"It wasn't easy," I replied. "But I was told you were the expert to talk to when it comes to arsenic poison and the effects it has on the human body."

The toxicologist began rattling things off effortlessly.

"Yes, you could say I'm an expert on arsenic. I'm proud to say I'm one of the foremost arsenic experts. I've studied arsenic and its effects, unfortunately, for over sixteen years. I say 'unfortunately' because of the fact that arsenic has been and continues to be used to cause human suffering and a very painful death. Arsenic is a poison that has been used to kill people since the time of Napoleon Bonaparte and probably even before that.

"Arsenic is tasteless. It is odorless. A person doesn't know that it has been ingested until they start having severe cramps accompanied by nausea, vomiting, and diarrhea. The severity of the attack depends on the dosage of the arsenic that was administered. And depending on the amount of arsenic a person was given, when the effects are felt it is usually too late and death usually occurs hours afterward and sometimes a few days later. Dimacaperol and Pencillimine are the only two medicines that are used to treat arsenic poisoning, and this must be administered immediately after diagnosis of arsenic poisoning. Arsenic poisoning is a very painful and miserable way to die. It's probably worse than the gas chamber or electric chair. If a person hated another person real bad, then that would be the way to kill them. It is a horrible way to die. I wouldn't wish it on my worst enemy."

After talking to Dr. Pirl, I called the Alabama DA's office. In the widely publicized arsenic murder case, the DA had exhumed the body of Marie Hilley's husband and found arsenic in his body. "We're still getting people calling about that murder case," DA Joe Hubbard said. "From time to time reporters still call. I'm sorry to hear that arsenic is still being used to commit murder. From what I hear, being poisoned by arsenic is a horrible way to die, with so much stomach trouble and all. If we can be of any help, give us a holler."

"Thank you for your time, Mr. Hubbard. I'll let you know how things turn out."

As I hung up, I was wondering where to go with my investigation. My phone rang. It was my daughter calling. She excitedly told me about an arsenic murder case that had recently been solved in the Dallas area. After talking to my daughter, I started calling Dallas. I finally located the investigator who had broken the Richard Lyons arsenic murder case in Dallas. I talked with the detective for quite some time. He told me that he had heard about the Sternadel arsenic murder. He said he would be glad to talk to Sheriff Bogard and Texas Ranger Bill Gerth and offer them any information and assistance they might need.

After speaking to the Dallas investigator, I called Bogard, who put me through on a conference call to Gerth. I informed the lawmen about the Dallas investigator and the arsenic murder case he had recently solved. They said they would contact the detective.

"Right now we're in the process of getting a subpoena for the financial records and phone records of Debbie and Tony Baker going back a year and a half before Jerry's death."

They thought that Debbie and Tony Baker, with Lou Ann's help, had stolen more than the $38,000 that they already knew about.

"We'll know more when we get the records from the bank," Gerth said enthusiastically. "Just keep your prayers going strong. We could use a couple more miracles. The good Lord has come through for us so far."

"He sure has," I replied. "He sure has!"

A few days later, I had a vivid dream about Jerry. The dream was so real that it startled me awake. In the dream, I was driving a blue car. Jerry was dead, but he was sitting over on the passenger side of my car. The sky overhead was a beautiful turquoise blue. Jerry remarked how beautiful the heavens were. Somehow I knew I was dreaming and thought it was strange that Jerry was speaking this way, because I had never heard him mentioning anything of beauty while he was alive. In the dream, I was driving down a road, when all of a sudden the car went

out of control and began plunging down a steep hill. I instantly knew
we were going to die, although in the dream Jerry was already dead.
As the car started plowing down the cliff, Jerry started praying, "God
save us! Jesus, help us." I could not recall the last time I had heard Jerry
pray. I was always the one who prayed, not Jerry. But in my dream, it
was Jerry who was praying.

Before Jerry finished his prayer, the car started flying through the
air as though it was an airplane and landed safely on the ground. Becky
and Sandy ran over to greet us. They had big smiles on their faces. That
was when I woke up. I was not sure what the dream meant, but it gave
me a good feeling. I thought about how Jerry suffered horribly when he
was in the hospital. I knew Jerry had time to see all the hurt, suffering,
and pain he had caused himself and others. Jerry knew he was dying
and had no one to turn to but God. I thought the dream meant Jerry
had prayed for God's redemption before he died and God had forgiven
Jerry his sins.

The next morning, I was sitting at my desk pondering the time
that seemed to fly by without any significant new developments in the
murder case. I looked down at the yellow legal pad that I constantly
used to write down pertinent information from my research. I noticed
I had written Cowley's Rat and Mouse Poison over and over on one
page of the legal pad. *What am I doing?* I thought. *I'm focused on this
one when it could be any kind of arsenic. I'm wasting my time on this one
poison.* I sat wishing I knew the name of the poison that had been used
to kill Jerry. I started to tear the page off the tablet, but for some reason,
I couldn't bring myself to discard that page.

I sat at my desk, staring at the words Cowley's Rat and Mouse Poison.
Finally, I placed the yellow legal pad inside my desk drawer, but I couldn't
get that particular poison off my mind. I called the EPA and got the
registration number and other information on Cowley's Rat and Mouse
Poison. I found out the manufacturer of the arsenic poison was S. L.
Cowley in Hugo, Oklahoma. I looked up the phone number. I learned
that Mr. Cowley had passed away, but Mrs. Ruby Higginbotham had

taken over the business. I called the EPA again and requested the license number and address for Cowley's Rat and Mouse Poison from their computer programs. I was thunderstruck when personnel from the EPA called me back with the information I had requested.

The lady from EPA said, "The only address I have on Cowley's is P.O. Box 666."

"Did you say P.O. Box 666?" I questioned.

"Yes, the address is P.O. Box 666. The company voluntarily surrendered its license back in 1988. When I called you, I couldn't help but notice that the prefix in your phone number is 666."

"Yes, ma'am, I've had the 666 phone number for a long time now. It is a constant reminder that I have to fight the devil every minute of every day."

"I'm glad to hear that's why you have the 666 prefix in your phone number. But I'm sorry I could not be of more help. Good luck in your research. I hope you find what you're looking for."

"Thank you. I appreciate your help. I'll pass this information on to the sheriff."

My heart was flip-flopping over the address. I wasn't sure what it meant except it was one more sign we were fighting the devil. It was good against evil. I quickly called the sheriff and told him what I had found out.

Sheriff Bogard replied, "That P.O. box number is scary, Jeannie. I've been meaning to say something to you about your phone number. Guess this is the time to do it. I've been wondering with you being such a devout Christian and all, why your phone number starts with 666."

"Like I told the lady from the EPA and everybody else who asks, my phone number is a constant reminder that I have to fight the devil every minute of every day."

"Could be we're up against something bigger than we thought."

"It sure seems that way," I responded. "I'm thankful we have the good Lord on our side. I still feel in my heart, we will find the arsenic that was used to kill Jerry."

"Well, being in law enforcement all these years, I've been fighting evil for a long time. But this is the first time I have come almost face to face with the devil. We're going to win though. We've just got to keep our faith. A lot of things could happen. I believe if we could get a new district attorney, we could see a lot more things going in our favor. But this is one of the strangest and hardest cases I've ever come across. Keep me posted, Jeannie. Ten-four."

I hung up the phone thinking that somehow, the postal address was one small step closer to solving the case and one giant leap in winning the fight against the devil.

In November 1991, my daughter was due to deliver her baby. I wanted to be with her for the delivery and help with the baby afterward. I made reservations to fly to Texas.

My granddaughter was born on November 5, 1991. I stayed in Grand Prairie for a couple of weeks and helped care for the baby.

A few days before Thanksgiving, I called Bogard, telling him I would be driving to Henrietta the next day.

"Good," he replied. "There's somebody I want you to meet when you get here."

The receptionist notified the sheriff that I had arrived and was in the lobby.

Sheriff Bogard's voice boomed over the intercom, "Send her on back!"

Proceeding down the hallway and walking into the sheriff's office, I immediately saw a nice-looking, well-dressed fellow wearing dark-rimmed glasses sitting with the sheriff.

"Come on in, Jeannie. I want you to meet the gentleman who is going to run against Jack McGaughey. He's the answer to our prayers. I want you to meet Tim Cole."

Tim Cole was elected DA and prosecuted Debra Baker

Tim Cole was born on February 24, 1959. He was a native of Saint Jo, Texas, and the son of a Church of Christ minister. He graduated from the University of Texas Law School in 1988 and was admitted to the Texas bar the same year. He worked as an assistant DA in Wise and Jack counties before announcing his intention to seek the seat of district attorney for the 97th District.

My first impressions of Tim were very positive. He seemed to have enthusiasm and determination. Hopefully, Tim Cole would make a good district attorney. Everyone knew the only chance we had of moving the arsenic murder case forward and getting it prosecuted was by getting a new district attorney elected.

I watched as the sheriff showed the aspiring candidate two piles of folders full of cases. The thirty-two-year-old attorney picked up and carefully studied each case file. He held up a folder, "Sheriff, this guy should already be back in prison. Why wasn't he prosecuted?"

"You got me!" Sheriff Bogard replied as he picked up a different folder. "This case right here is even stronger than that one. It just goes to show you what I've been talking about."

Both men were busy going through the case files, so I excused myself and drove over to the courthouse. As I walked up the sidewalk, I thanked God for sending us Tim Cole.

Copying the last of the court papers that I needed, the court clerk said, "You might just be the next Angela Lansbury and solve the Jerry Sternadel case."

"That would be nice," I replied. "But we're pretty sure who murdered Jerry. All we need is a district attorney who will prosecute the case."

The clerk responded, "Maybe this new guy will do something once he's voted in. A lot of people are counting on him in this next election. It's about time Clay County had somebody representing us who will bring criminals to justice."

"I wholeheartedly agree. Thanks for your help." I left the courthouse and headed back over to the sheriff's office. I met Chief Deputy Paul Bevering, who was on his way out the door.

Deputy Bevering was a tall, slim man. He carried the gun in his holster like he knew how to use it. He reminded me of Chester Goode, Marshall Matt Dillon's deputy on *Gunsmoke*.

In December, I received a call from Sheriff Bogard. It took me aback when he said he had decided against seeking election to a fifth term as sheriff. The good news was that his chief deputy, Paul Bevering, would be running for the post. "Law enforcement is in my blood. My term as sheriff will be over in 1993. But, I'll probably stay on as a deputy. (What the sheriff did not tell me was that he had just been diagnosed with lung cancer and was going to start radiation and chemotherapy treatments.)

"We received some interesting information from Ken and Kathleen Harney. They told us they had gone on a few trips to Ruidosa, New Mexico, with Jerry and Lou Ann Sternadel. The Harneys said Lou Ann stayed on the phone with Debbie Baker the entire trip. The Harneys thought that was strange. They came in and gave us a statement. Why don't you call and see what you can find out? I'm sure you know this, but Bill Gerth and I are both handling the investigation and we share everything, just in case one of us dies or gets killed. We sure don't want this case dying with us."

During the week, I telephoned the Harneys. They repeated to me what they had told the sheriff. But Ken Harney added, "Jerry made the remark, 'I'm going to have to get rid of that fat woman.' We had no idea why Jerry said that."

The Harneys told me they went to the hospital several times and visited Jerry. "On one occasion, we saw one of Jerry's doctors pick up a saltshaker and ask Lou Ann if she was sprinkling it on everything Jerry ate. At the time, we didn't know what 'it' was. We believe it was Dr. Humphrey who made that remark to Lou Ann."

Kathleen said, "When Jerry first went in the hospital, I asked Lou Ann if she wanted me to stay so she could get some sleep. Lou Ann replied, 'No, Debbie's here. She has everything under control.' I was just trying to help Lou Ann out, but I guess she didn't need my help."

Ken said, "A month or so before Jerry started getting sick, he left to go to town to check on a job. I had just started working on a project, when he suddenly drove back up. He said he felt the wheels vibrating on the truck, turned around on the highway, and came back. He asked me to check out the tires and wheels. On a couple of wheels I noticed the lug nuts were missing, and the lug nuts on the other wheels were loosened to the point they almost fell off when I touched them. I told Jerry about the lug nuts, and he got very upset. He went straight to the mechanic who had serviced the vehicle the day before. The mechanic told Jerry he was positive he had tightened the lug bolts on the wheels when he rotated the tires. Jerry always drove at high speeds. It seemed to me that someone had purposely removed some lug nuts and loosened the others. I don't know it for a fact, but if Jerry had died in a car accident, it wouldn't have been suspicious."

Ken and Kathleen Harney were good friends of Jerry Sternadel

On election night in 1992, Sheriff Bogard called throughout the night giving me box-by-box results. The good news was Tim Cole won the seat for district attorney. He would take office in January 1993. The bad news was Paul Bevering wound up in a runoff, but everyone was optimistic that he would win and become the new sheriff in 1993.

That winter, for some unexplained reason, I started noticing self-storage warehouses. Whenever I went grocery shopping, to the mall or just for a drive, no matter what route I took, I saw a storage warehouse. I was mesmerized and spellbound by these warehouses. But I couldn't understand my sudden fascination. The oddest sensation came over me that storage warehouses meant something, and whatever the something was had to do with Jerry's murder.

A feeling began to gnaw at me that I needed to go visit my ex-husband's grave. I had not been to the Wichita Falls cemetery since the

Fourth of July in 1990, when my daughter and I put flowers on Jerry's grave. At that time, there wasn't even a grave marker on the burial site. The next time I flew to Texas, I would go to Crestview Cemetery and visit his grave.

Tombstone on Jerry Sternadel's grave at Crestview Cemetery

Sign from beyond the Grave

On May 18, 1992, I was on a commercial airliner flying to Texas. I planned on meeting up with Sheriff Bogard, Texas Ranger Bill Gerth, Chief Deputy Paul Bevering, and Tim Cole. But the first thing I was going to do was visit Jerry's grave.

The airline flight from Long Island to Dallas–Fort Worth was smooth and on time. I picked up a rental car at the airport. My immediate plan was to drive to Wichita Falls, stop off at Crestview Cemetery, and then go to dinner with my son, Sandy.

The first thing I noticed at the cemetery was Lou Ann's name engraved on the tombstone alongside Jerry's name. I was appalled that Lou Ann had had the audacity to put her name on the grave marker, but what could I do? Lou Ann was Jerry's wife when he died. To rid myself of the tension I was feeling, I started walking around the cemetery. When I got back to Jerry's grave. I observed ants crawling on it.

I recalled the day Jerry was buried almost two years earlier. I thought of how Jerry knew he was being poisoned to death and begged for help but no one would help him. The murder case was still no closer to being solved or having an arrest made. I was helping with the murder case investigation, but now I wanted to help Jerry.

An overwhelming sensation came over me that Jerry was reaching out to me from the grave. I felt my ex-husband wanted to leave the black hole he was buried in. Looking down at the mound of dirt, I was thinking of the arsenic-mummified body within the grave. I said, "Jerry, if your spirit wants to go with me, and it is okay with the Lord, then you're welcome." I stayed at the grave for a short time, said a prayer, and walked to my rental car. I drove away from the grave site with a strange feeling that I was not alone. I quickly dismissed the thought.

Before I left the cemetery, I stopped off at the office to tell them about the ants on my ex-husband's grave. The custodian made a note and said he would put some poison down. Again, poison would be used in connection with Jerry.

As I pulled onto the highway, I still had a relentless sensation that I wasn't alone. I sensed a "presence" in the car. Dismissing the notion, I picked up my cell phone and punched in the numbers for my son. "I'm in Wichita Falls. I'll be there in five minutes. Let's go out to eat."

Sandy was standing outside his apartment when I pulled up. After a kiss and a long hug, he said he would unload my luggage before we went to dinner.

I tossed my son the car keys. "Thanks. The bags are in the trunk."

Sandy took the keys and walked around to the back of the car. He questioned, "Mother, did you just come from the cemetery? Were you at Daddy's grave?"

"Yes, I was at the cemetery and visited your dad's grave."

"Get your camera quick! Take a picture of the license plate. Hurry, Mother, hurry, before it disappears!"

I had no idea what my son was talking about, but I quickly grabbed my camera from the front seat and raced to the back of the car.

"Look!" Sandy said as he motioned toward the license plate on the rental car.

Sign from beyond the grave

I took one look at the license plate and gasped in surprise. The letters and numbers displayed on the license plate were a sign from beyond the grave.

"Daddy's birthday is February 18. That's how I knew you were at Daddy's grave. Daddy is not in the grave, not now. He left the cemetery with you."

For a moment I was speechless and stood staring at the IGO218.

"Mother, I know this a sign from Daddy. Why else would the license plate say I GO 2-18? You always told me you see signs on license plates. Look at the date. Do you think the date of June '92 means anything? Next month is June and this is 1992. Mother, this is freaking me out!"

I stood looking at the license plate. "Honey, I have a funny feeling that some kind of evidence is going to turn up in June. Since I rented the car in Texas and the license plate is from Oklahoma, this makes me think the evidence has something to do with Oklahoma. I don't know what the evidence is, but it's going to be something big. Big enough to break your daddy's murder case wide open."

"Oh, Mother! I sure hope you're right. Now, I'm beginning to believe in signs too. Are we both crazy?"

"No, sweetheart, we're just seeing the sign the good Lord is giving us. This license plate is a huge sign. I'm taking a picture to capture it on film for everyone to see."

I flew back to New York a couple weeks later. I wasn't alone on the flight. A "presence" was with me. I could feel Jerry's spirit just as surely as I had felt Bobby Sternadel's spirit before he passed to the other side. How long the "presence" of my ex-husband would stay with me, I did not know.

Storage locker where arsenic was discovered

On June 8, 1992, I received a phone call from Sheriff Bogard. He sounded enthusiastic and eager to talk. "Jeannie, for two years, you have been telling me not to give up on finding the arsenic. And I kept telling you Debbie and Lou Ann threw the poison away. Well, I've got some real good news."

I quickly said, "I can't wait to hear what it is."

"Well, Bill Gerth and I think we have found the smoking gun."

"The smoking gun?" I asked.

"Yep. We received a telephone call from a storage warehouse in Wichita Falls. The manager said he was unable to locate the person who had rented a storage locker and the rent was long overdue. So he decided to open the locker and sell the contents. Confiscating and selling the contents of lockers for overdue storage bills is a common practice. Well, the manager opened the locker and saw Jerry Sternadel's name. He knew Sternadel as being a man who was murdered. He remembered seeing the story about Sternadel's murder on television and in the newspaper. The manager said he called the warehouse lawyer, Ron Poole, and then called me. To make a long story short, we went to the warehouse and started poking around. We found an interesting-looking item that turned out to be a bottle of arsenic."

"Did you say you found a bottle of arsenic?"

Bogard answered, "Yep! Sure did! It's locked up safe and sound in my office."

"Sheriff, I just knew they didn't throw the arsenic away and somehow you would find it. I just knew it! Was there a name on the bottle?"

"Hold on while I get the bottle. I'll have to get the keys and put on my glasses so I can read the label."

"I'll hold on as long as it takes." I didn't wait for long.

"Okay, this is what's on the label: COWLEY'S RAT AND MOUSE POISON—BATCH #9987. MANUFACTURED BY S. L. COWLEY AND SONS MANUFACTURING CO., HUGO, OKLAHOMA. The back of the bottle lists the active ingredients as ARSENIC TRIOXIDE, 1.5%—TOTAL ARSENIC, AS ELEMENTAL, ALL IN WATER SOLUBLE FORM, 1.14%."

"Sheriff, did you say Cowley's Rat and Mouse Poison?"

"That's the label on the bottle, Cowley's Rat and Mouse Poison."

"That is the arsenic poison I've been researching. I can give you the EPA number, the name of the manufacturer, the address, the phone number. I can tell you everything about Cowley's Rat and Mouse Poison." *Instantly,*

*I remembered writing Cowley's Rat and Mouse Poison over and over on the
yellow legal pad. Now I understood why I couldn't bring myself to throw that
page away.* I said, "Sheriff, this has got to be divine intervention!"

Bogard replied, "I know a lot of people were praying for us to find
the arsenic."

"Thank God! Those prayers were answered! Sheriff, what else can
you tell me?"

"Jeannie, remember all this is confidential information. We found the
bottle of arsenic in a locker in Wichita Falls. Bill Gerth, Paul Bevering, and
I didn't waste any time responding after being notified by the warehouse
manager. The name on the rental agreement for the storage unit was
Kathy Simmons. The address listed for Kathy Simmons was one that
we immediately recognized as being Debbie and Tony Baker's address
in Holliday, Texas. The locker was originally rented back on February
21, 1990, and the rent was paid up at that time for two years. Somehow,
somebody forgot to pay the rent when it came due on February 21, 1992.

"There were boxes on top of boxes of records and cancelled checks
in the locker. We were poking around when we came upon a plastic bag
half full of correspondence mailed to Jerry Sternadel on June 12, 1990,
the day he died. That's where we found the bottle of arsenic. It looked
like the eight-ounce bottle originally held about six inches of white
liquid, but there was only about one inch of liquid remaining inside
the bottle. It just might be the arsenic they used to poison Sternadel.
We listed it as evidence right away. We're sending it off for analysis and
fingerprints.

"Gerth and I had been at the storage warehouse for about thirty
minutes. We were sitting in the office when the phone rang. We heard
the manager say, 'Sorry, lady … it's too late! The police are here now.'

"We questioned the manager about the call. He said, 'It was a
woman who said she had rented the locker. She stated she was out of
town. She wanted to take care of the past due bill, and pay the rent up
for another year. She sounded desperate, saying, 'Oh my God! Let me
rush you a cashier's check.'

"Funny thing, though ... Ron Poole was Lou Ann's criminal attorney and the lawyer for the warehouse. Gerth and I will subpoena the phone records. But, I'll bet you the woman who made that call to the warehouse was either Lou Ann Sternadel or Debbie Baker. That phone call may be the nail on the coffin."

I was so elated I could barely contain myself. "Thank you, Sheriff. Thank you for calling me. I just can't thank you enough."

"Of course, I'd call you. You've been with us from day one. Now, how about giving me that information you say you've got on this arsenic, so we can follow up on it."

Bogard and Gerth wasted no time contacting the police captain in Hugo, Oklahoma, who said he would talk to the Cowley men living in the area to see if either of them knew anything about S. L. Cowley and Sons. The lawmen began concentrating their efforts to find out where the bottle of arsenic had been bought and who might have purchased it.

Surprise and disappointment was an understatement, when the DA notified Bogard of his decision not to prosecute the case, even though the arsenic had been found. McGaughey told the sheriff that even with the discovery of the arsenic poison, he still did not have sufficient evidence to bring an indictment in the murder case.

"Well, keep the faith, Jeannie. I know it's hard. If I didn't have you encouraging me from time to time, I might even consider throwing in the towel myself. Maybe we need to think about hiring a private eye."

Remembering Jerry had hired a private eye to follow me around when we were separated made me think the sheriff's notion might be a good idea. I didn't know anything about hiring a private detective. But then I hadn't known anything about arsenic or investigating a murder before Jerry was poisoned to death, either.

One night I just happened to be watching the program *Investigative Reports with Bill Curtis* on A&E. The private detective on the episode seemed very impressive. The next day I began researching Bill Dear.

On June 9, I telephoned the Federal Bureau of Investigation in Quantico, Virginia. I spoke with John Douglas, chief of the investigative support unit. Mr. Douglas was very helpful, giving me names of FBI experts regarding violent crimes and psychological profiles.

On June 14, I concluded my research on the private investigator I had seen on A&E. I was hoping Jerry's murder was the kind of case William C. Dear thrived on. But first I needed to contact the sheriff.

Sheriff Bogard said, "Well, that would be great, if you can afford it."

By the end of June, I was flying to Texas to meet Bill Dear at his office in Dallas.

Standing six feet, three inches, Bill Dear cast a long shadow. He wore big gold rings and alligator cowboy boots but still appeared humble.

"I guess the good Lord has been good to me. He allowed me to make a decent living and see my son grow." He proceeded to tell me about himself, his detective agency, and some of his cases.

Bill Dear said he was credited with having a sixth sense, but he didn't think it was so. "I think I am intuitive. But for me to think like the victim or the killer, I must do things I feel were done by them. It is my only way of developing the characterization and finding a way of solving and understanding the crime. If I sit and think about it before I go to bed, I will dream about it all night long. It's like a camera with the film rolling back and forth, back and forth. All of a sudden I will wake up in the middle of the night and think of something that I did not do. I'll quickly write it down and then go right back to sleep. How could I solve the crime if I didn't live it, breathe it, and feel it? That's why a lot of cases never get solved. It's like looking at something, but you can't see the forest for the trees."

He said he always wanted to be a policeman. "As a fifteen-year-old paperboy, I witnessed a robbery and followed the getaway car on my bicycle. I watched the suspects pull their vehicle in at a house that happened to be on my paper route. I wrote down the address and reported the crime to the police. I was in the newspaper and in big trouble. A car tried to mow me down ... twice. The robbery suspects were trying to scare me out of testifying, but justice prevailed. After that, I was hooked on solving crime."

Mike Hammer was one of Bill Dear's literary icons. At the beginning of Bill's career, he did low-level detective work and then moved up to doing accident investigations for attorneys. From that point on, he started getting jobs by word of mouth. He won national media attention when he successfully solved the quirky case dubbed Dungeons and Dragons. After that case, he never had to hunt for another one. The television show *Unsolved Mysteries* had brought him into the limelight with the case of a wax-museum owner poisoned by strychnine that had been put into a bottle of Nyquil. The coroner rejected the possibility that the museum owner's death was a suicide and ruled it a homicide.

In Dear's office, I noticed a photo of Bill toting a machine gun while dressed in Elliott Ness–style garb, a clip from *Playboy*, newspaper headlines, letters of praise, and official citations. I liked what I saw and heard. I said, "The good Lord has been good to me too. I believe he sent me to you." I proceeded to tell him everything I knew about my ex-husband's murder.

"What you have told me about the case is compelling. When I get a down payment, we'll take the case."

I wasted no time in making out a check. Bill Dear and his detective agency began their investigation.

On July 5, 1992, investigator Chris Stewart started reviewing the records and report. A couple of days later, Mr. Stewart traveled to Henrietta, Texas, where he checked records and the probate file of Jerry Sternadel. The file showed that the judge had granted every motion filed by any attorney representing the widow, Lou Ann Sternadel, concerning the disposition of and the management of the estate of Jerry Sternadel. The administrator of the estate, Lou Ann Sternadel, had sold the plumbing business, cattle, horses, and real estate properties at a greatly reduced value.

Stewart then visited the Clay County sheriff's office. Sheriff Jake Bogard was out having his chemotherapy session but had left a message for the investigator to contact District Attorney Jack McGaughey.

Stewart met with McGaughey in Montague, Texas. The DA said the investigation was still active and being pursued by Sheriff Bogard and Texas Ranger Bill Gerth. The DA also stated that the lab was processing the most recent evidence found in the Saf-T-Lok storage building rented by Debbie Baker under an assumed name. The bottle of Cowley's Rat and Mouse Poison had been sent to the lab and was being checked for fingerprints, and the boxes of financial records removed from the storage facility were being analyzed. McGaughey stated that Bogard and Gerth had presented information related to the investigation on two occasions to the grand jury. But McGaughey had not formally requested an indictment be handed down by the grand jury due to his opinion that the majority of the evidence was circumstantial and did not directly tie Lou Ann Sternadel and Debbie Baker to the poisoning death of Jerry Sternadel. The DA stated that when Tony Baker met before the grand jury, he continuously pleaded the Fifth Amendment. McGaughey said his primary interest, at this point, was to track the victim's physical symptoms with the level of arsenic in his system on a daily basis from May 23 until June 12, 1990, when Mr. Sternadel died.

McGaughey stated that he needed to determine when the arsenic poison entered Mr. Sternadel's system, when he began exhibiting the symptoms of arsenic poisoning, when the body fluid samples were taken and analyzed, and when the laboratory reports came back to the physicians at the hospital. The DA stated he could refer the investigator to an arsenic consultant in the Dallas area and would provide a letter of authorization at a later date. McGaughey said he was interested in connecting one of the three suspects to the acquisition of arsenic and to its insertion into the juice the victim had consumed at his residence.

McGaughey said he considered Debbie Lynn Baker, Tony L. Baker, and Lou Ann Sternadel the primary suspects. He said he had the impression the bottle of Cowley's Rat and Mouse Poison that was possibly used in the murder of Jerry Sternadel had been obtained or acquired in the area of Paris, Texas. He noted that Lou Ann Sternadel's mother, Barbara Ford, and Lou Ann's aunt, Jo Ann Flippen, also resided in Paris, Texas. McGaughey said there had been some unsubstantiated rumors that Lou Ann's father had died under somewhat mysterious circumstances, exhibiting before he died symptoms similar to those observed in Jerry Sternadel before he died in 1990. (The same could be said for Debbie Baker's father who died in 1975 and Debbie Baker's mother who died in 1977. Both were in their early forties and exhibited some of the same symptoms before they died.) McGaughey said he felt the investigator should contact Sheriff Bogard and Ranger Bill Gerth for more pertinent details concerning the past investigation on the murder of Jerry Sternadel.

Our next stop was the Sternadel ranch to speak to Jerry's son, who was still living there. Sandy informed us that any conversation we had with him would have to take place in the presence of his grandmother—Jerry's mother, Marcy. At Marcy's home, certain inconsistencies in the case were clarified. Marcy and Sandy also provided documents for the investigators.

On Wednesday, July 8, 1992, investigators met again with Bogard and Gerth. Points of importance were clarified, suggestions were made concerning the direction of new investigative efforts, and background investigations on personalities were divulged. The two men told the investigators they would be happy to share any and all previous investigative information with us after receiving written authorization from the DA.

The investigators then traveled again to Montague and met with McGaughey, who agreed to provide a written letter of authorization for the investigators to discuss and review the file, which they brought back to Bogard.

The investigators then traveled to the Wichita Falls Department of Public Safety with a copy of the letter of authorization for Bill Gerth. There they reviewed four three-ring binder notebooks and discussed the official investigation. Gerth answered questions and provided background information, theories on various aspects of the investigation, and suggestions for new avenues of pursuit on the investigation.

On July 9, Stewart returned to the Wichita Falls Department of Public Safety office to continue his discussion with Gerth about documents obtained from Marcy and Sandy. Afterward, the investigators returned to their accommodations to organize and prepare for interviews of individuals.

Stewart went to see Deidre (Debbie) Williams, a nurse who was on duty during Jerry's stay at Bethania Hospital. Ms. Williams stated that she did recall Lou Ann Sternadel and Debbie Baker at the hospital. It had seemed unusual to her that every time anyone came to visit Jerry, Debbie Baker was either in the room or standing in the doorway of the room.

The investigator traveled to the residence of Glynda Garland*, a good friend of Jerry's, who declined to provide the investigator with a written statement. She did agree to discuss her observations and opinions from May 1, 1990 to July 1, 1990. She had known Jerry for most of her life and called him Sterny. She stated that Jerry and her husband had worked together in the past. They were family friends and had occasional social contact together as well. Garland said Jerry had come to her home approximately the third week in May of 1990 with his Doberman pinscher. Jerry had provided her with a Doberman puppy and wanted to compare the two dogs from the same litter. Approximately fifteen minutes later, Lou Ann Sternadel arrived at the Garland residence. Jerry had a brief discussion with Lou Ann and left with his dog.

Garland said that Jerry was like a second daddy to her and she used to tease him about being an old miser with his money. She said Jerry usually called her by the nickname Gal. Jerry remarked to her that he was having problems with his kids and that "they were not worth a shit." Jerry's son, Sandy, was not interested in the plumbing business, and Jerry had problems with his daughter, Becky. Garland stated that Jerry had to have things his way, no other way, and that he really wanted both Sandy and Becky to have a college education before working in his plumbing business. Lou Ann Sternadel had told Ms. Garland in the past that Becky was a "piece of shit."

Garland said she heard that Jerry was in the hospital in late May and early June. She contacted Lou Ann and was informed that they thought Jerry had a virus but he would be going home in a couple of days. Later on that week, Garland called the Sternadel residence, and Debbie Baker answered the telephone. Debbie stated that Jerry had come home from the hospital but then got sick again and had returned to the hospital. Garland contacted Lou Ann at the hospital. Lou Ann told Garland that they thought Jerry had hepatitis. Garland said she called the hospital the

next day and was told that Jerry had gotten worse. She then called Lou
Ann who told her Jerry was back in the hospital but was better.

Garland said when she went to see Jerry in the hospital on the first
of June, he didn't seem to recognize her at first. He was very subdued.
He was not joking or kidding around with her like he usually did. Jerry
just stated, "Okay, well, whatever," and goodbye very lethargically, not
engaging in his usual banter. The only coherent thing Jerry said to
Garland was when he asked her, "How is the puppy?"

Garland's husband came back into town on June 4 and inquired
about Jerry. When she informed her husband that Jerry wasn't doing
very well, he decided to call the Sternadel residence. Sandy answered
the telephone and informed Mr. Garland that they were taking Jerry
back to the hospital. Sandy said his dad's condition had gotten worse.
He was vomiting, had diarrhea, and was hallucinating. He said his
dad thought there were snakes in his bed at home. Garland went to
the hospital to visit Jerry in the ICU. Lou Ann and Debbie Baker were
sitting close together talking when she arrived. Lou Ann told Garland
that Jerry had some type of weird syndrome called Guillain-Barré.
During the conversation, Lou Ann continuously referred to Jerry as
being her "honey," her "baby," and her "darling." Debbie asked Garland
if she wanted to see Jerry, and Garland indicated that she did. Baker
escorted Garland down the hall to the room. When Garland saw Jerry,
she couldn't believe how bad he looked and how much his condition had
deteriorated. He was not coherent and was rocking back and forth in the
hospital bed. He was restrained, with his arms and legs tied down to the
hospital bed, and he was thrashing back and forth and side to side.

Garland heard Jerry ask Debbie Baker to cut him loose, and Debbie
just joked with him about the matter saying, "Yeah, Jerry, we'll get to
it in a minute." But Debbie never did cut Jerry loose. Garland couldn't
take the sight of Jerry suffering in such anguish; she began crying and
left the room. She returned to the hospital morning, noon, and night on
each day thereafter. But she never actually went back into Jerry's room
to talk to or see him. She said she overheard a conversation between

Becky and Marcy about getting Jerry to Dallas to have a different doctor determine what the problem was and cure his condition.

Garland observed that every time anyone came to visit Jerry on his last stay in the hospital, Debbie would escort the person to Jerry's room and would remain inside the room or just outside the room throughout the entire visit. Two days before Jerry died, Garland was present during a consultation by Dr. Humphrey with the family. Humphrey stated that high levels of arsenic had been found in Jerry's system. Lou Ann said she was totally puzzled about how Jerry could have gotten arsenic into his system. Dr. Humphrey stated that, since arsenic was odorless and tasteless, Lou Ann could shake some out of a saltshaker onto someone's food and the other person would not know that they had ingested arsenic.

Garland said that on the night of June 11, she was leaving the hospital at about 11:00 to go home. She saw Debbie Baker coming across the parking lot toward the hospital. Debbie asked her if the doctor had been in to see Jerry and questioned her as to what the doctor had said. "What did the doctor say? Will Jerry live?" Garland replied that it did not look good and that she didn't think Jerry was going to make it. She told Debbie the doctor had stated Jerry's low blood pressure did not look good.

Garland noticed some papers in Debbie's hand. She observed the name Parker Square Bank at the top of the paperwork. Debbie went on into the hospital and Garland went home.

The next day, when Garland returned to the hospital she heard Lou Ann make a comment about needing to get a loan so they could make the plumbing company payroll.

During the day on June 12, Dr. Murthy told Garland that Jerry's condition did not look good. The urologist said he had not made a clear diagnosis but did not feel that Jerry could last much longer.

After Jerry died, Garland said that Lou Ann briefly gave the impression she was falling apart emotionally but a short time later was joking and laughing with Debbie Baker. Debbie never showed any emotion other than being very, very nervous. All Debbie did was pick at her false fingernails. Sandy and Becky, Jerry's son and daughter, were both very distressed. Garland said she believed Sandy had been given a tranquilizer.

The next day, Garland told her husband that she suspected Debbie Baker was involved in the death of Jerry Sternadel because of her extremely nervous condition. Garland felt that something was wrong and that something was going on between Debbie Baker and Lou Ann.

The day Jerry died, there were several friends of his at the hospital. Garland went with Becky back into Jerry's hospital room while his body was still there. Garland tried to console Becky when she saw Debbie try to give Lou Ann a speckled nerve pill. Debbie was almost to the point of forcing Lou Ann to take the nerve pill. Jerry Wood's wife, Erline Wood, told Lou Ann not to take it.

Becky did not want to leave her father's bedside. Lou Ann came into the room and was trying to force Becky out of Jerry's hospital room. The two exchanged harsh words. Becky accused Lou Ann of killing her dad. Out in the hall, Kathleen Harney told Garland that before Jerry died he had told her that somebody was trying to kill him.

After Jerry died, Garland went to the funeral home. Lou Ann told her that she wasn't sure she was going to have enough cash to pay for the funeral. Garland assured Lou Ann that she would be happy to make up any shortfall. Later, Lou Ann told Garland that she had acquired the money but didn't say from where. The evening before Jerry's funeral, Lou Ann asked Garland to sit with her at the front of the funeral home. Lou Ann told Garland that she did not want Jeannie Walker to see Jerry Sternadel in the coffin. Lou Ann said Jeannie Walker was in town and that she had seen her in a car outside the funeral home. Lou Ann told her that she was staying in the front of the funeral home watching for Jeannie Walker in order to prevent her from entering into the funeral home.

Debbie Baker was also sitting next to Lou Ann. Lou Ann commented to Debbie, "I cannot get far away from you, can I?" After the grave site service, Becky told Justin, Garland's son, that she and her mother, Jeannie Walker, had requested the coffin be opened after the service so

Becky could place some personal items into her father's coffin. Justin accompanied Becky for the coffin opening. Tony and Debbie Baker stayed after the grave site service and watched the grave tender as he opened the coffin. Garland was sitting in her car waiting for Justin when Tony and Debbie Baker walked over to her. The Bakers demanded to know what Becky and Jeannie Walker were doing at the coffin. The Bakers insisted on answers. "Why are they hanging around the coffin? Why is the coffin opened up? Who is that guy hanging around the cemetery with Becky?" Tony Baker became very upset when Garland told him it was her son, Justin, standing by Becky. Tony Baker made a lot of vile comments about the situation to Garland.

The investigators inquired whether Garland knew anything about the arsenic. Garland suggested the investigators consider subpoenaing pharmacy records for Lou Ann and Debbie from Gordon Pharmacy. She stated that Sandy had personally told her he had observed Lou Ann and Debbie spoon-feeding Cran-Apple juice to Jerry at home before he entered the hospital and died. Sandy told Garland he had heard his dad tell the women he did not want the juice and the women telling his dad that he needed it, to take it and to drink it.

Garland said after she learned that Cowley's Rat and Mouse Poison may have been used in killing Jerry, she contacted Clay County Sheriff Jake Bogard to inform him that she had acquired a bottle of the same arsenic solution from an older black male employee of Wichita Feed Store. Ms. Garland said she was at the store discussing a problem she had with squirrels in her attic, and the employee stated he had something that would take care of this problem. The employee went home and came back with a bottle of Cowley's Rat and Mouse Poison that he had used at home to kill a wood rat. This bottle was not in stock for sale at the store at that time but was part of some old stock that had been pulled from the shelves due to EPA regulations and kept by the business to eradicate rodents in their warehouse. Garland turned the bottle of Cowley's Rat and Mouse Poison over to Clay County Deputy Paul Bevering, who came to her residence to pick it up.

Investigator Villanueva met with Joy Lewis, manager of Wichita Feed Store located at 301 Indiana Street in Wichita Falls. Lewis had worked for her father, Ira Crottinger, for approximately fifteen years at this location. Lewis stated that the feed store had carried Cowley's Rat and Mouse Poison up until 1989. At that time, the rat poison was taken off the shelves in response to new FDA regulations. Ms. Lewis checked the store's invoices regarding sales of this poison to see if any was sold to anyone connected to the Sternadel ranch. No documents were located. However, Ms. Lewis stated that items sold on a cash basis were not invoiced. The feed store had originally purchased ten to twelve cases of this rat poison either directly from the manufacturer in Hugo, Oklahoma, or Tufts & Son in DeSoto, Texas. On the second trip to the feed store, the investigator was able to obtain an eight-ounce bottle of Cowley's Rat and Mouse Poison. The bottle was brought from the residence of an employee. Wayne Foster had taken the rat poison home for his own personal use after it was taken off the shelves. Ms. Lewis said she would try to establish whether the manufacturer had assigned batch numbers before shipment.

The investigator had a conversation with Jimmy Foster, who had worked for Wichita Feed Store for fifteen years as a feed mill supervisor. Foster was familiar with the Sternadel death and knew the employees of the Sternadel ranch. Foster was aware that the feed store did carry Cowley's Rat and Mouse Poison, as he had taken some off the shelf to use in and around the feed mill. To his knowledge, he had not sold, traded, or given away any of the poison in question to anybody. He said his brother, Wayne, was more aware of the business dealings that took place in the sales department.

Investigator Villanueva interviewed Wayne Foster, who had been employed with Wichita Feed Store in Wichita Falls, Texas for approximately fifteen years. Both Wayne and his brother, Jimmy, are employed at this location. Their father was also employed there until 1960. Mr. Foster stated he made trips to the Sternadel ranch on several occasions to deliver feed and supplies and was able to identify the employees physically and by name. During his visits to the Sternadel ranch or on the occasion of ranch employees coming into the feed store, he never observed any of the arsenic rat poison being sold to any of the parties connected to Sternadel's operation. Foster said that after Cowley's Rat and Mouse Poison was taken off the shelves, he took three eight-ounce bottles to his residence for his own personal use. The batch number on the bottle of Cowley's Rat and Mouse Poison Foster gave to the investigator did not match or coincide with the batch number on the bottle of arsenic found at the storage facility. Also, the eight-ounce bottle of arsenic found by the lawful authorities at the storage locker had a price sticker of $2.97 with the price and dollar sign imprinted on the initial price label, whereas the bottle in Foster's possession had a handwritten price tag of $1.87.

The investigator contacted Tambra Thornton regarding her statement to Texas Ranger Bill Gerth. One point needing clarification was regarding the fact that Thornton had contacted a private investigator to discuss Jerry Sternadel's poisoning. Thornton stated that because of Jerry's poor health, she was worried he was infected with the AIDS virus. Therefore, she contacted Cliff Duncan, a personal friend. Duncan, being very suspicious, suggested to Thornton that she obtain numerous mason jars with lids to get samples of the liquid from the carpet-cleaning machine for further observation. Thornton said Kent Kaser cleaned the carpet inside the Sternadel residence while Ms. Thornton went to the Sternadel barn and groomed several horses. Kaser did not keep a sample of the liquid. She didn't enter the Sternadel residence on the day in question, June 12. On June 12, after Kent Kaser cleaned the carpet, both Thornton and Kaser returned to the hospital and learned that Jerry had passed away. Thornton said she heard Dr. Bartel directly ask Lou Ann and Debbie Baker whether they had poisoned Jerry. Thornton stated that Lou Ann was very calm when asked the question, while Debbie became nervous and acted strangely, running to the elevator and leaving the hospital. At that point, Lou Ann walked over to Thornton and started asking her about a horse. It was apparent to her that the horse was more significant to Lou Ann than her husband's death.

The investigator obtained information that Lou Ann and her daughter, Holly Maag, had lived at Apartment 209 in the French Quarter Apartments in Wichita Falls but had moved to 2517 Summer Tree Lane, No. 2063, in Arlington, Texas, on approximately June 25, 1992.

The investigator interviewed Richard Mize, an investigative reporter for the *Times Record News,* located at 1301 Lamar in Wichita Falls, who had written an article about Jerry's death. Mize stated that he kept only the article and did not have any notes from his story. He further stated that he became knowledgeable of the Sternadel death from Sheriff Jake Bogard and Texas Ranger Bill Gerth. To Mize's knowledge, no one with the paper had any additional information for a news article.

A telephone call was placed to the residence of Margaret Vehon, nursing supervisor at Bethania Hospital. Vehon rudely stated that she could not talk to the investigator and hung up without further explanation.

The investigator received a telephone call from the Bethania Hospital loss prevention manager, who stated that due to pending litigation against the hospital from the children of Jerry Sternadel, it would be impossible for any of the current hospital staff to discuss any aspect of Jerry's treatment or death with the investigator. The investigator was referred to Glynn Purtle, the attorney representing the hospital.

Purtle stated that due to the letter of intent filed by Jerry Sternadel's family concerning a wrongful death action against Bethania Hospital, he could not authorize any current hospital staff member to be interviewed. The investigator inquired if authorization could be obtained to interview Bethania Hospital staff members after the statute of limitations had expired on litigation involving the wrongful death suit. Mr. Purtle stated that he had no intention of authorizing any interviews with the staff concerning the criminal aspects of the case, even after the statute of limitations on the civil litigation had expired.

The investigator then traveled to Paris, Texas. A written request was made for the death certificate of John Henry Ford, the late husband of Barbara R. Ford and the father of Lou Ann Sternadel. Ford had died eight years earlier. It was rumored that he had exhibited some of the same symptoms exhibited by Jerry prior to death.

Stewart traveled to Hugo, Oklahoma, to the residence of Wilburn and Ruby Higginbotham on Ballpark Road, north of Hugo, Oklahoma, in a rural area. Mrs. Higginbotham stated that they had discontinued production of Cowley's Rat and Mouse Poison by voluntarily surrendering their license to produce the material to the EPA in 1988. She stated the average shelf life of the poison was approximately two years and after that it would normally be withdrawn from the shelves. She said there was an evaporation problem with the stock, and the older the product got, the stronger the arsenic became.

Mrs. Higginbotham stated lot numbers or batch numbers were required to be stamped on every bottle of their product sold in Texas or Louisiana and that the batch numbers were simply the month, day, and the two digits of the year that the product was mixed and bottled. The batch number 9987 that was stamped on the bottle of arsenic found in the storage locker indicated this batch was mixed on September 9, 1987. Mrs. Higginbotham stated that one batch would make up five hundred cases of twelve bottles per case with eight ounces of 5 percent arsenic fluid in each bottle. She said the primary distributor in the local area of Hugo, Oklahoma, and Paris, Texas, was Bunch Wholesale of Texarkana. She stated that all shipping invoices from Cowley's to Bunch Wholesale would have the batch number on both the shipping and billing invoices. She stated they did not have a wholesale distributor in the Wichita Falls area. She said she would try to locate the shipping records of Batch No. 9987 for the period of time in question.

The investigator traveled back to Wichita Falls and made contact with Jerry Woods at the former Sternadel residence. Woods had purchased the residence from Lou Ann and was in the process of remodeling at this time. Woods said that Jerry Sternadel was very domineering toward his family and employees and that Jerry had a lot of enemies within the community. However, he had no doubt in his mind that Lou Ann and Debbie had poisoned Jerry to benefit from his estate. Woods stated it was common knowledge that Jerry was having an affair with Lou Ann's daughter, Stella, and that even Lou Ann knew it. Woods believed Lou Ann tried to get even with Jerry because of it. Woods said he witnessed Jerry abusing Lou Ann at a friendly card game. In Woods's opinion, Lou Ann had both motive and intent. Woods said he and Jerry were in the horse business to make a profit. Woods clearly stated that he did not use Cowley's Rat and Mouse Poison at his facility nor had he ever used it.

The investigator traveled to the Saf-T-Lok warehouse in Wichita Falls and spoke to the manager, Robert Bailey. Bailey said that on June 4, 1992, he found cancelled checks and bank statements belonging to the Sternadel estate in storage unit 629. He said there were also numerous containers of personal items belonging to Debbie Baker in the unit. Bailey said the managers at that time were Mr. and Mrs. Templeton, who resided in the Lake Texoma area. Bailey said the Templetons were related to him. Mr. Templeton had rented the locker to a woman, who said her name was Kathy Simmons. Mr. Bailey stated that a woman fitting the description of Debbie Baker made payments on the storage unit on two occasions. However, Bailey was unable through a photo lineup to identify Debbie Baker as being the one who had rented the storage unit. At this time, the storage unit had been secured pending release from the authorities, and the investigator took photographs of it.

Investigator Stewart traveled to Paris, Texas, to inquire at local farm and ranch stores as well as feed and pet stores that might have handled the Cowley's Rat and Mouse Poison product.

The businesses did not have the product in their store or warehouse during the period of time of 1987 to 1990. Investigator Stewart contacted other businesses in Paris, Texas, and determined that these businesses had never stocked Cowley's Rat and Mouse Poison.

Contact was made with Vicki Wise at Bunch Wholesale in Texarkana, Texas. A request was made to check their shipping invoices to determine if Batch No. 9987 of Cowley's Rat and Mouse Poison had been distributed to any of the local farm and ranch stores in the Paris area. Wise was very cooperative and eager to help. She stated that the owner, Betty Bunch, would be back the middle of the week, but she would personally do some research and get back in touch with the investigator.

Contact was made with Ruby Higginbotham who had located the old records for 1987. She stated that Batch No. 9987 had been shipped to Tufts Wholesale Distributors in De Soto, Texas, on October 19, 1987. She also said a shipment had been sent on March 24, 1987, of a batch made on December 12, 1986, to Tufts & Sons in Arlington, Texas. (Lou Ann Sternadel had brothers in Arlington.)

Investigator Stewart made a note to follow up with Vicki Wise at Bunch Wholesale, Mr. Ray at Estes Chemical Company, and Sue Raney at Lamar Seed & Pet Store.

By the end of August, I had the report in my hands. One disturbing piece of information I gleaned from the investigative report was that Sheriff Jake Bogard had lung cancer. Finding out this devastating development upset me greatly.

A week later, I mailed a letter to District Attorney Jack McGaughey asking him to step aside for a special prosecutor. In September, I received an answer from the DA declining to step aside. His letter stated that I was bound to know he had not been reelected and a new district attorney would assume his duties on January 1, 1993. The DA also stated it would have been in his political interest to seek an indictment in the Sternadel murder and that his "foot-dragging" delayed the case long enough for new evidence to come to light.

On September 25 and 26 a benefit roping event was held in Henrietta, Texas, for Sheriff Jake Bogard.

On October 13, I was on the phone with Dr. Jorg Pirl, the expert toxicologist, who explained that an exhumation was the way to get analytical evidence to show a person had been fed arsenic and died from arsenic poisoning. The doctor said a lab could plot data and find out when arsenic was received and how much.

After talking to the toxicologist, I immediately called Sheriff Bogard and Bill Dear. I told the men what the expert said about an exhumation. They both agreed there was a strong possibility that Jerry's body might have to be exhumed.

On October 15, I called the last known place where Tony Baker had worked in San Antonio. I found out he had quit the company, but that he and his family still lived in San Antonio. A man by the name of Lenny said he was a good friend of Tony's and knew where he lived. After getting the address, I passed it on to Bogard and Dear.

On November 3, Chief Deputy Paul Bevering won the runoff election for sheriff of Clay County. I called Bill Dear and asked him to go meet with the new sheriff and district attorney. I also asked Dear to meet with Jerry's mother and my son to discuss the possibility that Jerry's body might have to be exhumed. As requested, Dear went with Chris Stewart to Henrietta to visit with Paul Bevering and Tim Cole. They also traveled to Wichita Falls to visit with Sandy and Marcy to discuss the possibility of exhuming Jerry's body.

A couple of weeks later, I contacted the lawyer I had retained on behalf of my children for the wrongful death suit against Bethania Hospital and the doctors. I told the attorney not to pursue the lawsuit. I felt the nurses and doctors might come forward and help with the criminal investigation if they didn't have a civil lawsuit hanging over their heads.

Late one afternoon, Sheriff Bogard called. "Jeannie, did I ever tell you how I met my wife, Wanda?"

"No, Sheriff, you never did. But I would love to hear the story."

"Well, I met Wanda in a bowling alley. I was in Burkburnett. I was hungry and looking for a place to eat. I went into a bowling alley because it was the only place I could find. Wanda was in there bowling. Sparks flew immediately. We were married at the Cheyenne, Wyoming, courthouse at twelve noon on July 27, 1962. Wanda and I have been sweethearts ever since. The thing is, my daughter got married there 20 years to the day after we were married.

"I was born on the RO Ranch near the Texas Panhandle on May 5, 1935. The creek was up the day I was born so my folks couldn't get to town. My grandpa was a cowboy. My brother, Dusty, was a cowboy. Dusty was kicked in the chest and killed by a horse in 1985. I was a rodeo cowboy before I married. But, that didn't provide security for a family man so I went to work punching cattle. Later on, Wanda and I were on our way to visit my folks and happened upon a sheriff scouting for a deputy. I took the job. That started my career in law enforcement. Well, now you know a little bit about me."

On January 7, 1993, I called the district attorney to discuss the progress of the murder case. DA Tim Cole said, "I'm in the process of organizing right now, but I will be contacting the rest of the family and you very soon."

After a couple of months passed, I still had not heard anything. On March 18, I called the district attorney inquiring how the murder case was developing and when he would be presenting evidence to the grand jury.

He informed me that he would be calling the family together for a meeting on March 26. At the family meeting, the DA advised that he would be presenting evidence against Debra Baker to the grand jury and asking for an indictment.

On March 30, I called Bill Dear, asking him to travel to Wichita Falls to meet with Texas Ranger Bill Gerth and Sheriff Paul Bevering.

On April 30, I received an unexpected early morning telephone call from Jake Bogard. "Jeannie, I just wanted to tell you, I've enjoyed talking to you and working with you. I know I can count on you to keep up our fight to get Lou Ann and Debbie Baker. I know Bevering and Gerth will stay after them, too. I don't have anything new to tell you except I consider you a dear friend. Well, I've got to go. I love you, Jeannie."

When I hung up the phone that morning, I had an ominous feeling Jake Bogard was saying goodbye. I knew he was very ill, even though he and I had never discussed his illness. For some reason, he did not want me to know how sick he was, so I never let on that I knew about the cancer. I felt the sheriff was a real rarity. I admired and respected him greatly. I was afraid I would never get to talk to my good friend again.

On May 8, 1993, Jake Bogard died in the hospital in Henrietta from complications of lung cancer.

I called Bill Gerth after Jake's funeral. Bill said, "Jeannie, we lost a good lawman and a good friend. Jake's last words to me were, 'Bill, make sure Lou Ann and the Bakers don't get away with the murder of Sternadel. Bring 'em to justice.' Jake's death is a big setback for the case. We may know who did it, and how it was done, but we still have to prove it. This case is like a snowball rolling down the hill—the farther it rolls, it just gets bigger and bigger. It may take time to bring them to justice, but there is no time limit on murder."

On May 11, I called to extend my condolences to Sheriff Paul Bevering on the loss of his longtime partner and friend. Bevering said, "We are all going to miss Jake. When he was in the hospital and knew he was dying, he told us to go get Lou Ann and Debbie Baker. And that's what we plan on doing. We're just finalizing a few details before we make an arrest. The grand jury will be meeting next week to consider the evidence and question witnesses. Debra Baker is subpoenaed to appear. We know she will take the Fifth Amendment on all the questions. But she'll still be indicted. I'll keep you posted."

On May 13, 1993, the Clay County grand jury rekindled the arsenic murder case to review new evidence that had surfaced since they had last met and heard the case in 1991. Debra Baker appeared before the grand jury on May 14. She took the Fifth Amendment on every question. DA Tim Cole requested and received an indictment of Debra Lynn Baker. Sheriff Bevering informed Debra Baker she could not leave the courthouse until the grand jury decided whether or not they needed to recall her.

At noon, I received a phone call from Sheriff Bevering. "Jeannie, I thought I would be the first to tell you the good news. Debra Baker is being arrested for murder as we speak. My deputies are booking her at this very moment. She'll be spending tonight in jail. Debra and her husband, Tony, were sitting on a bench in the hallway of the courthouse. They were laughing and kidding around, as if the grand jury investigation was a joke. When the Bakers heard the grand jury had reached a decision, they started gathering up their belongings to drive back to San Marcus. I walked up to Debra Baker with my deputies and arrested her as she was preparing to leave the courthouse. The judge set her bond at $500,000."

I was elated at hearing the good news. But I couldn't help but wonder why the DA had left Lou Ann out of the picture. After thanking Sheriff Bevering, I immediately phoned Tim Cole and questioned him on why Debbie was the only person indicted.

Cole answered, "We do have other suspects, so we could be asking for indictments of other people at a later time. The investigation is continuing with regard to the other suspects."

After Debra Baker's indictment, former DA Jack McGaughey, who had lost the 1992 election and begun a private law practice in Nocona, Texas, told a reporter, "There just never was sufficient evidence for an indictment. There were several reports out when I left office." He said he assumed the information from those reports must have provided the evidence that was needed for the new district attorney to pursue the case against Debra Baker. "She was not the only suspect. I wouldn't be surprised if additional indictments are forthcoming."

Sheriff Bevering told the reporter, "I don't believe Debra Baker acted alone. We believe there is at least one other person involved in the murder of Sternadel." The sheriff added he felt other indictments could be down the road.

Debra Baker was formally indicted for murder in Clay County. But she also had a felony charge of forgery against her in Hays County. When the judge in Hays County learned she had been charged with murder in Clay County, he immediately postponed accepting her guilty plea on the forgery charge and sentencing until after her murder trial.

On May 15, I arrived in Texas, rented a car, and immediately drove to Henrietta, where I was planning on reviewing the mug shot of Debra Baker. At the Clay County jail, I watched Baker on the TV monitor as she walked around and around in the exercise area. After leaving the jailhouse, I traveled to Wichita Falls to meet with newspaper reporters and editors of television stations to discuss the media coverage of the case.

Fourteen days later, I flew back to Long Island.

On May 30, District Court Judge Roger Towrey appointed Roger Williams of Nocona, Texas, as the attorney for Debra Lynn Baker.

I began corresponding with Baker, asking her to plead guilty and turn in her accomplices. I also informed her of a $5,000 reward I had posted. A couple of weeks later, the DA called me requesting that I stop sending letters to Baker, and I complied.

On August 24, a pretrial hearing was held for Baker. Judge Roger Towrey lowered the bond to $150,000. Debra could not make bail and remained in jail.

On September 15, Baker's bond was lowered to $50,000. Lou Ann was seen coming out of the bail bond office. It seemed she had posted the cash bond for her friend, because Debra Baker was released from jail that day.

A couple months later, I called DA Tim Cole to find out what was happening on the case. He told me he was interviewing potential witnesses for the murder trial and that jury selection would begin on January 15, 1994. "Your son, Sandy; Jerry's mother, Marcy; and Jerry's brother, Jim, will all be subpoenaed as witnesses."

"Are you going to subpoena Lou Ann?" I asked.

Tim Cole replied, "The widow, Lou Ann Sternadel, will be subpoenaed, but I am sure I will have to declare her a hostile witness."

I informed the DA I would be attending the murder trial.

Clay County Courthouse in Henrietta, Texas,
where the murder trial was held

The Murder Trial

On Saturday, January 15, 1994, the sun came up over the horizon spreading a beautiful orange glow throughout the sky. By noon, on the bright sunny day, my plane was departing from Long Island's McArthur Airport. I was anxious and excited about the upcoming murder trial. It had been almost four years since my ex-husband was murdered.

The DA had said the trial would last from ten days to three weeks. Jury selection was to begin on Tuesday, January 18. He was hoping the process of picking a jury would last only one day but couldn't promise anything in that regard.

My flight was on time and uneventful. After exchanging hugs and kisses at the airport, my daughter and I headed to Wichita Falls.

Because of the publicity, 225 potential jurors were summoned to the 97th District Court in Henrietta, Texas, on Tuesday, January 18, 1994. By the end of the day, the number had dwindled to 89. It took the lawyers one and a half days to pick the eight men and four women seated on the jury.

Testimony was expected to begin on Wednesday afternoon.

I made reservations at a motel in Wichita Falls for the duration of the trial. However, Jerry's mother suggested that my daughter and

I stay with her. "Why waste money when you don't have to? You and Becky are perfectly welcome to stay with me. I've got twin beds in the back bedroom. I won't take no for an answer!" Out of respect for Jerry's mother, I cancelled the motel reservations.

On the morning testimony was to begin, my daughter and ex-mother-in-law rode with me to the Clay County courthouse in Henrietta. I was driving slowly around the courthouse square looking for a parking space when my sharp-eyed daughter noticed a prime parking space right in front of the courthouse. I began driving to the spot. Suddenly, a car came out of nowhere and zoomed into the parking space.

Becky gasped, "Mother, look at the license plate of that car."

Marcy said, "Who would put that kind of license plate on their automobile?"

Becky questioned, "Mother, does this mean Debbie Baker is going to get off?"

I eyeballed the plate. I knew that number far too well. "It means we are fighting the devil. But he won't win. I'll find another parking spot."

Marcy said, "Only the devil would put those numbers on their plate."

I was driving round the courthouse square again when Becky exclaimed, "Look, Mother, a car just pulled out over there! Go get that spot."

Driving toward the open space, I quickly realized it was the same spot the car with the 666 license plates had zipped into a few minutes earlier. But now the automobile was gone.

"Why on earth would anyone pull into a parking space and leave a minute later?" Marcy questioned.

"Maybe it wasn't a car at all, MoMo. Maybe it was a mirage!" Becky responded.

"Well, I saw that car. I know I didn't imagine it!" Marcy replied.

"Nevertheless, I'm taking this space," I said, pulling my car into the parking spot. "We should already be inside the courthouse. We need to talk to Tim Cole before the trial starts."

"Mother, I'm scared! Did you see the driver of that 666 car?"

"No, I didn't think about looking at the driver. I was too busy looking at the license plate. If the devil was trying to scare us, he succeeded. But we are going to win this fight. C'mon, ladies, we've got a trial to attend."

The DA and my son were standing just inside the courthouse vestibule. After cordial greetings, we walked up the winding staircase to the second-floor courtroom. On the way up, the district attorney told us that he had asked prospective jurors how they would feel trying someone who was a party to murder, because the jury selection was his only chance to ask questions during the trial and receive answers. He said that he told the prospective jurors that he felt from the beginning that more than one person was involved in the murder. "Even though Debra Baker is the only person who was charged with the murder, my theory is that Debra Baker and Jerry's widow were accomplices in a conspiracy to murder Jerry."

I asked him if he could furnish me with the names of the witnesses he planned on calling. Within a minute or two, he brought a copy of his witness list over to me, saying, "Obviously, there have been no conspiracy charges, but this investigation is not over. Any other person involved could be indicted at a later date."

Becky, Sandy, Marcy, and I took seats in the courtroom with the rest of Jerry's family. Lou Ann was nowhere to be seen. Rumors were flying that she was not going to show up at the murder trial for her husband's killer because she was living it up in the Bahamas with a married man.

Debra Baker was sitting at the defendant's table located on the left side of the courtroom. She was laughing and joking with her husband and son, who were seated on the front row right behind her. She winked at and waved to people in the courtroom, as if the murder trial was a joke. Suddenly, she gave out a loud laugh and exclaimed, "Not a chance!"

Debra Baker's courtroom behavior was outrageous and repulsive. The sight and sound of her loud snickering gave me a sick feeling in the bottom of my stomach.

The courtroom was dead silent as the jury walked in and took their perspective seats. The court was now in session.

Judge Roger Towrey asked for the plea of the defendant.

Debra Baker stood up and said, "Not guilty."

Roger Williams, Debra Baker's court-appointed attorney, immediately made a motion for a mistrial, "Debra Baker is being tried as a party in Jerry Sternadel's death. But no other person is charged in the death. And that is grounds for a mistrial."

The judge denied the motion.

The trial began with DA Tim Cole outlining his case against Debra Lynn Baker during his opening statement to the jury.

"Debbie Baker was part of a plan to murder her former boss by lacing his food with arsenic. The reason, the motive, for the murder was the oldest in the world—old-fashioned greed. Jerry Sternadel was killed for his money. By all accounts, Jerry was a successful businessman, who built a substantial clientele in his business. He raised and raced thoroughbred horses at tracks in New Mexico and Oklahoma. The defendant, Debra Baker, was Jerry's secretary and bookkeeper for about seven years before his death. She was responsible for keeping track of all the accounts, prepared checks and paid all the bills. Over the years, the defendant and Jerry's wife, Lou Ann Sternadel, became very close friends. Many said they were very much like sisters, confiding in one another and constantly spending time together. Debbie Baker came and left the Sternadel residence as she pleased. She would often walk to the house from the plumbing office behind the Sternadel home to talk to Lou Ann Sternadel or have lunch, or drive to Wichita Falls to pick up their lunches. Jerry lived in the home with his wife, Lou Ann; his son by a former marriage, Sandy; and his stepdaughter, Holly Maag."

The prosecutor slowly walked around the front of the courtroom.

"Jerry Sternadel was a hard man to work for or live with. He could be quite harsh to his employees and his family. Witnesses are going to tell you that he was very demanding toward the defendant, so much so that many people wondered, and some even asked Debra Baker on occasion, why she stayed. The answer was she stayed for Lou Ann—and for the money. Sometime during 1989, things began to go wrong with the business. Even though Sternadel's business was as good as ever, for some inexplicable reason, suppliers began to have checks returned from the Sternadel account. Payroll checks began to bounce. It almost seemed that there was never enough money, even though the money continued to flow into the business. The defendant would scramble to try and cover the hot checks, begging the holders not to tell Jerry Sternadel. In 1989 alone, over $40,000 was taken from the business accounts in the form of checks made out to the defendant's husband, Tony Baker, and deposited in the defendant's personal bank account at Parker Square Bank in Wichita Falls—checks written by the defendant and signed by Lou Ann Sternadel.

"Texas Ranger Bill Gerth would eventually discover scores of such checks totaling tens of thousands of dollars over a three- or four-year period, amounts which the defendant explained away as 'loans' from Jerry. A large portion of the profit was being drained away, and as you might expect, the scheme began to unravel. In early 1990, Jerry Sternadel was coming closer to the truth and was preparing to do something about it."

Debra Lynn Baker in court with her defense team

Clay County Court in session with defense attorney and
DA arguing a point

District Attorney Tim Cole walked over to the jury box, looking
squarely at the jurors as he continued.

"On May 22, 1990, Jerry Sternadel ate a lunch of taco salad, as
he often did, brought to him from Taco Bell. Less than half an hour
later, he was deathly ill, vomiting with gastrointestinal distress, which
continued through the next day. On May 23, he was admitted to
Bethania Hospital's intensive care unit, where he remained until being
released in improved condition on May 29, only to return with new
symptoms on May 30, baffling the doctors and hospital staff who were
treating him. Jerry once again went home on June 2, and by June 4, his
intense symptoms had returned as he lay in bed at home. By June 12,
Jerry Sternadel was dead from what doctors knew to be a massive dose
of arsenic—fed to him in the liquids that he was given for dehydration
by the women, who pretended to care for him. Two days later, on June
14, Lou Ann Sternadel filed for probate of her husband's will. She was
the sole beneficiary of the estate and inherited an estate worth close to

half a million dollars—an estate that was quickly liquidated and turned into cash. Financial dependence of the defendant, Debra Baker, and her husband, upon money from Lou Ann Sternadel continued even after Jerry died and even after the defendant moved to South Texas."

Tim Cole remained standing in front of the jury box as he said, "Dozens of witnesses are going to describe all the circumstances which show the defendant's guilt. You will hear about her actions before Jerry's death, at the hospital, which she seldom left, and after Jerry's death. Finally, you are going to hear about the bottle of arsenic poison, which was found in a storage unit in Wichita Falls in June 1992—a storage unit that was rented by the defendant under an assumed name, even before Jerry died."

Walking toward the defense table where the defense attorney and the defendant were sitting, the prosecutor summed up, "I suspect that the defense is not going to dispute that Jerry Sternadel was murdered by someone close to him with arsenic poison. But he will try to convince you that you cannot find the defendant guilty because no one saw her pour arsenic into a bottle of juice or food. There is no eyewitness to that fact. However, I submit to you that once you have heard and seen the evidence against the defendant, and once you know the circumstances of Jerry Sternadel's death, that one missing fact will not matter to you, because you don't need an eyewitness. You will be convinced beyond a reasonable doubt that the defendant, Debra Baker, is guilty of murder."

In his opening statement, Debra Baker's attorney, Roger Williams, set the tone for the testimony he would be presenting. He began by saying, "The widow, Lou Ann Sternadel, is not on trial for the murder of her husband, although District Attorney Tim Cole would ask you, the jurors, to believe that Lou Ann Sternadel and my client, Debra Lynn Baker, plotted the plumber's death."

When the defense attorney finished his opening statement, the DA started calling his witnesses.

Jerry's mother, Marcy Sternadel, was the second witness. It was difficult for the prosecutor to have to do this to the victim's mother, but he showed Marcy a picture that was taken at the autopsy and asked her to identify her son so he could submit the photo as evidence. Jerry's mother was overwhelmed and devastated when she saw the horrid photo of her dead son with tubes in his mouth and nose and IV lines inserted and attached to his arms and feet. Tears welled up in her eyes as she slowly said, "Oh, what a horrible picture."

Tim Cole asked, "Is this your son, Jerry Sternadel?"

Marcy slowly answered, "Yes, it is. But it's a terrible, terrible picture of him."

Marcy described to the jury how her son's family had been wrapped up in sexual scandal and feuding. She testified how she had lectured her son about an infatuation he had with his stepdaughter. She said she scolded her son about a home he had purchased for another woman, who was his mistress. She described her son's widow as a manipulator, who didn't care that her husband had bought another woman a home. "I told Lou Ann that I would leave Jerry, if I were her. I told her she didn't have to put up with it. But she said she wanted to."

Roger Williams repeatedly questioned Marcy about lawsuits she and other family members had filed against Jerry's widow, Lou Ann Sternadel.

Marcy said the lawsuits were eventually settled. She had received $30,000. "I wanted to get to the bottom of this." She stated that the suits had been filed after former District Attorney Jack McGaughey refused to file charges in the murder case. Williams implied through his questions that the rest of the family had filed the suits to get at Jerry Sternadel's estate, which was left entirely to his widow, Lou Ann.

When asked about her son's assets, the victim's mother said she did not know how much her son was worth. But she described him as a plumber who owned several valuable racehorses and also cattle. Marcy testified she had felt it was odd that Debbie Baker was with the family so much. "I thought it was kind of funny. In the hospital, Debbie and Lou Ann were always off to themselves, talking and whispering. I don't know what they said." She also said that during her son's illness, family members questioned Debbie Baker's presence and attentiveness at the hospital. She stated she found Debbie and Lou Ann's behavior very strange. She testified that she had questioned Lou Ann and Debbie about how Jerry went into Bethania Hospital three times, feeling well enough to be released and then relapsing when he went home. She recalled her son often drank Cran-Apple juice because at one time he had had kidney stones and the Cran-Apple juice was supposed to help. She testified, "Jerry loved Cran-Apple juice. He was the only one out there in his family who liked it."

The trial ended for the day with Marcy Sternadel's testimony.

Later that evening at Marcy's home, she and Becky watched TV, while I sat at the dining room table scrutinizing the prosecutor's witness list.

I identified the people I knew.

- Bill Gerth—Texas Ranger who investigated the murder case with Sheriff Jake Bogard.
- Paul Bevering—Chief Deputy, later sheriff, who inherited the case from Sheriff Bogard.
- Robert Bailey—The manager of the storehouse warehouse who called the police.
- Dr. Roger Humphrey—personal physician and primary doctor who attended to Jerry's overall care at Bethania Hospital.
- Dr. Danny Bartel—Neurologist who cared for Jerry and assisted Dr. Humphrey and other physicians at Bethania Hospital.
- Kent Kaser—friend of Jerry, who cleaned the carpet at the Sternadel home for Lou Ann Sternadel on June 12, the day Jerry died.
- Tambra Thornton—groomed horses for Jerry and occasionally cleaned the Sternadel home with her partner, Kent Kaser

- Ken Harney—job foreman and good friend, who rented property from Jerry.
- Kathleen Harney—Ken Harney's wife and good friend of Jerry.
- Jerry Gamble—State Plumbing Inspector and good friend of Jerry.
- Harold Newton—salesman at Morrison Supply where Jerry bought plumbing materials.
- Ron Sugamosto—friend and business associate of Jerry's from Ruidosa, New Mexico.
- Dr. Thomas Kurt—expert witness and toxicologist from Dallas, Texas.
- Thomas Bradley—teenager, visitor at the Sternadel ranch, who accidentally drank juice containing arsenic poison.
- Stella Milburn—daughter of Lou Ann and stepdaughter of Jerry.
- Barbara Ford—mother of Lou Ann and mother-in-law of Jerry.
- Lou Ann Sternadel—widow of Jerry Sternadel and murder suspect.
- Ruby Higginbotham—current owner and relative of manufacturer of Cowley's Rat and Mouse Poison.

Putting the witness list aside, I walked into the living room where Marcy and Becky were sitting on the couch looking at photo albums full of old pictures. I sat down to join them.

Marcy glanced over at me. "I am so ashamed of myself for letting that lowlife, Lou Ann, come into my home and letting her stay over here when Jerry was in the hospital the last time. Lou Ann sat right here on my couch. She just kept saying, 'Oh, my poor baby. My poor baby's just gotta get well.' It just makes me sick thinking Lou Ann and Debbie Baker were feeding Jerry poison all that time. I let that so-and-so sleep in my extra bedroom on one of the twin beds. I don't know if I'll ever forgive myself."

"Marcy, don't torture yourself like this. You couldn't have known what Lou Ann and Debbie Baker were doing. Nobody knew until it was too late."

At bedtime, I told my daughter I would sleep in the twin bed by the window closest to the street and she could sleep in the twin bed next to the wall. Becky and I talked for a short time before turning in for the evening. Once the light was turned out, Becky was soon fast asleep, while I lay in bed rehashing the testimony of that day.

I thought I sensed movement at the end of my bed. It felt as if something was tugging at the sheet covering my feet. I promptly dismissed the notion, thinking my foot was shaking from nervous energy of the hectic day's activities. At that very moment, I felt something touching my foot and tugging on it. I sat upright, looking at the foot of the bed. The outside street lamp shed a faint light into the room enabling me to catch a glimpse of what it was, if anything. I gasped when I saw tiny creatures crawling on my bed covers. Low mumbling sounds were coming from ugly dwarfish creatures dressed in black, as they furiously tugged on the sheet. I quickly kicked the cover off the bed sending the miniature beings tumbling to the floor. But the things quickly regained their balance, climbed back up onto the bed, and started tugging furiously at my foot. It was then that I heard rumbling noises coming from the floor of the bedroom. I looked toward the sound. I became immensely frightened by what I saw. There was a black hole in the middle of the floor with scores of the little ugly creatures crawling out of the dark underground. The tiny creatures on my bed gathered together and started tugging on both of my feet. I realized the little devil-like creatures were trying to pull me off the bed and toward the ominous hole.

More and more tiny elf-like demons crawled out of the black opening and ran toward the bed. The menacing sight struck terror into me. Instinctively, I began praying, "Lord Jesus, please help me." As I prayed, the little devil creatures thrust their arms into the air, mumbled something, and began running and jumping off my bed into the black hole. I watched as all of the little devils descended back inside the black hole, and the opening immediately closed up and disappeared. I sat on the bed trembling with fear. Although I was wide awake, I wasn't sure if what I had seen was real or unreal. Was I hallucinating? And if I was hallucinating, then what was causing it? I never took any drugs. I was averse to even taking an aspirin.

What had happened was like something coming from an unreal world of monsters and fairies. But the tiny demons I had witnessed were not fairies. They looked as if they were creatures from hell. I was afraid to go to sleep. I felt if I dozed off, the tiny devilish monsters would come back. I got up from the bed and tiptoed to the middle of the room where I had seen the black hole in the floor. There was no evidence of it. I breathed a sigh of relief and walked into the living room. I sat down on the couch. I was exhausted but stayed awake all night. Every once in a while, I would get up and look into the back bedroom to make sure my daughter was safe. It was a blessing when the sun finally dawned.

"Did you have a good night's sleep?" Marcy asked as she walked into the living room that morning.

I just shrugged and said, "It could have been worse."

At the murder trial on Wednesday, January 19, DA Tim Cole presented testimony about the storage locker where the bottle of arsenic poison had been discovered. James Shelton, the man who originally rented the locker to the defendant, had died. Cole called the current Saf-T-Loc warehouse manager to the witness stand. Robert Bailey did not rent the locker to the woman who called herself Kathy Simmons. But he was the manager who had cut the locks off the five-by-five-foot locker, unit 629, and had discovered letters and statements belonging to Jerry and Lou Ann Sternadel and Debra and Tony Baker inside. There was even an eight-by-ten photo of Debra Baker in one of the boxes, along with correspondence addressed to Debra Baker's address in Holliday, Texas.

The last person to testify on Wednesday was Dr. Charles Odoms of the Southwest Institute of Forensic Science in Dallas, Texas. The forensic expert testified that Jerry Sternadel's corpse contained more than four times the lethal amount of arsenic that it would take to kill a person. The medical examiner said traces of arsenic were found in the two-liter Cran-Apple juice bottle that was brought to the lab. Dr. Odoms stated that he believed the victim was poisoned at least three different times leading up to each hospitalization with the arsenic poison finally causing his death.

On Wednesday night, I had the same horrifying experience with the tiny demons coming out of the opening in the floor. But the pitch-black hole opened up even larger as more and more tiny creatures crawled out into the room. Once on the bed, the devilish things began violently tugging on my feet, trying to pull me off the bed and into the hole. Again, my prayers caused the mumbling little demons to run and jump back into the black pit.

Marcy and Becky Sternadel, Jerry's mother and daughter, reading trial coverage in newspaper

At the trial on Thursday, January 20, the prosecutor called Jerry Sternadel's personal family physician. Dr. Roger Humphrey said he thought it was unusual that Debra Baker, who was not a member of the family, had spent so much time at the hospital. Dr. Humphrey remarked that he noticed Debra Baker and Lou Ann Sternadel seemed to be especially close and Debra Baker was often present during conferences with the family.

The physician testified that Jerry had been hospitalized on three occasions. The first was on May 23, 1990, when Jerry came to the emergency room suffering from nausea, vomiting, diarrhea, abdominal cramps, and muscle weakness. The doctor stated that he had diagnosed and treated Jerry Sternadel for an intestinal infection, his condition improved, and he was released from the hospital on May 29. He stated that Jerry returned to the hospital the next day, May 30, suffering from similar symptoms, along with hallucinations and a swollen abdomen. The doctor said he suspected something other than an infection was causing his patient's illness. Jerry's family doctor said that he called in specialists in other medical areas, and they ordered a series of laboratory tests for possible heavy metals or other toxins that might be causing the illness. Dr. Humphrey testified that the numerous lab results revealed Jerry had ingested arsenic. He said on the second hospital visit Jerry again recovered sufficiently to be released from the hospital but was readmitted on June 5 with the same recurring symptoms plus multiple organ failure related to arsenic poisoning. The doctor testified that when Jerry was admitted for the third and final time, he had so much arsenic in his system that the doctors ruled out any chance of survival. (The doctor did not explain the increase in arsenic levels. Wasn't it obvious that his patient was being poisoned? Did he think Jerry had ingested the poison by accident and was continuing to ingest it by accident? Why didn't he go looking for the source of the arsenic? I was hoping to get some answers. But Cole ended his direct examination without asking these questions.)

During cross-examination by the defense attorney, the family physician described his patient as being mentally unstable and violent. Dr. Humphrey testified that Jerry Sternadel had to be strapped to the bed, and notes made by the nurses indicated Jerry was hallucinating and saying things about people trying to kill him.

Dr. Danny Bartel, the neurologist who attended to Jerry Sternadel in the hospital, took the witness stand. He testified that Jerry told him from his hospital bed that Debbie and Lou Ann were poisoning him. But the doctor stated, "The time he pointed his finger at his wife and said, 'That is the woman who is trying to kill me,' was a delusional statement made from a delusional man."

Jerry's friend Kent Kaser also testified that Jerry told him from his hospital bed that Debbie and Lou Ann were poisoning him. Kent went so far as to say that he witnessed the two women taking an unknown substance out of a paper cup and placing the substance into Jerry Sternadel's mouth. He stated that on a previous visit to the hospital, Jerry had motioned for him and his girlfriend, Tambra Thornton, to come into the room where Jerry told them, 'Those women are trying to kill me.' Kent testified as to what Jerry had told him as he pointed at the two women, "He said they were giving him, ah, a bunch of shit, is what he told us." In his testimony, Kent Kaser stated, "Lou Ann said, 'He's being crazy or silly.'" He testified that Lou Ann made that statement just before she sent for a nurse to tranquilize her dying husband. He also testified that Debbie Baker called Jerry a "mean son of a bitch" and an "asshole." Kent said that after he heard all this, neither he nor his girlfriend were allowed by Debra Baker or Lou Ann to enter the hospital room again.

Debbie's attorney repeatedly asked medical witnesses to explain the psychotic side effects of arsenic poisoning. It seemed that both the prosecutor and the defense attorney were trying to use testimony to give credibility to the words of a dead man.

The DA continued to get witnesses to testify as to Jerry's mental stability on June 11, 1990, the day before he died. The prosecutor had already established that a man suffering from psychotic episodes during arsenic poisoning could still continue to be competent up to a certain point, that point being June 11, 1990.

Probably the most damaging testimony on Thursday came from Jerry's job foreman, Ken Harney. Harney began his testimony by recounting the day his boss had become ill after eating lunch with Debbie and Lou Ann. He testified that he left Jerry at noon when Jerry went to the house to eat lunch with the two women. When he returned about an hour later, he found Jerry very ill. The foreman said Jerry told him he thought he got food poisoning at lunch, which caused him to vomit repeatedly. Harney stated that sometime later that afternoon, Jerry was taken to the hospital for the first of his three admissions. Harney also testified about directing officers to a trash pit behind Jerry Sternadel's home where they recovered a Cran-Apple juice bottle that was later verified to contain arsenic poison. (The previous day, an expert witness, Dr. Charles Odoms, had testified that arsenic poison had been found in a Cran-Apple juice bottle.)

Harney stated that when Jerry returned to work after his first trip to the hospital, he and Debbie fought over fruit juice. Ken said that when he arrived at the plumbing office behind the Sternadel home, he heard Debbie say to Jerry, 'You've got to drink this.' He stated he saw Debbie try to get Jerry to drink something.

"I believe it was apple juice. There were ice cubes scattered among the rocks of the gravel driveway. Debbie Baker turned and said, 'Get him to drink something. He's dehydrated.' I told Debbie, I can't get Jerry to drink anything. You know him better than that."

The defense attorney hammered at Jerry's morality, while the prosecutor piled up people who pointed fingers at Debra Baker.

On Thursday night, I experienced another terrifying episode with the tiny hellish creatures. There were hundreds of the demonic critters. Once again, my prayers pushed the devilish little monsters back into their dark abyss.

Jerry Gamble and other witnesses waiting to testify

On Friday, January 21, the district attorney called Jerry Gamble, the state plumbing inspector, to the witness stand. Gamble had employed my husband when Gamble had his own private plumbing business. The two men had become good friends and eventually business competitors when my husband started his own plumbing business.

Gamble testified about a visit to his friend's hospital room in the intensive care unit. He described the sight of his friend, who was seriously weakened by illness. He testified that Jerry's hands and feet were strapped to the hospital bed. He repeated Jerry's words, "Gamble, you gotta help me. You gotta cut me loose, get me out of here." Gamble said that he told Jerry he would return later in the afternoon, but that did not satisfy his sick friend. "He said, 'It will be too late, Gamble. I'll be dead by then.'"

Gamble said he remembered Jerry nodding toward the door of his hospital room, where Debra Baker and Lou Ann were silhouetted. He stated his friend said those two women were trying to kill him. Gamble testified that Jerry pointed an accusing finger at Debra and Lou Ann and said, "Those two women are trying to kill me. There's $35,000 missing and they took it. They're trying to kill me."

Gamble said he left the hospital room and informed the two women of the accusations Jerry was making. He said Jerry's wife promptly summoned a nurse, who gave Jerry a tranquilizer.

Defense Attorney Roger Williams began trying to put doubt in the jurors' minds about Jerry's mental stability. During his cross-examination of Gamble, Williams reminded Gamble of another part of his conversation with Jerry. "Didn't he ask you, 'Is there blood all over me?'"

Gamble answered that Jerry had asked him that question. "There was no blood, but that was Jerry's only nonsensical statement during the visit."

Witnesses for the prosecution at the courthouse
waiting for their chance to testify

Although Lou Ann was not on trial, the DA was linking her to Debra Baker through the testimony of the witnesses.

The next prosecution witness, Harold Newton, a salesman with Morrison Supply, testified, "It seems like every time you saw Lou Ann, you saw Debbie." His Wichita Falls business had supplied Jerry Sternadel Plumbing with plumbing materials and equipment. Newton stated that Jerry had purchased $300,000 annually in plumbing supplies from Morrison Supply. Newton described Jerry as a meticulous businessman who always paid his bills by the tenth of the month to take advantage of the 2 percent discount. The salesman said about six months before Jerry's death, his company's checks started bouncing. Newton said he notified Jerry's bookkeeper, Debra Baker, when the first check came back. The salesman testified that Debra said there was a bookkeeping error she was trying to get corrected. He said Debra promised to bring a cashier's check to Morrison Supply to make the payment good and pleaded with him not to inform her boss. The salesman testified that checks bouncing on the plumber's account continued to occur each month until Jerry's death, and each time Debra would ask him not to tell Jerry. The salesman thought Jerry was very demanding. He said that at times, when he showed up at the plumber's office, he would find Debra crying and saying that Jerry had scolded her.

During cross-examination, Newton testified that he witnessed several shouting matches between Jerry and Debra. The salesman said that despite the problems with insufficient checks, the account was always paid in full. He stated that he honored Debra's request and never told Jerry about the company checks bouncing.

He recalled a visit to the hospital when he was sitting with Debra and Lou Ann. He stated that Lou Ann asked him what plumbing supplies contained arsenic. He said that when Debra heard Lou Ann ask him that question, Debra became "nervous and tense" and got up and walked to the other side of the room. Newton also said the two women seemed to be good friends and were together constantly.

The DA was successfully linking Debra with the hospital and monetary inconsistencies but had not linked her to the arsenic poison doses that had killed Jerry.

During later testimony, Ron Sugamosto, a friend and business associate of Jerry's from Ruidoso, New Mexico, stated that he and Jerry had bought and raced horses together. Ron described his friend's volatile relationship with his wife, Lou Ann, as he told of arguments between them. He also testified that Jerry once made a serious comment about getting rid of Lou Ann and Debra during a conflict over the purchase of a horse. He testified that both women had misled him when he called to ask about Jerry's condition in the hospital by telling him that Jerry was improving when actually "Jerry was almost in a coma."

Roger Williams asked the witness, "You didn't think you could put anything over on him?"

Sugamosto replied, "Jerry was trusting, you know what I mean? You probably could, if you got close to him."

Other vivid testimony came from Thomas Bradley of Fayette, Missouri. The young man had spent a month in the Wichita Falls area and worked with Jerry's stepdaughter, Holly Maag, at Uncle Lynn's Catfish Restaurant. Bradley testified there was a party one night in early June 1990 at a fellow worker's apartment. Holly allowed him to sleep in her sister's bedroom so he wouldn't have to drive back to Nocona, where he lived. The young man said when he arose the next morning he saw Holly and Sandy Sternadel cleaning the house in preparation for Jerry's return home from the hospital. He said he asked for something to drink, and they invited him to help himself to whatever was in the kitchen. He testified that he went to the refrigerator and poured himself a glass of Cran-Apple juice. He said he took two swallows of the juice and his throat started burning. "I felt it burn all the way down my throat and into my stomach." He recalled that within ten to fifteen minutes he had diarrhea and was vomiting. He immediately suspected food poisoning. "I felt like I was dying." He said Holly drove him to the clinic where he was treated for a viral infection. He said that two or three days later he still felt poorly. He stated that after he returned to Missouri, he was contacted by the sheriff's office and instructed to undergo a series of medical tests. The young man testified, "The tests proved positive for arsenic poisoning."

During cross-examination by Williams, Thomas Bradley said he had no idea what might have happened to the juice bottle. He said he had never seen Debra Baker prior to his courtroom appearance.

On Friday night, hundreds of tiny, fiendish creatures crawled out of the black hellish pit. They started tugging on my feet as if they were in a wild feeding frenzy. More little demons poured out of the hole, raced up onto the bed, and began tugging on my hands and feet. My prayers did not deter the little devil monsters. I continued praying, as more and more of the creatures poured out of the bottomless pit. They were crawling all over me. I gave a loud cry, "Jesus, help me! Cast these demons back into hell!" Instantly, the creatures jumped off the bed and hurriedly descended back into the black hole.

My daughter stirred awake. "Mother, I was having a horrible dream. I dreamed little tiny men were coming out of the ground and dragging you into a deep, black pit. Then, they started coming after me. I heard you yell, and I woke up. I'm too scared to go back to sleep. Can I sleep with you in your bed?"

"Let's go sleep in the living room. There'll be more room for the two of us on the couch."

The next morning Becky kept talking about the vivid nightmare she'd had. That afternoon, I told my daughter about the little creatures and the black hole. Over the weekend, my daughter and I slept on the couch in the living room. I contemplated going to a motel for the rest of the trial, but I felt Marcy's feelings would be hurt. So I decided to continue to stay at Marcy's home for the duration of the trial.

On Tuesday, January 25, only one witness took the stand, Texas Ranger William Gerth. He described an interview he conducted with Debra Baker a week after the poisoning death of Jerry Sternadel on June 12, 1990. "I thought she was about to confess."

Williams's objection to Gerth's words was sustained, but the statement already had had its effect on the jurors, who were seated only a few feet from the lawman.

The DA asked Gerth another question about his first interview with Debra Baker as part of his investigation into Sternadel's death. Gerth said Debra had been calm in answering his questions and told him she had daily access to the Sternadel house. When he asked her about a two-liter Ocean Spray Cran-Apple juice container in the Sternadel refrigerator that might have contained arsenic, her mood changed. "Her entire demeanor changed. She became very solemn. She crossed her arms and started rocking back and forth, back and forth." The Texas Ranger crossed his own arms and imitated Debra Baker's actions.

He testified, "It was that dramatic. Evidently, Baker had not heard that Thomas Bradley had gotten sick soon after drinking from the juice bottle." Gerth testified that her surprise at the news of the boy drinking juice from the Sternadel refrigerator almost coaxed Debra to admit guilt. But instead she went to the ladies room to compose herself. Gerth stated that later in the interview, Debra told him that she might have been responsible for Sternadel's death. "She told me she may have given Jerry Sternadel the lethal dose. That just came up at the end of her statement ... she was not visibly rocking at that point. She was very, very reserved."

In his cross-examination, Williams pointed out that Debra Baker's mention of the "lethal dose" came after Debra had been told of the Thomas Bradley incident. The defense attorney was trying to convince the jury of Debra's realization that she might have unwittingly contributed to Jerry's death. Williams stated that his client had signed a statement in which she said on June 4, 1990, the day Jerry went into the hospital for the final time, that she had given Jerry 7UP, water, and juice because his doctor had told him to drink plenty of liquids.

Cole was hammering away at Debra's guilt and her embezzlement of thousands of dollars from Jerry.

Gerth testified that there were a total of fifty-five checks from Jerry's bank account made out to Tony Baker, Debra's husband. He stated that a $1,250 check made out to Tony Baker was dated June 13, 1990. But the bank refused this check because Jerry Sternadel's bank accounts had been frozen.

Checks and photocopies of checks recorded on a poster-sized list were entered as evidence by the prosecutor and passed from juror to juror. The final tally included forty-eight checks written on personal or business accounts of Jerry Sternadel made out to Tony Baker or Tony Baker's used car dealership, Midwestern Motors, and totaling $66,528.46. The checks were dated beginning in May 1986, up until five days before Jerry Sternadel's death on June 12, 1990.

Gerth stated that the financial relationship between Lou Ann and the Bakers continued even after Jerry Sternadel's death. In July 1991, Lou Ann became a partner with Tony Baker in a trucking business named Red Bird Express.

On cross-examination, the defense attorney showed the jury checks written from Debra and Tony Baker's account made out to Lou Ann or Jerry Sternadel totaling $5,761.25 and written between June 1989 and April 1990.

The DA continued to link Debra Baker to the arsenic poison. He also showed the jury that Debra had the opportunity and the motive to kill her boss. But Cole still had not mustered up an eyewitness to the actual act of poisoning Jerry.

The next witness called to the stand was a medical director with the North Texas Poison Center in Dallas. Dr. Thomas Kurt testified that he believed three large doses of arsenic were administered to Jerry between May 23, 1990, and June 12, 1990. The doctor stated the large doses of arsenic poison killed Jerry Sternadel.

Bottle of arsenic and Cran-Apple juice entered as evidence

Earlier testimony had brought into evidence the eight-ounce bottle of arsenic poison that had been discovered in a storage facility in Wichita Falls, Texas, along with business and personal papers and personal items from both the Sternadel and Baker families. The bottle of Cowley's Rat and Mouse Poison was about three-quarters empty. The label read COWLEY'S RAT AND MOUSE POISON MANUFACTURED BY S. L. COWLEY AND SONS MANUFACTURING CO., HUGO, OKLAHOMA. The label listed the active ingredient as ARSENIC TRIOXIDE—1.5%; TOTAL ARSENIC, AS ELEMENTAL, ALL IN WATER-SOLUBLE FORM, 1.14%.

Dr. Thomas Kurt testified that the three-quarters amount of arsenic poison missing from the eight-ounce bottle would have been enough to make up three lethal doses.

The DA suggested that the first dose of arsenic poison had come in a taco salad served to Jerry by Debra Baker in May 1990.

Dr. Kurt testified, "If I were going to do it [kill someone], I'd mix it [arsenic poison] with about an ounce of picante sauce and I'd pour it on." The medical director said the hot sauce would have disguised the unpleasant, bitter taste of the other ingredients in the rat poison. Dr. Kurt stated, "Cranberry juice has the same effect in disguising an unpleasant taste. Cranberry juice is sometimes used to help hospital patients take bitter-tasting medicine."

The defense attorney recalled Clay County Sheriff Paul Bevering to the stand. Williams asked only one question. "Was Lou Ann Sternadel ever arrested, charged, or indicted for any offense in connection with the death of Jerry Sternadel?"

Sheriff Bevering answered, "No."

The defense attorney later told a questioning reporter that getting Sheriff Bevering's testimony on record during the prosecution's case did not necessarily have bearing on the current trial, but he said it might come up in the case of an appeal or in future motions concerning the murder case.

When Sheriff Paul Bevering left the witness stand, the state rested its case.

The first witness for the defense was Wichita Falls attorney Stephen Shelton. Shelton had represented Lou Ann when her claim to her husband's $320,000 life insurance settlement and property were contested by a lawsuit filed by Becky and Marcy. Shelton said that the two women had sued Lou Ann for damages alleging "Lou Ann Sternadel caused Jerry Sternadel's death either alone or in concert with another." Shelton testified that the lawsuit was settled out of court. He had brought to court a copy of the settlement that was eventually reached. He was ordered by Judge Roger Towrey to disclose the information. According to Shelton, of the $320,000 Lou Ann gained from Jerry's life insurance policy, Becky was given $100,000, Marcy was given $30,000, and Sandy was awarded $20,000. Shelton testified that Sandy had not participated in the original lawsuit but was allowed part of the settlement at Lou Ann's request.

Later in the trial, Lou Ann's lawyer called witnesses to try to show that Jerry had had a volatile nature and a poor relationship with his children.

"He was aggressive," Jerry Woods said. "He was a womanizer." The one-time friend and business associate also testified how Jerry had cheated people on business deals and beat his son. "Jerry Sternadel had an affair with his stepdaughter, Stella Milburn. That's when my wife and I broke off our personal relationship with Jerry and Lou Ann Sternadel."

During the trial, Debra continually made notes or watched the witnesses and joked with the few people who had come to lend her support.

One witness the defense called to the stand almost brought the courthouse to a standstill. The courtroom became eerily quiet when Defense Attorney Roger Williams called Jerry Sternadel's stepdaughter, Stella Milburn, to the stand. Williams asked Stella why as a seventeen-year-old, she had left the Sternadel house in Dean, Texas, where she had lived with her mother and stepfather.

Even the chatty trial observers were speechless and sat riveted to their seats as they carefully listened for the young lady's answer. The buzz of the fluorescent lights was the only sound in the courtroom.

Stella Milburn squirmed around on the witness stand. She stared back at the defense attorney with a blank look, finally whispering, "I don't know how to say it."

The defense attorney prompted the witness, "Was it because of the actions of your stepfather?"

"Yes."

Williams continued, "Was it because he sexually molested you?"

"Yes!" she answered loudly.

All of a sudden, Debra started rocking back and forth in her chair. She began shaking as though she was deeply distraught. She gave out a loud convulsive sob. Debra supposedly became so overcome with emotion at hearing Stella Milburn's testimony that she began letting out piercing, high-pitched wails.

The sounds of Debra Baker's ear-splitting prolonged wails echoed back across the wooden benches and throughout the courtroom. The defendant had kept her composure throughout the many days of testimony, joking and laughing. But now she appeared to be inconsolable as she rocked back and forth, back and forth in her chair sobbing and moaning.

After two more questions, District Attorney Cole suggested a recess.

After the jury filed out of the courtroom for a short recess, Debra barely made it to the back of the courtroom, as she seemingly was on the verge of collapse. Her moans and sobs grew louder and louder as supposedly she could no longer keep her emotions in check when she heard the testimony from Lou Ann's teenage daughter about being sexually assaulted.

(Before Jerry's murder, Stella and her husband, Marty Milburn*, were allegedly struggling to make ends meet while she went to nursing school. After Jerry died, Stella and her husband moved into a lavish and extravagant house that Lou Ann allegedly paid to have built for them in Paris, Texas, in 1991.)

Stella continued with her testimony after the short recess. She testified about the summer of 1992 when she was living in Paris, Texas. Stella said her mother had spent a lot of time at the Bakers' home in Wimberley, Texas. She also testified that her mother was always calling her from Wimberley when Lou Ann was living with the Bakers. She stated that her mother lived with Debbie and Tony Baker during May and June 1992. She testified that her mother personally dialed many of the telephone calls made from the Bakers' telephone the summer of 1992. This was verified by phone records, which also showed a phone call made from the Bakers' home in Wimberley to the Saf-T-Lok warehouse in Wichita Falls on June 4, 1992.

(It was on June 4, 1992, that an unidentified woman called Saf-T-Lok warehouse in Wichita Falls trying to pay the overdue rent on Unit 629. However, the authorities were already at the warehouse after being called by the manager who had found Jerry's personal belongings in Unit 629. The bottle of arsenic poison was also found in Unit 629.)

Stella testified that she went to the store with her mother and saw her purchase two glass bottles of "cran something" for her stepfather after he returned home from his first trip to the hospital.

After Stella left the witness stand, the defense called Lou Ann's mother. Barbara Ford testified she was at the Sternadel ranch on June 13, the day after Jerry's death. Barbara Ford stated she helped empty two glass bottles of "cran something" down the sink. She said one of the bottles she emptied down the sink was full and the second one was almost full.

On cross-examination by District Attorney Tim Cole, Barbara Ford said her daughter and Debra Baker had always been very good friends. She stated Lou Ann and Debra Baker grew even closer in the controversial days after Jerry's death.

"So you wouldn't say anything that would hurt either one of them?" Cole questioned.

"Frankly, I don't know anything that would hurt either one of them," Barbara Ford immediately responded. The old woman eyed the jurors when she said that Jake Bogard was sitting on her doorstep early one morning. "He told me he wouldn't leave until I talked to him. The nosy sheriff just kept sitting there like he owned the doorstep. I finally told him that Sandy Sternadel had poured out a brand new bottle of Cran-Apple juice down the sink and another bottle that was nearly empty, and then he rinsed the Cran-Apple juice bottle out." She also said that Jerry would always give her money and pay for her vacations. "Jerry knew that I didn't have the money for vacations, so he made sure I could go. Jerry was free with his money."

Cole asked Barbara Ford if her granddaughter, Stella Milburn, had ever told her that Jerry had molested her. She replied that her granddaughter had told her, 'He never laid a hand on me.' Barbara Ford also said Jerry denied ever touching Stella.

She testified that her daughter, Lou Ann, had stayed for a while in Wimberley, Texas, with Debra and Tony Baker, but she did not recall for how long.

Roger Williams used other witnesses to take aim at some of the evidence that the DA had stacked up against his client. Taking the witness stand was a private investigator Williams had hired for the defense. Randy Littlefield was a former investigator with the Wichita County DA's office. Littlefield testified he examined the boxes that had come out of the Saf-T-Loc warehouse in June 1992. He said he went to the warehouse and looked at the boxes that the sheriff had seized and concluded that Debra Baker had been framed. "There was no mail for Kathy Simmons. It was just all piled in together. Not how I would store it." Littlefield stated each box held junk mail, personal mail, business receipts, and blank checks. In the private investigator's mind, the consistency of the disorganization in each of the boxes "raised red flags."

On cross-examination, Tim Cole asked, "Your theory is that somebody took all of that stuff, put it in there along with the bottle of poison to frame Debbie Baker?"

"I would say it could be, yes, sir," Littlefield answered.

Cole asked Littlefield if somebody hurriedly throwing things in boxes to move them would also be "consistent" with what he found in the boxes.

Littlefield stated, "I would say it could be, yes, sir."

By the time Tim Cole finished cross-examining Randy Littlefield, there were enough holes in the defense's privately hired investigator's story to drive an eighteen-wheeler truck through it.

The defense called a Wichita Falls gastroenterologist who helped treat Jerry during his three trips to Bethania Hospital. Dr. Konappa Murthy told the jury about some of the episodes during which Jerry had become confused and agitated. During the prosecution's cross-examination, Dr. Murthy read from the nurses' reports about having to wipe away white secretions around Jerry's mouth and nose during the latter stages of his poisoning and during Jerry's last trip to the hospital. (Kent Kaser had earlier testified he saw Debra and Lou Ann putting cotton swabs into Jerry's mouth in the hospital.)

**Jerry Sternadel's mother, Marcy, and daughter, Becky,
waiting in courthouse lobby with another witness**

On Friday, January 28, Eugenia Seaborne, an accountant for
Redbird Express, took the witness stand. Seaborne testified that
Redbird Express was a trucking company partnership formed in 1991
by Tony Baker and Lou Ann Sternadel. The bookkeeper said that Tony
didn't have the money for a trucking business, so Lou Ann loaned
him the money he needed. Seaborne said Tony and Lou Ann were
partners in the trucking business and their 1992 personal salary was
$31,000. Seaborne said the company was supposedly losing money
every year; in 1992, they lost about $10,000. Seaborne also testified
the trucking company was started with a capital outlay of $42,324
that was provided by Lou Ann. This money included Lou Ann's half
of the start-up money, and the other half was in a loan that Lou Ann
made to Tony Baker at 9 percent interest. Seaborne said the money
was used to buy an eighteen-wheeler truck. The accountant testified

she helped Debra Baker set up the bookkeeping system for Redbird Express.

Eugenia Seaborne was the final witness for the murder trial.

The defense and prosecution both rested their cases immediately after the accountant's testimony.

It had been a long and grueling eight hours on the last day of testimony. It was announced that the court would reconvene at 9:00 AM on Tuesday, February 1, 1994. At that time, both sides would give their closing arguments. The prosecutor and the defense attorney said the murder case could be handed to the jury as early as Tuesday afternoon.

The episodes with the little devil creatures had ceased a few days earlier, so my daughter and I went back to sleeping on the twin beds in the back bedroom at Marcy's home. For a couple of nights, I had been getting a good night's sleep.

That Friday night, I was exhausted, as were Becky and Marcy. The trial was taking a toll on all of us.

My daughter was with her husband at a motel, and Marcy had retired earlier that evening. I was resting on the twin bed, rehashing all the testimony of the trial. The room was dark, except for the dim glimmer of the streetlight. It was very windy outside. I began listening to the rustling of the trees and the beat of the chimes hanging in Marcy's backyard. I was enjoying the melodious sound. Suddenly, the ringing resonance of the chimes stopped. Even so, I could hear the wind gusting through the branches of the trees. The window screens began rattling and shaking from the strong wind. Out of nowhere, a huge shadowy figure emerged, swooping downward from the ceiling. The thing landed right on top of me, pinning me to the bed. I gasped in horror at the sight of the grotesque creature with piercing eyes the color of flaming red-hot pieces of coal. The monster began pawing and sexually assaulting me. The heavy weight of the beast was making it difficult for me to breathe. I sensed the demon was Lucifer. I had met the Prince of Darkness before, a long time ago, when the Evil One had

tried to take my life at Lake Arrowhead dam. I knew my only hope
was to pray. I began saying the Lord's Prayer. "Our Father, who art in
Heaven, hallowed be thy name."

The creature snarled and snorted, then it morphed into a hissing
serpent, coiling itself around my arms and legs and squeezing me, its
tongue darting in and out, showing its elongated fangs.

I continued the prayer, "Thy kingdom come, thy will be done on
earth as it is in Heaven."

The creature transformed itself again. It grew and sprouted four
thick legs with horny toes, a long tale, and a neck. It had a broad head
with pointed ears, horns, and a fire-breathing mouth.

The depraved demon from hell changed into even more beasts. All
at once, the demon's frustration turned to rage and fury.

I could feel the evil brute's power penetrating my brain and affecting
my mental faculties. Knowing I must keep praying or the wretched
beast would ravish my body and surely kill me, I closed my eyes and
used all my might to regain control of my memory. "Father Almighty,
I repent of my sins. Please help me."

The supernatural demonic creature pressed even harder and harder
against my body. It was squeezing the life out of me. I was suffocating.
The words to the prayer slowly came to me, "Give us this day our daily
bread "

The wretched spirit became even more infuriated. It tossed its head
back in anger. It lunged at me with great intensity and pressed with a
great deal of strength against my body.

"And forgive us our trespasses, as we forgive those who trespass
against us. Lead—"

The monster was again blocking my power to visualize the words.
I knew in my heart there wasn't much time left. I could feel my life
force ebbing away. I cried out, "Lead us not into temptation." The
words continued to flow from my mouth, "but deliver us from evil.
For thine is the kingdom, the power, and the glory. Forever and
ever, Amen."

Suddenly, the evil beast of Satan jumped off me and disappeared back into the dark tomb of hell.

Instantly, I started gasping and coughing. Slowly, I began breathing air into my lungs and expelling it. Straightaway, the chimes started ringing. I knew I was going to be okay. I was completely exhausted and drained but very thankful to God for saving me once again and keeping the Devil from taking my life.

On Sunday morning, I went to worship service at St. Paul Lutheran Church in Wichita Falls with Marcy, Becky, and her husband. I said a prayer asking the good Lord to protect all of us from the evil that was in Marcy's house.

Later, Becky's husband returned to Grand Prairie. That night, I was very weary and tired, but I stayed in the living room long after my daughter and my ex-mother-in-law had retired. Becky kept coming into the living room and asking me to come to bed. I finally relented. Although I was afraid to go to sleep, I was so mentally drained and physically exhausted that I could barely keep my eyes open. Before long, sleep overcame me. I had a dream that the Devil was trying to suffocate Marcy. Around six o'clock in the morning, I heard moans coming from Marcy's bedroom. Almost immediately, I jumped out of bed and raced to her bedroom. I started shaking her, "Marcy, wake up!"

Marcy stirred awake and sat upright in her bed. "Oh, Jeannie, I am so glad you woke me. I was having the worst nightmare. I felt like I was suffocating. I dreamed the Devil was trying to choke me to death."

Over coffee later that morning, I told Marcy and Becky everything about the experiences I had been having in the back bedroom. All three of us went out shopping. We went to different stores and purchased every cross we could find. When we returned to Marcy's house, we got out a hammer and nails and hung a cross or a crucifix in every room.

**Jeannie waits for trial to resume with her daughter,
Becky, and son, Sandy**

The trial was set to resume at the Clay County Courthouse in Henrietta on Tuesday morning, February 1, 1994. However, the presiding judge, who was overseeing the murder trial, fell ill from a virus. A retired judge from Wichita Falls was summoned to fill in for Judge Roger Towrey. Court was called to order later that morning with Judge Calvin Ashley on the bench.

Debra's attorney, Roger Williams, stood up and began his closing argument. He told the jurors that the DA would ask them to "get on a slippery slope and go down" in assimilating the evidence against his client. "There are gaps in this case wide enough to cause a reasonable doubt." Williams told the jury there was no scientific proof that the arsenic that had been in the eight-ounce bottle of Cowley's Rat and Mouse Poison was the same arsenic that killed Jerry Sternadel.

He reminded the jurors that the burden of proof rested with the prosecution and that any presumption of innocence would be enough for the jury to acquit Debra Baker. Williams cited several points in the trial that could give rise to "reasonable doubt." He told the jurors their job was to decide "from the evidence beyond a reasonable doubt" if Debra Baker was guilty as charged. "The devil is in the details," he said.

While Williams did not directly accuse any of the witnesses of lying, he cautioned the jurors to consider that their stories came from different perspectives, which could slant their viewpoint. "I don't have to ask you to believe that any witness lied. The prosecution's entire case was built on a hypothetical chain of circumstantial evidence."

The defense attorney posed questions to the jury about why the prosecution did not subpoena the murdered man's widow or other people most associated with the household. He walked over and stood in front of the jury box. Looking directly at the members of the jury, he asked, "If Sternadel was such a shrewd businessman, how could he not notice the thousands of dollars that the prosecution claimed was stolen from the plumbing business over a five-year period? We are not talking about maybe, probably, or even possibly. The prosecution cited greed as the primary motive for the murder. But Debbie got no gain from this. Don't put somebody else's guilt, pain, or benefit on Debbie. Debbie didn't get the insurance money. Don't make Debra Baker a scapegoat in this case, just to satisfy the community."

Roger Williams finished his closing argument and sat down.

District Attorney Tim Cole stood up and walked over to the jury box.

"Do justice. The case has been built for you. When you look at it all, Debra Baker is guilty. The pieces of evidence should be thought of as strands of a rope. A single strand of a rope can be broken by a child ... but add more strands to the rope and eventually, it can hold the weight of a man ... more strands and it becomes a cable, which can support a bridge. Judge the evidence on the whole ... that's what this case is all about."

Cole rekindled questions surrounding the testimony of a private detective hired by the counsel for the defense. The private eye had theorized that someone planted the bottle of arsenic poison and some personal belongings that belonged to Debra Baker in the storage locker to set her up. "How could that be? Evidence showed that Debra could steal money from the plumbing business because "she controlled the books." Shortly after Jerry had discovered what was going on, he became ill after eating a taco salad brought to him by Debra. Debra and Lou Ann were the only persons who had access to that meal before it was served. Although Jerry had mistreated Debra, "she waited on him hand and foot." It was fear of what Jerry might say that kept Debra close to him at the hospital. Friends testified that Jerry was coherent at the hospital when he begged them to loosen his restraints and help him escape from the two women he said were stealing his money and poisoning him. Even as sick as he was, Jerry had put it all together."

The DA told the jury it was a common defense tactic to shift the focus of testimony to persons other than the defendant on trial. "In this case, the defense worked to focus on Jerry Sternadel, who was characterized as being tough on his family, employees, and business associates, in addition to being a womanizer who molested his stepdaughter."

Moving toward to the jury box, Cole walked slowly by each jury member. Looking directly at each juror, he asked, "Do you see the rabbit trails that are being taken? What real difference does it make what kind of person Jerry Sternadel was? Jerry Sternadel is not on trial here and neither is the family of Jerry Sternadel."

Cole rested his case on the weight of testimony that was offered about money missing from Jerry's bank accounts and the first poisoning in May 1990. "Jerry Sternadel became violently ill shortly after being served a taco salad by Debra Lynn Baker."

The DA continued looking at each jury member as he summed up his closing argument. "That poison had to be in that meal. And who had access to that meal? Just two people had access to that taco salad, Debra Baker and Lou Ann Sternadel. Ladies and gentlemen, the case has been built for you. When you look at it all, Debra Baker is guilty."

On Tuesday morning at approximately 11:00, the jury began deliberations. Lunch was brought to the jury room.

Later that afternoon, one of the jurors passed the bailiff a note stating the jury could not reach a verdict. Judge Calvin Ashley pressed them into giving it another try.

Tension ran high in the 97th District Court as the jury continued to deliberate. The courtroom was full to the maximum with Jerry's family and friends. Debbie's husband and teenaged son were also sitting in the courtroom, waiting for a verdict. Numerous spectators meandered in and out of the courtroom, as if they were playing musical chairs.

After five hours of sifting through the testimony of dozens of witnesses and exhibits, another note was passed out to the bailiff.

The jury had reached a verdict.

People who had exited the courtroom and were waiting downstairs in the courthouse lobby clambered hurriedly back into the courtroom. Judge Ashley warned everyone in the courtroom about any outbursts before he told the bailiff to escort the jury into the courtroom.

The jury of four women and eight men silently walked into the courtroom and took their seats in the jury box without displaying any kind of emotion.

The whole courtroom went quiet. There was no noise except for the sound of the rotating blades of the overhead fans that created a current of air for cooling and ventilation.

Judge Ashley asked, "Has the jury reached a verdict?"

The foreman stood up and said, "Yes, Your Honor. We have reached a verdict."

The judge asked the foreman to read it. The foreman glanced around the courtroom before looking down at a piece of paper he was holding in his hand.

"We, the jury, find the defendant, Debra Lynn Baker, *guilty* of first-degree murder."

At the announcement of the guilty verdict, Debra began sobbing hysterically. Then she let out a high-pitched scream. Further back in the courtroom, sounds of relief and soft crying could be heard coming from Jerry's family and friends.

The judge polled each juror, one after the other, asking if this was his or her verdict. The jurors replies of "Yes" were barely heard above Debra Baker's loud sobs.

Marcy, Becky, and Jeannie elated at guilty verdict

Immediately after the jury was polled, Debra's teenaged son jumped up from his seat. Like a shot from a gun, he scaled the court rail directly in front of him and rushed over to his sobbing mother to embrace her. He let out a sharp cry. "I'm losing her."

The teenager clenched his teeth as he answered different questions from the defense attorney, who was trying to calm him down. Then the boy turned and looked squarely at me, his face distorted with rage. He jumped the rail and lunged at me and was almost upon me when an alert security officer grabbed him, stopping the attack. The angry teenager tore loose from the officer, jumped the court railing, and raced toward the jury box. There was a flurry of activity in front of the jurors as court officers and deputies surrounded him. They contained the seething young man and promptly escorted him to the door and into the vestibule.

Once Debra's son was safely outside the courtroom, the bailiff began his task of bringing order back to the courtroom. When everyone had calmed down, Judge Ashley instructed the jury to return to the courthouse the next morning to consider the punishment phase.

We learned that the sentence for first-degree murder could range from five to ninety-nine years in prison and a fine up to $10,000. Debra remained free on bond.

TV crews had their cameras trained on Debra Baker. Her son went berserk again, flying into a seething rage and attacking the nearest television cameraman, who was standing near the winding staircase. Just as suddenly, the teenager lunged forward and grabbed a newspaper reporter, aggressively accosting the unsuspecting man. Cameras continued rolling as security officers, a deputy and two bystanders desperately tried to restrain the enraged young man. The angry boy tore loose from the men and teed off on another reporter, who was innocently walking down the staircase. Court officers and sheriff's deputies quickly gathered to prevent him from another attack and promptly accompanied him out of the courthouse.

That evening, TV coverage showed the footage of the scuffle with Debra's son. However, what was not shown in the coverage was the boy attacking others. Debra had made sure her son was sitting in the front row right behind her every day of the trial in her effort to solicit sympathy from the jury. I grew very concerned that jury members watching the footage would feel sorry for the boy. The jury was warned by the trial judge not to watch television coverage or read about the trial. But I was betting the jury members would see the segment showing the teenaged son and would empathize with him and be far too lenient with his mother, whom they had just convicted of first-degree murder.

My stomach churned. I tossed and turned all night. The morning sunrise couldn't come soon enough for me. The murder trial was the only thing on my mind as I walked into the kitchen, turned the lights on, and made some coffee. It was 4:30 AM.

I thought about the one person who was conspicuously absent throughout the entire trial. Lou Ann had been nowhere to be seen. The mere thought of the widow not showing up at the murder trial of her husband's killer made me see red.

Lou Ann had not shown up even to support her daughter, Stella, who testified that she had been sexually molested. I was told during the trial that Lou Ann was basking in the Bahamas with a man who was married to one of the witnesses for the prosecution. It was my opinion and everybody else's that Lou Ann would also be a no-show at the sentencing. Some felt that she was afraid of being arrested. Everyone knew she was a suspect in the murder case and possibly a coconspirator in the murder.

Jeannie greeting her son, Sandy, before court reconvenes for the sentencing of Debra Baker

Wednesday, February 2, 1994, was the day of the sentencing, and the courtroom was full to overflowing. Television crews and newspaper reporters were everywhere.

The DA made a persuasive statement about his circumstantial case. "Jerry Sternadel was given three doses of arsenic rat poison by Debra Baker before he finally died at the hospital from extreme arsenic poisoning."

Williams then made a provocative statement. He presented the jurors with the idea of giving his client probation instead of a prison term. "Because the defendant, Debra Baker, has never before been convicted of a felony, she is eligible for probation under state law." After hearing that, everyone in the courtroom audibly gasped and began softly whispering.

After the prosecutor and defense attorney had finished their statements, Judge Ashley gave the jury sentencing guidelines and instructions. The bailiff then escorted the jury members as they walked single file to a room at the back of the courtroom. A couple of deputies locked the door to the jury room and took their respective places standing guard at the door. Getting up from my seat in the courtroom, I moved a little closer to the back room where the jurors were deliberating.

An hour and a half into the jury's deliberations, loud rumblings could be heard coming from the jury room. The growing voices of discontent coming from the room indicated that the jury was having a hard time agreeing on a sentence. However, it took them only four hours to make their decision.

As the jurors walked back into the courtroom. I instantly noticed three members walking with their heads down. That didn't look like a good sign.

The judged asked the jurors for their decision on the sentencing of the defendant.

The jury foreman stood up in the jury box and glanced around the courtroom. Then he looked directly at the defendant, Debra Lynn Baker, and said, "Ten years probation and a $10,000 fine."

Nobody in the courtroom could believe what he or she had just heard. The courtroom was so quiet and hushed that a person could have heard a pin drop.

All of a sudden, Debra Baker gave out a loud, silly laugh. She was literally laughing in the face of the jury and showing open contempt for the murder victim, as well as the victim's friends and family. Her loud cackling left the spectators in the courtroom with a feeling of disdain and hopelessness. In essence, Debra Baker had just gotten away with murder.

My happiness with the guilty verdict melted into intense pain and utter disappointment. The word probation kept bouncing around and around inside my head. The punishment meted out by the jury was impossible for me to comprehend.

Debra Baker and her husband, Tony, overjoyed
after Debra received probation from the jury

Downstairs in the hallway of the courthouse, camera crews turned their lenses on the devastated prosecutor. Cole said, "My general reaction is that I'm not quite sure why I'm in this business when a thing like this happens. The jury has made their decision, and I have to abide by it. But I think the sentence is a travesty of justice."

Soon the cameras were turned on me. "We are obviously very disappointed with the jury's decision to give Debra Baker probation. But I know Debra is so evil she will do something to violate the terms of her probation and she will wind up in prison."

All Jerry's family and friends and even the spectators at the murder trial were in shock and disbelief when they left the courtroom at the end of that day. No one could believe the jury convicting Debra Baker of first-degree murder had turned around the next day and given her nothing more than probation as punishment.

I was standing outside the courthouse with my son, daughter and Jerry's mother and brother. We all spotted Debra Baker at the same time. She was with her husband and son. They were walking across the street from the courthouse, supposedly on their way out of town.

When Debra saw us looking at her, she yelled out very loudly. Her words were vulgar and downright sleazy. Then she laughed loudly and flipped us the finger.

The sight of Debra's obscene gestures and filthy comments infuriated me. I wanted to yell something back at the disgusting woman, but I kept quiet out of respect for my children and Jerry's mother and brother.

I spotted Thomas Bradley walking out of the courthouse. I trotted over to the young man who had been accidentally poisoned with arsenic. "Thank you so much for testifying. I am so sorry you became an innocent victim and poisoned with arsenic just because you were friends with Lou Ann's daughter, Holly."

Thomas said, "Holly was not my friend. Actually, I didn't know her very well. I met her once at my stepsister's wedding and occasionally saw her at the restaurant where we both worked. This all happened at the beginning of the summer, and I didn't know many of the other workers. I am just hoping that I don't have long-term side effects from the arsenic."

I told the young man I was hoping and praying for the same thing. I asked if I could keep in contact with him and his family.

Thomas said that would be fine with him.

Jerry Sternadel's widow, Lou Ann, was a no-show at the trial

After the murder trial and the upsetting sentence, people began saying, "If you want to commit a murder and get away with it, then commit the murder in Clay County." Some jurors were ridiculed and almost accosted when irate citizens of Henrietta, Texas, saw them in town a couple days later.

A few days after the trial ended, I called Tim Cole. "How did Debra Baker wind up with probation? It is my understanding that first-degree murder is the worst thing a person can be convicted of."

Tim Cole wasted no time in answering my question. "Debra Baker got probation because of a loophole in Texas law that allows people who commit murder to get probation. The loophole was originally meant for first-time offenders and for women who were abused or raped and then murdered the person who abused or raped them. It was not meant for this kind of case. The best thing I can tell you is for you and your family to do everything you can to get the loophole closed before Lou Ann is brought to trial."

I took the DA's advice and began contacting congressional representatives to learn about the flaw in Texas law that allowed probation for first-degree murder and how to get the loophole closed. I contacted all of Jerry's friends and asked for their help in getting the law changed. I knew it might take time and a lot of effort, but this was another thing I would not give up on.

I would do everything I could to get justice for Jerry. Getting a petition on the Internet was one way. (http://www.petitiononline.com/jwbs218/petition.html)

As was expected, Debra Baker's attorney did not waste any time after the murder trial in filing an appeal. He filed on February 16, 1994. One of the arguments in the appeal was that the same circumstantial evidence that had convicted Debra Baker applied to Lou Ann. The appeal stated that there were other people, in particular Lou Ann, who had motive—specifically, the $330,000 in life insurance—and even greater opportunity to commit the murder.

Thomas Bradley accidentally drank juice containing
arsenic poison that was meant for Jerry Sternadel

The Innocent

homas Bradley was an innocent victim, a young man at the wrong place at the wrong time.

He happened to be visiting Jerry's stepdaughter, Holly Maag, and helped himself to juice in the refrigerator at the Sternadel home. After drinking the juice, he became seriously ill from arsenic poisoning. His life would change forever.

In 1990, Thomas was nineteen years old. He lived in Boonville, Missouri, but took a job in Wichita Falls, Texas, for the summer. The innocent gesture of drinking a glass of juice almost cost him his life. One side effect he initially suffered from the arsenic poison was shingles.

On June 15, 1990, the Clay County Sheriff's office received a telephone call from Mrs. Russell Bradley of Nocona, Texas. Mrs. Bradley stated she heard about the investigation of a poisoning concerning rancher Jerry Sternadel. She said her grandson, Tommy Bradley, had spent Friday night on the first of June at Jerry Sternadel's house and, the next morning, had gotten very sick after drinking some juice from the refrigerator. She told the county authorities that her grandson was taken to the Wichita Falls Clinic where he was treated for a virus. Lou Ann Sternadel had come to the clinic for about five minutes and told

Shirley and Jerry O'Neal, her grandson's mother and stepfather, not to worry about the bill.

Deputy Bevering advised Mrs. Bradley that he needed to talk to her grandson. Later that day, Bevering received a phone call from Tommy Bradley, who was back in Missouri, confirming what his grandmother had told the deputy.

On June 17, Deputy Bevering talked with Shirley O'Neal, the mother of Tommy Bradley. Mrs. O'Neal stated she would send the admitting slip from the Wichita Falls Clinic that her son had received when he was admitted on June 2. Tommy's mother said she would be talking to her son later in the day and that he had an appointment with his doctor on June 18. She agreed to ask her son to sign a medical release for a copy of his medical records from his doctors in Missouri and would have them sent to the Clay County Sheriff's office.

At Debra Baker's murder trial in Henrietta, Texas, on Friday, January 21, 1994, the now twenty-two-year-old victim took the witness stand and gave vivid testimony for the prosecution. Thomas testified that he had consumed arsenic poison and lived to tell his story.

He told about spending a month in the Wichita Falls area and working with Jerry Sternadel's stepdaughter, Holly Maag, at Uncle Lynn's Catfish Restaurant. He testified there was a party one night in early June at a fellow worker's apartment. Holly Maag had allowed him to sleep in her sister's bedroom rather than him having to drive to Nocona, Texas, where he lived. He gave an articulate account of how when he arose the next morning he saw Holly and Sandy cleaning the house in preparation for Jerry's return home from the hospital. Tommy said he asked for something to drink and was invited to help himself to whatever was in the kitchen. He testified that he went to the refrigerator and poured himself a glassful of juice. He said he took two swallows of the juice. "I felt it burn all the way down my throat and into my stomach." He recalled within ten to fifteen minutes he had a bout of diarrhea and severe vomiting. He suspected food poisoning. "I felt like I was dying." He stated he was taken to the Wichita Falls Clinic and treated at the clinic for what the doctor thought was a viral infection. He said he felt poorly for two or three days. After he returned to his home in Missouri, he was contacted by the sheriff's office and instructed to undergo a series of medical tests. "The tests proved positive for arsenic poisoning."

During cross-examination, Bradley said he had no idea about what might have happened to the juice bottle. He also testified that he did not personally know Debra Lynn Baker and had never seen her prior to his courtroom appearance.

Thomas finished his testimony at the murder trial and left the courthouse. What he could not leave behind were the unknown, lasting effects of the arsenic poison.

Later, Thomas Bradley told me, "Not knowing these people, I still feel the sentence that this woman received was unjust. She should have been sent to prison for the crime."

As for Debra Baker, the first-degree murder conviction she received would carry the same penalty as forgery. Hays County, Texas, brought felony forgery charges against her on February 17, 1994. A routine pre-sentencing investigation by Hays County turned up the murder charge against her in Clay County. Therefore, the official sentencing on the forgery case in Hays County was delayed until after the verdict was reached on the murder charge in Clay County.

Debra Baker pled guilty in Hays County to signing her boss's signature on two checks in 1992, totaling $3,200 and made out to Red Bird Express, a business run by her husband, Tony, and Lou Ann Sternadel. She originally agreed to ten years deferred adjudication in return for her guilty plea.

On April 17, a hearing was held in Hays County on Debra Baker's plea bargain whereby the judge accepted her plea and sentenced her to ten years of probation.

Finding out a prison term was not mandated for Debra Baker on the forgery charge, I took it upon myself to speak with an official from Hays County. Assistant District Attorney John Costello said,

"It is true that 207th District Judge Robert T. Pfeuffer did not mandate a prison term for Debra Baker. The basic feeling was that if Debra Baker was not going to jail for a murder in Clay County, then she wasn't going to jail for forgery in Hays County. Debra Baker was supposed to sign the plea bargain agreement on February 17, but the court did not get to Baker's case before she had to leave for her first day at a new job. Judge Pfeuffer delayed the final paperwork. The April 17 hearing made the plea bargain official. According to the agreement, Debra Baker will serve the new probation concurrent with the Clay County probation and will be required to serve 160 hours of community service and pay back the $3,200 to her Hays County employer."

On January 3, 1995, the Second Court of Appeals in Fort Worth, Texas, gave its ruling on Debra Baker's appeal of the Clay County murder conviction. Judge Hicks ruled there was no error in the judgment of the trial court and affirmed the judgment. It was also ruled that the appellant, Debra Lynn Baker, pay all costs of the appeal.

I decided my next course of action was to try to get the story of Jerry's horrific murder into the public eye. I began contacting different television shows. In February, I did an interview with *Current Affair*. On April 15, the *Current Affair* producers were in Wichita Falls finishing up video interviews with my daughter and son. At that time, the producers received a disturbing call from their headquarters, informing them that a bomb had just destroyed the Federal Building in Oklahoma City. The film crew rushed to Oklahoma City.

Current Affair aired the story on the arsenic murder of Jerry Sternadel and the murder trial of Debra Baker in June 1995.

On July 25, I posted a $10,000 reward for information leading to the arrest and conviction of people involved in Jerry's murder.

Representative Scott Hochberg of Houston introduced House Bill 685 (relating to prohibiting jury-recommended community supervision for a defendant convicted of murder). The bill was referred to the Criminal Jurisprudence Committee and never came out of the committee. I asked the legislator to resubmit the bill to change the loophole in the Texas law.

In December, I flew to Texas to spend Christmas and New Year. After the holiday, I planned on contacting jury members to find out how they had come to sentence Debra Lynn Baker to nothing more than probation after they had convicted her of first-degree murder.

The Jurors Speak

In January 6, 1996, I began contacting the jurors. Some did not want to talk about the trial. However, some were glad to discuss their role. A couple members of the jury agreed to be interviewed anonymously, while a few others agreed to be interviewed on camera and on tape.

I found out some very interesting tidbits from the jurors.

One juror, who wanted to remain anonymous, told me that right after the murder trial he talked to District Attorney Tim Cole. The prosecutor told him that he didn't think Debra Baker's case was winnable and that he was lucky to even get her convicted. The juror didn't understand why the district attorney had said that. "Tim Cole didn't want to drag out the case, so he didn't present other witnesses in the trial. Every time the defense brought something up, Tim Cole closed them out. What I found interesting was the phone call from a woman at the Bakers' house in Wimberley, Texas, to the storage shed in Wichita Falls wanting to pay the past due rent. We learned from testimony that Lou Ann Sternadel was at Debbie Baker's house at that time. So that meant both women (Debbie and Lou Ann) had to be in on it (the murder). The storage shed is where the arsenic poison was found. The jury foreman felt Lou Ann Sternadel was setting Debra Baker up.

"Gary Monty* jumped up and volunteered for foreman of the jury as soon as we walked into the jury room. All the Henrietta people wanted him to be foreman, but it was just the Henrietta people. From the bag of evidence taken from the storage shed, it was easy to tell that Debbie Baker never paid bills on time. Bags from the storage shed contained Debbie Baker's personal stuff and her photo. The jury was adamant about voting guilty on the murder charge. The jury foreman said to us, 'Why don't everybody go home and sleep on this.' But the jury wanted to vote on it. We all kept going back to the box with the arsenic and the time line. The more I went over it, all the circumstantial evidence added up. The statement by the dead bookkeeper [Andrew Coker] saying money was missing. We all thought both women should have been on trial. There was plenty of evidence that both women tried to cover up the disappearance of the money. All the statements and the check testimony convinced me that they were stealing money. The money was missing. All three things, the statement on the money missing by Jerry Sternadel, all the checks from the bank account, and the fact that Debra Baker was hiding everything supported the fact that she was stealing money.

"The older man from Joy went to sleep during the check testimony. But the more I went over it, all the circumstantial evidence added up. The physical evidence pointed to Debbie Baker. I had the feeling something was going on between Lou Ann and Debbie Baker. The defense lawyer was throwing everything against Lou Ann. That day we all felt the same way and voted guilty and were going to send Debbie Baker to prison. But the next day, the jury foreman started pushing probation and changed people's minds. The people from Henrietta were set on probation because they felt sorry for the seventeen-year-old son of Debbie Baker. Everyone had a chance to say something on how they felt.

"First vote was 6-6. There was a lot of prejudice against the police force. Some of the jury wanted to take each piece of evidence on its own. But the more I went over it, all the circumstantial evidence added up. I felt like Debbie Baker should get twenty years. Some of them said I was a terrible person for holding out for prison time. It was a feeding frenzy. Then we had lunch.

"I felt like Jerry Sternadel wasn't a nice man because of the affair. But the man was tortured, unusual, and cruel. Other jury members felt sorry for Debbie Baker. I felt like if prison time was given to Debbie Baker that maybe she would give up Lou Ann. My first suggestion was twenty years. The jury foreman wanted to know how I could live with myself. The next vote was 8-4. Kimberly held out for sending Debbie Baker to prison and the man who drove the milk truck. The foreman was upset that he voted guilty on the murder charge, and now he wanted probation. I was the last holdout. The jury members wouldn't go back over the evidence. I feel sorry that probation was given. I was pressured into giving probation instead of prison."

I set up an interview with another juror, who also wished to remain anonymous.

"Every time Debra Baker was linked to the crime, so was Lou Ann Sternadel. When the rent was due on the storage locker where the arsenic was found, testimony indicated that one of the owners of the storage facility was Lou Ann Sternadel's lawyer. Shortly after the lawyer was notified of the past due rent by the manager of the storage facility, some woman called and tried to pay the rent. The call came from Wimberley where Debra Baker and Lou Ann Sternadel both were staying at the time the telephone call was made to the storage facility. So the wife of Jerry Sternadel was guiltier or as guilty as Debra Baker. When Jerry Sternadel died, no money was in his bank account, but money was stolen from Jerry. One guy thought Debra Baker was guilty from the start, but three people, including the foreman, thought Debra Baker was innocent and pushed into it by Lou Ann Sternadel. Two men and two women thought Debra Baker was innocent until they looked into the plastic bag containing a bottle of rat poison and saw pictures of Debra Baker and checks from Jerry Sternadel Plumbing and letters addressed to Debra Baker and Jerry Sternadel and Lou Ann Sternadel. Everybody felt the wife was guilty, and every time Debra Baker was linked to the crime by circumstantial evidence, so was Lou Ann Sternadel. Everybody felt the wife had the motive to get rid of Jerry Sternadel. For example: The affair with the stepdaughter and money from the life insurance.

"Some jurors were upset because they could not take notes.

"Testimony indicated there was enough arsenic poison missing from the rat poison bottle for three doses of poison that was given to Jerry Sternadel and enough to kill him. First time Jerry Sternadel got sick they [Lou Ann Sternadel and Debra Baker] kept him at home and then finally took him to the hospital. Second time he got poison and he got sick again. The boy, Thomas Bradley, spent a night at Jerry Sternadel's house and drank canapple juice out of the refrigerator and got sick and had to go to the emergency room. The boy had tests done, and they found arsenic. The DA said Debra Baker hid the Cran-Apple juice bottle. Testimony indicated Jerry Sternadel made life miserable for everybody. The jury instructions said she was guilty if she knowingly or intentionally caused death. We all felt the wrong person was on trial. The wife was guiltier. After the trial, one lady who was on the jury told me when she went to the bank she was jumped out by a person who thought it was horrible about the jury giving Debra Baker probation."

The next day, I contacted a friend and asked him to accompany me to help record juror interviews.

Terry Daily* and I met Artie Fant at the Dairy Queen in Henrietta, Texas.

I began the interview with Fant, a milk-truck driver, by asking him to tell anything he could remember about the murder trial. He stated that none of the jury members had known each other prior to the trial. The jurors had felt the wrong person was on trial. Fant said he was open-minded and thought DA Tim Cole presented the case well and did a good job. Most of the jury thought the sheriff's office didn't do their job well regarding the chain of custody of the Cran-Apple juice bottle and failing to take fingerprints. There was a problem with just who found the Cran-Apple juice container and with officers of the law not doing their job properly. While in the jury room, the jurors examined the plastic bag in which the bottle of arsenic rat poison had been found along with checks from Jerry Sternadel Plumbing and letters addressed to Lou Ann, Jerry, and Debra. Some jurors didn't believe Debra would have kept arsenic in the storage locker. They wondered why Lou Ann wasn't there to testify. Lou Ann taking the Fifth Amendment would have confirmed the conspiracy. "Why send Debra Baker to prison and not the widow? We decided to convict Debra Baker and give her a light sentence, and then we all expected the widow to be brought to trial. We thought the wrong person was on trial. Copies of checks made out to Debra Baker and Tony Baker confirmed conspiracy. Part of the money reverted back to Lou Ann Sternadel. We did not believe the money was a loan made by Jerry Sternadel. The evidence against Debra Baker only proved conspiracy of murder."

I questioned Artie Fant on why the jury gave Debra Baker nothing more than probation.

Jeannie thanking juror Artie Fant for granting an interview

"We decided she would get something but not take the whole fall. Debra Baker crying and wailing didn't evoke sympathy or change our opinion of her that she was a conspirator. The news cameramen got sympathy for Debra Baker when they showed how upset her son was. There was confusion in the jury over the verdict of reaching guilty of committing the crime. I always felt she was guilty of conspiracy. There was a concession when the guilty verdict was reached. We decided that Debra Baker would get something but not take the whole fall. The jury asked if there were options after reaching the guilty verdict. The judge sent back a paper with the choices we could make. The court bailiff brought the paper to us. Our choices were: life in prison or probation. If both of them had been on trial, both would have been convicted and sent to prison. I have been very upset over what went on inside the jury."

I informed Artie Fant that researchers had concluded more women than men used poison as their weapon of choice. I also told the juror that women who used poison to kill usually killed more than one person. And people who used poison did not throw the poison away. But researchers could not ascertain whether the poison was kept to gloat over or to be used again.

The next day, Terry and I interviewed another juror, LaVonda Wheeler, who was a local business owner in Henrietta.

"Tim Cole acted like a two-year-old with his toys taken away. (You can put that in your book.) I hope District Attorney Tim Cole has a lot more professionalism in his next trial. If you put me in the same situation, I would do the same thing. We did the best we could with what we had.

"I don't blame Debra Baker for using the emotional aspect, but she shouldn't have used her teenage son to get us to feel sorry for her. He was sitting in the courtroom every day. I won't ever serve on another criminal jury. I feel like I am a victim. If they give you probation to use as a tool, then it might be used. They should not allow probation for a murder charge.

"We all felt there was proof Debra Baker knew what was going on with regard to Jerry Sternadel being poisoned. But nobody saw her put arsenic poison in his food or drink. They never proved where the arsenic came from. Every time your reward comes out in the paper, I think about the trial. I can't sleep at night. I wonder whether Debra Baker can sleep at night. I know I don't!"

The next week, Terry and I drove out to a home on Hwy 79 to interview Dale Cope, who gave us permission to videotape and record the interview.

I started the interview by asking, "Was there anything outstanding about the trial that stood out in your mind?"

Dale Cope replied, "The thing that stood out ... I didn't understand why they had Debbie Baker on trial and they didn't have Lou Ann Sternadel on trial with her. That was the biggest problem everybody had. All the evidence they had, both of them were together. They bring one person to trial and not the other. I had a problem with that. I didn't understand it. They didn't explain it or nothing.

"And the sentence that she [Debra Baker] got ... was bad ... there were four of us who wanted to send her to prison. And when we said something ... there was three women who busted into tears crying and everything else saying, 'You can't do this to this woman 'cause she's not guilty.' I said, 'How can you say that! You just sat through that trial.' I think a lot of them had it in their mind that this lady is getting railroaded while the real one that committed the murder was out in the Bahamas. Every bit of the evidence they had showed both of the women were together, but they didn't bring both of them to trial. All the evidence was circumstantial. They had no physical proof that Debbie Baker actually did it, but she had to have something to do with it because she was there every time the guy got sick. It's hard to get true evidence of somebody pouring something into a drink unless somebody saw them do it. The evidence was purely circumstantial ... but enough circumstantial evidence will get a conviction.

"But see, when we went in there to convict her, there were five people that didn't even want to give her a guilty sentence. One guy—I don't know if you've talked to him, but he works at the hospital in Henrietta."

I asked the juror, "Do you know what his first name was?"

"I don't remember his name, but he was the foreman."

"Gary Monty was the foreman," I quickly replied.

"Yeah, that's him! He volunteered to be foreman. He jumped up and said, 'I'll take it!' Everybody goes, 'Okay.' 'Cause, see, some people from Henrietta knew him. But I didn't. He's the main guy who pushed to get her probation. See, he didn't even want to convict her. And he said, 'I'll give her a conviction if you'll let her off on probation.' I said, 'No, you're full of shit! If she gets convicted, she's going to jail.' Then, the next day, they came around and said, 'What do you want to give her?' There were four of us that wanted to send her to prison. There was three or four of them from Henrietta that wanted to let her go. They were the ones that got him in as the foreman. They said they wanted to give her a $10,000 fine with probation. I said a $10,000 fine ain't nothing. When I said that, there were women crying and screaming and throwing a fit. Everyone from Henrietta wanted to let her go. Well, the girl from out toward Windthorst … young girl … well, she wanted to let her go bad. She was one of the women that was screaming and crying. A blond-headed lady from Henrietta was really screaming and carrying on. See, I work with her husband. His name is Wheeler. I seen him later on, and he goes, 'Hey, don't worry about it. That lady didn't do nothing.' I said, 'What are you talking about? I'll regret this the rest of my life. We did something stupid!' He goes, 'No, you didn't.'

"That was the worst thing I ever been through. It was bad! I don't see how they can sit through a trial like that and then think she wasn't guilty. But … I mean … I learned a lot. I had never been on a jury so there was a lot I didn't expect to happen that did. It kind of blew me away."

Terry interjected, "I've got two questions. One is what were the women's reasons behind all this, and the other is why was the jury foreman pushing so hard for probation?"

"I didn't ever understand that. There were three guys that pushed real hard to get probation. They said, 'All it does is cost us money when we send them to prison.' Which it does cost the taxpayers money to send people to jail. And I said, 'Well, I'll tell you what! I'd rather be out walking free.' I said 'It ain't nothing like sitting in a little five-by-seven prison cell.' They wouldn't hear of it.

"If I had it to do over, I'd lock the jury and let the judge decide. After the trial, I went to the prosecuting attorney, Tim Cole, and I talked to him. I said, 'Hey, them people should never have had that decision in their hands. I said, 'I don't think any law-abiding citizen should go and tell how many years somebody should get for a crime. 'Cause you take a woman with a kid … and a husband. A lot of people don't want to say, 'Hey, I'm going to send you to jail for ten to twenty years.' Cause a lot of people can't get up and say that. Tim Cole said he was going to write Congress and do everything he could to get that loophole changed, but I don't know if he did or not."

Terry asked, "Do you recall about when it was that you talked to Tim Cole?

Dale Cope replied, "It was about two months after the trial."

Terry questioned, "So basically you think the women jurors were more concerned because Debbie Baker was a mother of a teenager."

"Yeah," he answered. "That's basically what they were hollering and screaming about. Well, a lot of them said that all she was convicted of was conspiracy to murder, and they didn't think she should get a sentence. But she was in a plot to kill somebody, and that's just the same as killing the person. I mean that man went through a horrible death. I walked out of the jury room and looked at that foreman, and I said, 'Boy, we screwed up. But it was too late then."

Terry asked, "What was his reaction when you said that?"

"He just went"—Dale made a face—"and then he just turned around and walked out and left and didn't say another word. But there was a couple of guys who didn't want to sentence her. This lady that lives right back here—I can't think of her name—she wanted to sentence her at first, but she fell real quick. But there were three of us who wanted to sentence, and eight people against us. I mean … they lock you up in a room, and they want a decision before you come out. They say, 'Hey, you either make a decision or you ain't coming out of that room.' And with everybody talking against you, you finally go, 'I don't care what you do.'"

I chimed in. "I would think the jury members are counting on you caving in. Especially when the majority is against what you think."

Cope responded, "Yeah, you're going to cave in. That's the way it was … the foreman and the other guy over at Henrietta. Some of the things that guy said about Jerry Sternadel being in a lot of shifty deals. I couldn't believe they would even have him on the jury."

I asked, "Do you remember that person's name?"

"I don't remember. I'm not too good at names, and I didn't talk to many of the other jurors. But there was an older man from Petrolia and a man who drove a milk truck. All three of us were trying to send her to jail. It was a bad deal. It took me quite a while to get over that. But I know if I go in on a jury again … I will not leave until justice is done right … 'cause I don't think it was done right. I even went up to them, and I said, 'If you let her go, you're letting Lou Ann Sternadel go too.' I said, 'Just send her to jail for twenty years and let her start talking. But none of them would listen."

I said, "It seems that the jury foreman was allegedly dead set against the guilty verdict and then really dead set against any kind of prison term."

"Oh, yeah! I sat through the trial, and I listened to it. When I walked into the room for deliberation, I thought there's twelve people all thinking guilty. But when we walked in, there were five people saying she was innocent. And I go, 'Where are you people coming from? Ya'll must not have sit in the same trial I did.' Then there were two guys who held out and said, 'If you'll give probation I'll say guilty.' I said, 'No way, I'm not giving probation.' It was bad.

Terry asked, "Did they give any reasons for wanting to give her probation?"

"No! Other than they said Debbie got pushed into it by money and Lou Ann Sternadel, and she got caught up in something she shouldn't have done. Most of them thought Lou Ann Sternadel did the conniving. Which I think it was done by both of the women, and both of them should have paid. But they both got off now, I guess. I couldn't ever figure out why they didn't bring Lou Ann Sternadel up on murder charges."

I replied, "That's what we are all trying to figure out."

Cope said, "It seemed that with every bit of the evidence presented, they had both of them. Once somebody mentioned that they put Lou Ann Sternadel in jail for four months. And I said, 'And, they let her go? And they don't even have her on trial.' And then when we came in thirty minutes later and asked, 'Did you ever have Lou Ann Sternadel in jail?' And they said, 'No!' And, I'm going, 'I don't understand this. First they said they did have her in jail, and then they said they didn't.' The defense attorney comes up and asked the sheriff on the stand if he ever had Lou Ann Sternadel in jail and he said no."

I responded, "I think the defense was trying to get the jury to focus on Lou Ann instead of Debbie Baker."

"I guess so," Cope said. "I don't know what they were doing. But I still haven't figured out why Lou Ann Sternadel didn't get brought up the same time with Debbie Baker. They should have had both of them in there together ... and then I think they would have got a long prison sentence. I mean, how can two people go get a man food and an hour later the man hits the ground sick, if both of the women aren't involved. They were the only two people there besides the guy who gets sick. Then he gets out of the hospital, and those two women take care of him, and then he goes back to the hospital sick. But they bring only one woman up for trial. That doesn't make any sense to me."

I said, "It doesn't make any sense to anyone."

The juror continued, "I don't know if she had enough money to get out of being tried or what. I heard the guy had one policy for a half million dollars in life insurance. But I didn't know what all she got. Everybody was talking about that $10,000 was gonna be hell on Debbie Baker. I said, 'No! She's got Lou Ann Sternadel backing her. Ten thousand dollars ain't nothing to that lady. To keep you out of jail, that's no money.' That's nothing when you got somebody with that kind of money backing you."

Terry inquired, "Did the jury buy the fact that all the missing money and all those checks were loans from Lou Ann to Debra Baker?"

"No! They felt that it was embezzlement. See, Lou Ann Sternadel was in on that too. If I was gonna get somebody, I'd get the main person. I wouldn't go for the low person. I'd go for the head person."

I asked, "Would you say that everybody agreed that Lou Ann Sternadel was the one who should have been on trial?"

"Everybody agreed on that," Cope answered. "Everybody agreed that Debbie Baker had something to do with it. But nobody could understand why Lou Ann Sternadel wasn't on trial for it too. She was the wife and had to know what was going on. I don't know if it is because it is a little town, but surely those people aren't that stupid. I kept on waiting, thinking they're gonna bring up Lou Ann Sternadel. But nothing has ever been done about her."

Terry responded, "Everybody we've talked to so far has said the same thing."

Cope said, "I told them. I said, 'If ya'll don't send this lady to prison, you're letting both of them go.'"

I asked, "With the evidence that was presented at the trial, if Lou Ann Sternadel had been on trial, would you have found her guilty?"

"Yeah!" the juror replied. "I think either one of them would have been found guilty or they should have been. I mean, they've got trials like the O.J. Simpson trial where he gets off."

I questioned, "Would you say Debra Baker getting probation was a travesty of justice?"

"Yeah, I do!" Cope answered. "I think it was a travesty of justice. I don't think they should be able to poison a man like they did and get away with it."

Terry questioned, "Would you say when ya'll got into that room, you felt bullied into a probation sentence?"

"Yeah … well, I'm not too good to sit in a little room and have a guard outside where you can't get out. You start feeling pressure, and I'm not one to sit in a room for very long. I go crazy, you know. And I'm sitting there listening to that for about three to four hours. Finally, I just go, 'Ya'll just do what you want to. It's nine against three.'

"Tim Cole asked me later, he said, 'Who was the main guy against sending her to prison?' I said, 'It was the foreman.' Tim goes, 'I like to have shit when I heard he was foreman.' I saw Tim at a track meet in Nocona, and he shook my hand and talked to me for a long time. I told him I thought he did a good job with what he had. Somebody testified at the trial that they saw Debbie Baker in the hospital taking this rag and putting it into Jerry's mouth and then putting it in this cup and putting it back in his mouth. They told us that they thought Debbie Baker was still poisoning Jerry in the hospital. I keep wondering why Tim Cole didn't put Lou Ann Sternadel on the stand."

I said, "Tim Cole told us he wasn't going to put Lou Ann on the stand because she was going to take the Fifth Amendment on every question."

"Well, I think he should have brought Lou Ann Sternadel to trial first or with Debbie Baker," Cope replied.

I asked, "What about Jerry Sternadel's deathbed statement saying Debbie and Lou Ann were killing him?"

The juror responded, "The defense attorney got up and said that he was out of his head and hallucinating when he said that. I mean, you can listen to parts of the testimony or you can listen to all of it. I think some of the jury just listened to the parts they wanted to hear. And I think the women on the jury had a problem with sending another woman with a kid to prison. I always believed you do the crime, you do the time! I mean, it's hard to get up there and say, 'I'm going to send you to prison for twenty years or a hundred years or whatever.' But if you stop and think about what they were doing—poisoning the poor guy—when you're trying to decide on a sentence ... All the other jurors were thinking about a mother of a young kid spending time. They weren't thinking about what she did to Jerry Sternadel."

"Was there discussion in the jury about Jerry Sternadel being a bad person?" Terry asked.

"There wasn't a lot, but there was some," Cope responded.

"Did you feel like, well, he deserved it?" Terry questioned.

"Well, I heard people say that. But I didn't know the guy, and I don't think anybody could have deserved that," Cope said as he shook his head.

I asked, "Would you say there was a feeling that some people were prejudiced against Jerry Sternadel?"

"Well, I heard people say something like that. Maybe not jury members, but I don't think that way. He didn't deserve that. I mean, it would have been better if she would have just walked up and shot him. It would have been a lot easier on him. I don't know anybody that needs to go through that cruel a death. You think about a crime where you go up and cut somebody up—that's horrible. But really, if you think about it hard enough ... I mean, he went through a lot worse than that. We looked at pictures of what he went through ... I don't know how they could have given her the sentence they did. I mean, I was involved in it, and it's took me a long time to get over it. I've regretted it.

"But you get that kind of pressure and they put you in a little room. But I don't think any citizen should be able to sentence people. I think that should be a set deal if you go out and kill anybody, it's a hundred years. I wish now that we would've just locked it down and let the judge decide. If I ever have to go through that again, that's what I'll do."

"Who was the last one to give in?" Terry and I asked in unison.

"It was the guy who drives a milk truck. I think his name was Artie. He was the last holdout for a prison sentence. I knew we wasn't gonna change them, and me and the older guy just threw in our hands at the same time."

I questioned, "When you were being considered for jury selection, did Roger Williams ask you if you came up with a guilty verdict would you consider giving probation?"

The juror responded, "Yeah! The defense attorney came up and said, 'Is there any way if somebody got convicted of murder, could you see probation?' And I said, 'Yes, like if my mother was ninety-five years old and she's brain dead and I went in and killed her, that'd be probation.'

"It's been a bad deal for me. I lay awake at night thinking about that for a long time. And you talk about catching hell. I caught hell at work. Everybody started saying if you want to kill somebody go to Clay County. When we came out with the guilty verdict, Debbie Baker's kid tried to attack us. The deputy had to step in between him and us."

Terry said, "Nobody should have been allowed to get that close to the jury."

I responded, "Debbie Baker and her family were down in the lobby of the courthouse sitting right alongside the jury members and everybody else. Debbie was walking around looking at the jury members and smiling at them. It was a real spectacle."

Dale Cope said, "Yeah! I didn't understand that! Debbie Baker would walk by us and smile. I thought, How can this lady sit here and smile after what she's done?"

I said, "The jury should not have been subjected to that. They should not have been around Debbie Baker or her family. The jury should have had a private place to gather for breaks or while they were waiting for court to start."

Cope replied, "Yeah, that's right! But, you know I just can't believe Tim Cole hasn't done anything about Lou Ann Sternadel and brought her to trial. I knew we screwed up when we didn't send Debbie Baker to jail. It was wrong giving her probation. I'm sorry about it. It should have never happened that way. It was a real travesty of justice."

The Continuing Fight for Justice

After interviewing the jurors, I flew back to New York. As the months and then years passed, I remained vigilant while I waited for Debra Baker or Lou Ann Sternadel to make the wrong move.

Jake Bogard had passed away, but I gave my word to continue doing everything I could to get justice in this case. Above all else, I keep my promises.

Every month, like clockwork, I called Debra Baker's probation officers in Hays County and Clay County to check up on her. I always got the same response from the probation officers: Debra Baker is doing everything she is supposed to do regarding the terms of her probation.

In reality, unbeknownst to Debra's probation officers and to me, in 1998 and 1999, Debra was giving and bouncing hot checks all over Hays County.

On April 24, 1999, Debra Baker wrote one hot check too many. One business (Walmart) took action and filed charges against her for theft of property by check.

On May 3, 1999, I learned that Lou Ann Sternadel and Tony Baker had dissolved their business partnership in the trucking company Red Bird Express.

On September 13, Debra Baker pleaded guilty in Hays County to the felony charge of theft by check.

On November 30, Debra Baker received deferred adjudication in Hays County for the felony charge theft by check. She was ordered to pay $905.22 restitution, a fine of $100 plus court costs and put on unsupervised probation for 180 days.

On June 15, 2000, Debra Baker was able, once again, to get someone to feel sorry for her. She was given a favorable discharge from the unsupervised probation related to the April 24, 1999, Hays County theft by check charge.

The theft by check charge was a felony and clearly violated the terms of her probation, both in Hays County and Clay County. But Debra's probation officers did not become aware of the fact that Debra Baker had committed another felony. Nor did I know Debra Baker had committed a felony and had therefore violated the terms of her probation.

But that all changed on November 30, 2001, when Sandy called and told me he had heard through the grapevine that Debra was not living up to the terms of her probation.

My son asked if I would check and find out whether Debra Baker had violated the terms of her probation. Sandy asked me to call the victim's advocate in Austin and see if he could help us. I immediately made the call and left a message.

On December 1, Ray Ramirez returned my call. Mr. Ramirez said, "I'll see what I can find out." Within a short period of time, he called me back. "Debra Baker is not complying with the terms of her probation. She is not paying the Clay County monthly fees. She also has not paid anything toward the $10,000 fine."

I asked Mr. Ramirez what I should do. I listened intently to his advice and thanked him for the information. Then I contacted Debra Baker's probation officer in Clay County and District Attorney Tim Cole and informed both men of what I had learned about Debra Baker.

Tim Cole told me he would check out the information I had given him. When he called me back, he said Debra Baker had a lot of health issues, didn't have a job, and didn't have the money to pay the fees or fine. "If Debra Baker does not have the funds to pay the fees, there isn't a lot I can do about it. The law allows an absolute defense for a defendant if they can't pay. It doesn't please me, but we can't send people to prison if they can't really pay their fines. You can't get blood out of a turnip."

It wasn't the answer I wanted to hear. A couple of days later, I learned from sources that Debra Baker and her husband both had jobs and were making very good money. I promptly called Cole. "I am certain once you check, you will find out Debra Baker has more than ample funds to pay the fees and fines if she wants to. She is violating the terms of her probation."

He asked, "Where are you getting your information from?"

I did not tell Tim Cole how I got the information, just as he did not tell me where he had gotten his information on Debbie Baker not having the money to pay the fees.

Cole said, "If I find Debra Baker has the funds to pay the fees and is in violation of the terms of her probation, I will file to have her probation revoked. She will be arrested by Hays County sheriff's deputies, after which Clay County deputies will return her to Henrietta. A hearing will then seek to learn why she is not paying her fine."

On March 18, 2002, Cole filed a motion to revoke community supervision of Debra Lynn Baker.

On March 22, an arrest warrant was issued for Debra Baker with regard to violation of the terms of her probation.

On March 27, Debra Baker was picked up at her residence in Martindale, Texas, by Caldwell County sheriff's deputies on charges she violated the terms of her probation. The news of Debra Baker's arrest was soon in the newspapers and on television stations.

My daughter told the reporters that she considered Debra Baker's arrest proof that "God answers prayers. We've waited a long time for this to happen."

My son said that Baker's arrest was a strong indication that the jury's verdict was a mistake. "I don't think ten years probation is justified. Now she has shown the jury she does not intend to comply with the ten years probation and the fine. I wonder what that jury thinks now."

I told the reporters I was thrilled by the news of Baker's arrest. "It smoothed over some of the anger I have felt since Debra Baker received a probated sentence for first-degree murder. And it restored my faith in the criminal justice system and the district attorney's office. I'm just hoping and praying her probation will be revoked."

Tim Cole told the reporters that Baker apparently had not been making payments on the fine and was failing as well to pay court costs and other financial attachments to her sentence.

Officials at the Clay County Sheriff's office said they would have to wait until getting an order from the courts but that once they got the official paperwork they would go to Martindale, pick up Baker, and bring her back to Henrietta. It was Easter week, and I was elated that Debra would be spending the holy holiday in jail in Caldwell County.

After the holy holiday, Debra Baker was transported from the Caldwell County jail to the Clay County Jail. On April 3, a hearing was held in the 97th District Court to learn why Debra was not paying her fine. At the hearing, Judge Roger Towrey set bond, which Debra promptly put up and was released from jail.

On April 9, I talked to Tim Cole, who said a hearing on the revocation of probation was scheduled for May. He said Debra was claiming she'd had a bad car accident in 1996 that had left her disabled. "Debra said she needed treatment for abscessed teeth and also needed another hip replacement."

On May 20, the hearing on Debra's violation of probation was postponed until August.

August 19, the revocation hearing was held at the Clay County courthouse in Henrietta. The judge revoked Debra's probation for violating its terms and sentenced her to nine years and 360 days in prison.

On September 27, Debra's attorney, Roger Williams, filed a motion for a new trial with regard to her probation revocation. Debra remained out of jail on bail.

The motion began a series of appeals by Debra in her frantic attempts to stay out of prison.

On September 29, I learned that House Bill 685 closing the probation loophole had died in legislative committee once again. Shortly after that, I received a letter from Texas State Representative Scott Hochberg regarding the legislation. In the letter, he said the bill had not made it out of the criminal jurisprudence committee. He suggested that my family and I contact state legislators to let them know of the public's interest in getting rid of the loophole.

In November, Debra received a new court-appointed attorney, James Rasmussen, to handle her appeals. He filed a petition for discretionary review. The discretionary review appeal hearing was to be held in Fort Worth, Texas. Debra remained free on bail.

Tim Cole filed a motion stating his reasons as to why Debra Baker's revocation should be upheld by the appeals court. January 9, 2003, was the deadline for Rasmussen to file the final appeal for Debra Baker.

On February 18, I nominated District Attorney Tim Cole for the Danny Hill Award. I felt that Cole deserved the prestigious award for all his hard work and diligence in getting Debra Baker's probation revoked. I also felt he deserved recognition for all the help he had given me and my family and other victims of crime.

The first day of April was a very sad day. I received the devastating news that Marcy Sternadel had died after her long and courageous battle from colon cancer.

On April 2, I flew into McAllen, Texas, where my daughter lived and worked. Early the next morning, Becky and I began the long drive to Wichita Falls for her grandmother's funeral.

Throughout the years after Jerry was murdered, Marcy had helped me whenever she could in the quest for justice for her son. She would sign letters and mail them to people I felt could help with the murder case. She also helped me nominate Cole for the Danny Hill Award. Although Marcy was very sick at the time, she signed the nominating letter that I sent her and dutifully mailed it. Marcy was diligent and conscientious and a tremendous help. My ex-mother-in-law and I had become good friends with one common purpose: getting justice for a person we had both loved.

I had just flown back home to Long Island on April 22, when I was notified that Cole was indeed chosen to receive the Danny Hill Award. There was to be an award ceremony on May 8 at the Omni South Park Hotel in Austin. Since I would not be able to get to Austin for the award ceremony, I asked my daughter to attend on my behalf.

Cole graciously accepted the award. In his acceptance speech, he told of how he had successfully gotten a murder conviction in the arsenic murder case only to see the convicted murderer given probation the next day. He gave me recognition as the person who had nominated him. He recognized Becky as the daughter of the murder victim. He also recognized his secretary, Patti Poe, for all her help. He said, "The Sternadel family has seen more highs and lows in the criminal justice system than any family should have to endure."

The Governor of Texas, Mark White, was in the audience. He shook his head in disbelief when he heard a Texas murderer had been given probation after being convicted of first-degree murder.

A few days after the award ceremony, I received a gracious letter from Cole thanking me for nominating him.

On May 15, the 2nd District Court of Appeals of Texas ruled against Debra Baker's appeal. It ruled that the judgment of the trial court had been affirmed, thereby turning down Debra's contention that an error had been made in the trial court's judgment. I made sure TV stations aired and newspapers printed the news of the decision and of Debra's imminent arrest.

On June 15, Debra's attorney filed a petition for discretionary review. Debra and her attorney were hoping a district judge would reconsider the 2002 motion to revoke her probation.

As much as Debra Baker was fighting to stay out of prison, I was steadfast and relentless in my crusade to put her in prison where she belonged. What seemed at first to be a done deal in seeing her finally incarcerated had turned into a long, winding process, as Debra had her attorney file one motion after another.

On July 15, Debra's petition for discretionary review was sent to a higher court.

On October 8, Judges from the Texas Criminal Court of Appeals refused her petition.

By October 15, I was on the phone with Tim Cole. He said Debra's next option was to file a rehearing. The chance that the judges would reconsider rehearing the case was slim. He said the court of appeals would issue a mandate on their ruling, and then the state would issue an arrest warrant for her. He said the mandate would be forthcoming within thirty days or less.

"The only recourse Debra Baker has at this point is to hire an attorney and file an appeal with the Supreme Court. But Debra Baker will have to pay for this attorney, because she will not get any more free attorneys from the state. Oh, by the way, I thought you might like to know Debra Baker's lawyer called me the other day. He said if I would make a deal with Debbie, she would give me information implicating Sandy Sternadel. I told him the only information I was interested in was Debra Baker telling the truth about Lou Ann Sternadel and her involvement in the murder of Jerry Sternadel."

I was happy to hear that Debra would not get any more court-appointed lawyers. But I even more pleased that Cole refused to let her implicate my son, Sandy, in the murder.

On October 16, I called the Court of Criminal Appeals. I was informed a notice of rehearing petition would have to be filed by

Debra's attorney by November 2, 2003. I immediately thought, *What a coincidence! November 2 just happens to be Lou Ann's birthday.*

On the first day of November, I learned from sources that Debra's attorney had made arrangements with the Clay County sheriff for Debra to turn herself in on November 3.

As predicted by Tim Cole, the Court of Criminal Appeals in Austin sent Debra's appeal package back to the Fort Worth Court of Appeals.

The third of November came and went, but Debra did not turn herself in as she had promised. I learned later that her attorney called Clay County Sheriff David Hanes and arranged for her to turn herself in on November 10.

On November 5, I learned the mandate was issued by the Court of Criminal Appeals in Fort Worth and was mailed to the district clerk in Clay County, Dan Slagle. I promptly called Slagle to let him know the mandate was on the way. Slagle told me that he would be on the lookout for it. He said he was actually looking forward to the arrest.

It had been more than a year since the court had revoked Debra's probation. Although I was confident she would soon be arrested, no one could say for certain when or where the arrest would take place.

On November 6, Slagle received the mandate from the Court of Appeals. Straightaway he took it over to the Clay County sheriff with a writ of attachment for the immediate arrest of Debra Lynn Baker.

Later that day, I became aware that Debra Baker was trying to borrow $15,000 from different people. Debra was telling her friends and relatives that she needed a loan to hire an attorney for an appeal. She was also saying the Clay County authorities were scared of her, since she could file lawsuits against them because of her bad health.

At 11:00 AM on November 7, I called the Clay County sheriff. I informed him that I knew Debra had made arrangements to turn herself in to him on November 10. I also said I had learned that Debra was doing everything she could to stay out of prison. I told the sheriff that Debra was trying to borrow $15,000 from relatives and friends on the pretext she needed the money to file appeals. I believed Debra was going to abscond with the money and hide out and that it would be hard, if not impossible, for the sheriff to find her if she did fly the coop. I enlightened the sheriff as to the fact that Debra was telling people that the sheriff wouldn't dare arrest her because Clay County was scared of lawsuits she might file against them because of her poor health. "Debra Baker is laughing at you and all the Clay County officials."

Sheriff Hanes said, "Let's see who has the last laugh, me or Debra Baker."

At 3:30 PM, on November 7, the sheriff called me. "My deputies are escorting Debra Baker back to Clay County from San Marcus, as we speak. The deputies said Debra Baker is sitting in the back of their squad car screaming and complaining."

Finally, I thought I could breathe a sigh of relief knowing Debra would be going to prison for poisoning Jerry to death. I asked the sheriff if he would let me know the exact day when Debra hit the prison system.

On December 1, 2003, I received the long-anticipated news from Sheriff David Hanes. "Jeannie, we are officially transporting Debra Baker to prison today."

I was relieved and happy, until I learned a few days later that because no weapon was listed as being used on the nature of offense, Debra was immediately put into the parole review process with the Texas Department of Criminal Justice.

The Victims

According to the *Texas Code of Criminal Procedure, Art. 56.01*, a victim of a violent crime is (1) someone who has suffered bodily injury or death or, (2) the close relative of a deceased person.

Jerry Sternadel was a victim. My family and I were victims. My children and my grandchildren no longer had a father or grandfather because Jerry was murdered.

On December 7, 2003, I contacted the Texas Department of Criminal Justice's Victim Services to learn how to proceed as a victim of crime. In particular, I wanted to know how to protest Debra Baker being released on parole. Armed with all the information, I began contacting family members so that they too could file protests and keep track of Debra. I even put ads in newspapers asking people for their help by sending in protest letters to TDCJ.

I, along with my family and friends, began the arduous task of writing letters of protest to the parole board asking them to deny parole to Debra Baker. We also wrote letters to the editor.

On January 5, 2004, I sat down and penned a victim impact statement to the Texas Department of Criminal Justice in Austin.

On Tuesday, May 22, 1990, Debra Lynn Baker gave Jerry Sternadel a taco salad that she laced with arsenic poison. A half hour later, Jerry was vomiting with intense gastrointestinal distress. He died after three different stays in the hospital. Massive doses of arsenic poison were fed to Jerry Sternadel in the liquids and food he was given by his caregivers, who pretended to be worried and concerned about his welfare.

The motive for the heinous murder was old-fashioned greed.

In simple language, Jerry Sternadel was poisoned and tortured to death. The pain, misery, and torment inflicted on this man should not happen to a dog, cat, rat, or any animal, let alone a human being. The heinous and evil acts that were planned and carried out are appalling, despicable, disgusting, and inhumane.

Debra Lynn Baker knew the victim's widow was the sole beneficiary of a million-dollar estate and life insurance policy worth almost half a million dollars. The victim, Jerry Sternadel, became aware that his bookkeeper, Debra Baker, and his wife were feeding him poison. He told many people that the two women were trying to kill him by feeding him poison and that they had stolen thousands from him.

Debra Lynn Baker and Lou Ann Sternadel told the hospital personnel they were sisters. When the victim tried to leave the hospital, he was strapped down to the hospital bed by putting leather restraints on both his hands and ankles. The victim became a helpless prisoner with no chance to defend and protect his life as the two women continued to administer poison to him until he finally died.

I have happy memories of Jerry Sternadel. He was so full of life. He had a twinkle in his eye. He loved the thought of having grandchildren and spending time with them. He had his whole life in front of him.

When he was murdered, he owned expensive quarter horses. His horses won races and contributed to his wealth. He planned on giving each of his grandchildren a quarter horse. He never had a chance to see his second grandchild. He didn't get to see his grandchildren ride horses. He didn't get to see them graduate from school or get married. He never got the chance to see his two adult children grow and mature into wonderful, caring human beings.

Debra Baker and her coconspirator killed Jerry Sternadel in a planned assassination. The arsenic poison was purchased well in advance. The bottle of arsenic was found in a storage unit that was rented months in advance by Debra Baker under an assumed name.

Debra Lynn Baker, who showed no mercy or compassion for her victim, received mercy from the jury who judged her. Leniency was shown to Debra Lynn Baker when, after being found guilty of first-degree murder by a jury of her peers, she was then given ten years probation for the crime.

Did Debra Baker appreciate the fact that her life was spared when the jury gave her clemency? No! She went on to commit other crimes, because she has no respect for human life or for the property of others. She believes she can get away with anything. After all, she did get away with murder when she was given probation for first-degree murder.

I am asking the parole board to extend mercy to the victim, Jerry Sternadel. I am asking for mercy for his children, for his grandchildren, and for all the friends and family members who loved Jerry Sternadel and miss him dearly.

I know keeping Debra Lynn Baker in prison for her heinous and evil actions will not bring back our loved one. But knowing that Debra Baker is finally going to pay for her wicked crime will bring a small amount of closure and a measure of justice. Justice and closure is what the victims of this crime desperately need in order to go on with their lives.

Debra Lynn Baker has shown no remorse for her immoral actions. She does not have a conscience and is a corrupt and depraved person. I am beseeching the parole board to keep Debra Lynn Baker in prison for the full term of her sentence so that she cannot inflict hurt and suffering on any other family.

Thank you.

Jeannie Walker

A few days after I wrote and mailed my statement to the Texas Parole Board, I received a telephone call from my granddaughter, Shana.

She said, "I am writing a letter to the parole board. I think I can write one without crying. I'll read you the letter when I get it finished."

Shana finished her letter and called me. "Grandma Jeannie, I'm ready to read you the letter I wrote. I wrote it out in longhand. Mommy is writing a letter too, but she's typing hers. I hope you like what I wrote.

My name is Shana Perkins. I'm the granddaughter of Jerry Sternadel. I am twelve years old and in the sixth grade. I watched my mother's interview on TV. But really, behind the scenes, my mom sits in her bedroom and cries, sometimes all night long. And for that I can thank Lou Ann Sternadel and Debra Baker. My grandfather was murdered before I was born. I don't know the exact date. I will never get to play games with my grandpa and ride horses or even talk to him. I always ask my mom to tell me stories about Grandpa Jerry, and when I hear them I wish and wish he was still alive. I also heard how he was killed. I don't know how anyone can be so cruel and hateful to do something like that. There has to be something wrong with them to kill someone with arsenic poison. Arsenic, by the way, is rat poison. How can someone be so sick? So my point of this letter is: Please keep Debra Baker in prison and please try to get Lou Ann Sternadel too, because if someone is that sick to kill a person with rat poison, that person does not need to be on the loose. How can we be sure they won't kill someone else?

Thank you.

Shana Perkins

After a brief silence, I said, "Sweetheart, your letter was so touching, it made me cry."

"Grandma Jeannie, Mommy said you are planning on writing a book about Grandpa Jerry and his murder. We're going to mail you copies of our letters. Make sure you put my letter and Mommy's in the book. And would you send a copy of my letter to the district attorney?"

"Don't worry, Shana, your letter will be in the book and the DA will get a copy."

When I received my granddaughter's letter, I made a copy and mailed it directly to Tim Cole.

I started receiving copies of protest letters that other people were writing and sending to the Texas Parole Board. One of those letters was from my son.

Dear Parole Board:

Debra Baker murdered my dad, Jerry Sternadel. She poisoned my dad to death with arsenic. She poisoned him over a period of a month to make sure he died. She has shown no remorse and has not even taken responsibility for murdering my dad.

My dad owned a prosperous plumbing business. He also owned and raced quarter horses. He loved his business and loved racing his horses. He worked tirelessly improving the business and taking care of the ranch. When he retired, he planned on leaving the business and the horse ranch to his only kids, me and my sister. Daddy worked as hard as he did so that when he died of old age, we would be well taken care of. Daddy was a millionaire by the time he was thirty-three. And it was all due to his hard work and determination.

Debra Baker took all this away from my dad and from my sister and me when she callously committed the premeditated murder of my dad. She planned my dad's murder well in advance. My dad found out about money that Debbie Baker was embezzling from him with the help of my stepmom, Lou Ann Sternadel. Daddy told me and other people about Debbie and Lou Ann stealing from him and that he told them he wanted the money back or he would go to the police and have Debbie arrested for embezzlement. He gave Debbie and Lou Ann a deadline to have the money back to him by May 31, 1990, or else he would go to the police. Instead of giving back the money they stole, Debbie Baker and Lou Ann Sternadel started feeding my dad arsenic poison in everything he ate and drank.

On May 22, 1990, Debbie Baker gave my dad a taco salad laced with arsenic poison when he sat down to eat lunch with her and Lou Ann. My dad was the only person who got sick that day. About thirty minutes after he ate the salad, he started having severe stomach cramps with nausea and diarrhea. He was sick all day and into the night. He was so weak I had to help him walk to the bathroom. At first, Daddy thought he had food poisoning, but it seemed funny to him that he was the only one who got sick. Debbie and Lou Ann supposedly ate the same food that Debbie Baker had gone to Taco Bell and bought in Wichita Falls.

The next morning, Daddy ate an egg and toast for breakfast that he fixed for himself. He went to work for a few hours. When he came home, he sat down to eat lunch with Debbie Baker and his wife, Lou Ann. Once again, right after eating, he got deathly ill. At 4:15 PM that day, May 23, Daddy was loaded into the car by his workers and taken to the emergency room. He was admitted for gastroenteritis and/or possible food poisoning. He was put in the hospital's intensive care and placed on intravenous fluids. He got better while he was in the hospital and was released on May 25. He came home feeling much better. Marcy Sternadel, my grandmother, stayed at the ranch most of the weekend with my dad.

On Tuesday, May 29, Daddy was real sick again. He said he got sick after he ate with Debbie Baker and Lou Ann. At 10:30 that night, Daddy was readmitted to the hospital. He had been nauseated, vomiting, and had diarrhea with severe stomach cramps. The doctor said that Daddy's symptoms were too severe, prolonged, and varied to fit in the category of food poisoning. The doctor said he was beginning to think it was some other toxin. Daddy started telling people Lou Ann and Debbie were feeding him something to either kill him or make him real sick.

On Saturday morning, June 2, a friend of my stepsister, Holly Maag, drank some Cran-Apple juice that was in our refrigerator. Debbie and Lou Ann told me and Holly that the Cran-Apple juice was for my dad only and that nobody else better be drinking it. Right after Holly's friend drank the Cran-Apple juice, he got real sick with severe stomach cramps, nausea, vomiting, and diarrhea. That afternoon, Daddy was discharged from the hospital. When Lou Ann arrived at the ranch with Dad, I told her about the boy getting sick after he drank the Cran-Apple juice from the refrigerator. I told Lou Ann that Holly had taken the boy to the Wichita Falls clinic. Lou Ann drove straight to the clinic where the boy was and paid all his medical bills. Lou Ann told me that the Cran-Apple juice must have gone bad and she was going to pour it out. Lou Ann said the Cran-Apple juice probably gave the boy food poisoning.

The next day, Sunday June 3, I saw Lou Ann and Debbie Baker giving Daddy Cran-Apple juice. I asked if it was that same Cran-Apple juice that the boy drank and got sick from.

Lou Ann and Debbie chimed in at the same time, telling me that they had thrown that Cran-Apple juice out and this was a fresh bottle of Cran-Apple juice. Soon after Debbie and Lou Ann fed Daddy the Cran-Apple juice, he started getting sick with nausea, vomiting, and profuse diarrhea. At 10:54 PM, I helped take Daddy back to the emergency room. He was in cyanotic condition. In the hospital, Daddy was telling anyone who was in earshot that Debbie and Lou Ann were killing him and that they stole money from him.

On June 12, 1990, my dad died from extreme arsenic poisoning. I won't ever forget that day. No matter how hard I try, I still see Debbie and Lou Ann laughing and joking at the hospital right after Daddy was pronounced dead. It was like they were having a big party.

I found out later from Sheriff Bogard and Texas Ranger Bill Gerth that the Cran-Apple juice container contained arsenic. They said when Debbie Baker brought them the Cran-Apple juice container that the outside of the bottle had mud on it but the inside had soapsuds in it, like someone had tried to wash it out. But they said the Cran-Apple juice container still tested positive for arsenic.

I know that Debbie Baker and Lou Ann Sternadel murdered my dad. Their motive was greed. Daddy had a $350,000 life insurance policy that Lou Ann got, and his estate was worth over a million dollars, which Lou Ann also got.

In January 1994, Debbie Baker was tried and convicted for the first-degree murder of my dad. However, the jury saw her crocodile tears and felt sorry for her, which is why the jury gave her probation for the murder. Probation for murder was allowed only because of a Texas loophole, which allows probation for murder. We are trying to change that loophole.

Debbie Baker was laughing on her way out of court that day. When she saw me, my sister, and my mother, she gave

us the finger as she mocked and laughed at us. It was another
heartbreaking day for us.

    I miss my dad very much. I miss riding horses with him.
I miss feeding the horses with him. I miss talking to him.
His death affected all of us. I moved away from Wichita Falls
because of all the horrible memories that were there. I live
in Austin now, but even the distance doesn't help me forget
the horrible way my dad was murdered. And I can't forget
how Daddy was begging everyone to help him and not let
him die when he was in the hospital. I can't forget how he
was strapped down to the hospital bed with leather restraints
on his hands and ankles. Daddy was strapped down at the
insistence of Lou Ann and Debbie Baker. I can't forget how
those two women pretended to care for my dad while all
the time they were feeding him arsenic in everything he ate
or drank to murder him. I can't forget how my dad asked
me to forgive him of any wrong he had done to me. I can't
forget how he looked at the hospital, how helpless he was,
and how much he wanted to live. Daddy was a strong man.
He could do anything. He didn't like to depend on anybody
for anything. When he was real sick, I would sponge-bathe
him, while all the time he was apologizing to me that he was
too sick to wash himself. I told him I didn't mind washing
him and helping him. But he felt bad that I had to do this
for him. My dad was a good man. He would do anything for
you, especially if he liked you.

    Daddy didn't deserve to be poisoned to death with rat
poison. And Debbie Baker does not deserve to be considered
for parole. She needs to come to terms with how she tortured
and poisoned my dad to death. She needs to stay in prison to
pay for her evil and cruel deeds. She committed other crimes
while she was on probation. And when she is released, she will
commit more crimes.

I am asking you to deny parole to Debra Baker. Please keep her in prison!

Thank you,

Sincerely,

Sandy Sternadel

When I finished reading my son's letter, my heart ached. I sat down and wept. But I knew this was not the time to cry my eyes out. I dried my tears and picked up the protest letter written by my daughter.

Dear Parole Board,

My name is Becky Sternadel. I am the daughter of the deceased victim, Jerry Sternadel. I cannot even begin to express the shock and devastation I feel because Debra Baker is up for parole review. A person like Debra Baker should have to "rot" in prison for the rest of her life. In fact, I believe she should have been given the death penalty. I believe if you commit a crime, the punishment should fit the crime.

Debra Baker is in prison for committing a premeditated murder. She is a murderer! My father was continually poisoned with arsenic until the poison finally killed him. He had enough arsenic in his body to kill an elephant. I believe Debra Baker did not act alone in this premeditated act and she should come forward and tell the truth so that justice can prevail. She has no remorse for what she has done and the grief she has caused our family.

I have two children. My daughter did not even get to know her grandfather because she was not born until after he was murdered. When my dad was in the hospital, I lived in Dallas, Texas, and was working as a parole officer. When I visited Daddy at the hospital in Wichita Falls, Debra Baker would come into the hospital room and watch me. Daddy would get better while he was in the hospital. But every time he went home, he would end up back in the hospital in a worse state than before. The very last time my father went into the hospital, he couldn't even walk and was vomiting everywhere. My brother had to call the next-door neighbors and a family friend to come help him get our dad back to the hospital. Several weeks after my dad was murdered, I found out that Daddy had tried to get out of the hospital to save his own life. He was screaming at the nurses that the two women were trying to kill him and he needed to get out of the hospital before they finally killed him. Debra and her accomplice convinced the doctors and nurses that my dad was hallucinating and didn't know what he was saying. My dad was still screaming when he was strapped down to the hospital bed by the hospital security team. Security men strapped my daddy's legs and his arms down to the hospital bed. When my dad continued to scream out, "They are trying to kill me," he was tranquilized so that he could not talk. While visiting my dad during the last days of his life, he was in a comatose state and looked like a dead person. His whole body was swollen. Can you imagine how you would feel if you knew someone was killing you and no one believed you? It is a horrifying thought!

Debra Baker watched my father suffer and plead for his life while she continually gave him arsenic to drink. Debra watched my dad's body deteriorate until all of his organs failed, his blood vessels collapsed, and then he died. Only an evil person would do this to someone and then watch him or her die in such a cruel manner. Debra was embezzling money from my father. He found out about the missing money and was going to do something about it. But unfortunately for him, he died from arsenic poisoning before he had a chance to go to the authorities. He was trying to do the right thing when he gave

Debra Baker a chance to give him his money back. However, Debra Baker didn't do the right thing. She killed him.

Debra Baker was convicted of first-degree murder. However, my family and I were devastated when she was only given ten years probation for first-degree murder. I believe the jury felt that Debra did not commit this crime alone, which is why they gave her probation.

I don't understand Texas justice when a murderer gets probation and a drug dealer gets ninety-nine years to life in prison. I don't think anyone understands how that can happen.

While Debra Baker was on trial for murder in Clay County, she was facing forgery charges in Hays County for embezzling money from another employer. Her boss in Hays County found out she was stealing money from him and turned her in. It is a very strong possibility that Debra Baker may have eventually murdered him as well. Fortunately for that man, he turned her in before she had a chance to do anything to him. After Debra Baker received ten years probation for murder, the court in Hays County had no choice but to give her ten years probation for forgery.

While Debra Baker was on probation, she violated the terms of her probation. Debra Lynn Baker has shown that she is a habitual criminal who will murder a person to get them out of the way. My father is a prime example of that. I thank God every day that Debra Baker's probation was revoked and she was put in prison. She has no respect for the law and no respect for human life. She is a danger to our society and should not be released on parole.

Please do not grant Debra Lynn Baker the privilege of being on parole. Please let justice prevail.

Sincerely yours,

Becky Sternadel

Once again, my heart was filled with sorrow and I was moved to tears. The pain my children and grandchildren were suffering caused me great anguish. In my heart, I knew God would help us overcome evil and replace the pain with peace and comfort. I set aside my daughter's letter to regain my composure.

Then I picked up the letter written by Jerry's brother.

I am writing to protest the parole of Debra Baker. This woman planned and carried out a heinous and callous act of poisoning my brother to death. To date, she has shown no remorse for murdering Jerry Sternadel. Debra Baker does not even acknowledge that she did, in fact, poison Jerry to death.

Jerry was looking forward to when he could retire and could spend time with his grandson. Jerry never knew he would have a granddaughter, who was born in 1991. He had his whole life in front of him. He made plans for the future. Debra Baker robbed my brother of his plans and his life. She committed other crimes while she was on probation. She has no respect for the law or for law-abiding and honest citizens. I am asking you to keep this woman in prison as long as you possibly can.

Thank you.

Sincerely,

Jim Sternadel

I received hundreds of letters from people who wrote to the parole board protesting Debra Baker's parole. One letter was from juror Dale Cope.

As a member of the jury on the murder trial of Debra Baker and now a friend of the family of Jerry Sternadel, I am hereby protesting the parole of Debra Lynn Baker.

Debra Baker cruelly poisoned Jerry Sternadel to death. She fed Jerry Sternadel arsenic-laced food and when Jerry Sternadel could no longer eat, Debra Baker started giving him arsenic in his juice. Debra Baker told Jerry Sternadel that he needed to drink the juice in order to keep from being dehydrated.

Debra Baker callously watched and waited for Jerry Sternadel to die from the arsenic poison she was continuously giving him. She showed no mercy when she cruelly took his life. I am asking the parole board to show no mercy to Debra Baker and deny all requests of parole and keep her in prison for the full amount of time allotted by the law.

Respectfully,

Dale Cope

A week later, I received a protest letter from Jerry's cousin.

This woman cruelly poisoned my cousin, Jerry Sternadel to death over a period of time. She even pretended to care for him while giving him arsenic poison. I have heard that arsenic kills very slowly and very painfully.

Debra Baker showed Jerry no mercy, but was given mercy when she was given probation for first-degree murder. She committed other crimes while on probation. She also failed to carry out the terms of the probation she received for the first-degree murder of my cousin. I am asking you to deny parole and keep Debra Baker in prison.

Thank you.

Gene and Lila Terry

I also received e-mails from friends protesting Debra Baker's parole.

Hi there, Jeannie.

We are doing fine and enjoyed seeing the sun today. A little rain was nice and we do need more but I still like to see the sun. Here is a copy of the protest letter I wrote. "As a friend of the Sternadel family, I am protesting parole of Debra Lynn Baker. Since she was convicted of poisoning Jerry Sternadel with arsenic over a period of time, I see this as premeditated murder, a crime to be paid. She was shown gracious mercy when given probation. To violate her probation is to walk on the mercy shown her. Her conduct indicates she shows respect to no one, not even the court of law. Society does not need this person walking the streets and working in the workplace, for just what would keep her from preying on another citizen? I am asking you to deny parole and keep Debra Baker in prison. Thank you for your consideration in this matter.

Respectfully,

Bob and Sarah Self"

Before long, I had a cabinet loaded with protest letters. I also knew many other people were calling TDCJ protesting parole for Debra. It felt good to have an outpouring of affection and public support.

On January 12, 2004, I just happened to stumble upon information about a newly formed Unsolved Crimes Investigation Team made up of Texas Rangers. The cold case squad began operating in March 2002. Their headquarters was in San Antonio. The squad was set up to help local agencies and local Texas Rangers with unsolved slayings and major felonies. One old case solved by the squad was that of a nine-year-old boy, Cory Weems, who was killed in 1994 by a stray bullet while eating ice cream on the porch of a relative's house. The cold case investigators cracked the case three years after Weems's death. The suspect, Kevin D. McFail, subsequently received a life sentence. The squad brought peace and closure for Louise Howard, the young boy's grandmother.

Another cold case solved by the squad was a murder committed in Bexar County. In that case, a sixty-eight-year-old woman had been raped and killed. The case remained unsolved for six years until the task force went back and reinvestigated. Within a month, a rape kit was found in the medical examiner's office that had never been processed. The rape kit evidence allowed investigators to compare DNA with that of potential suspects, which resulted in the killer's capture.

The squad had an excellent record of successes in old cold cases.

I learned the commander of the squad was Lt. Gary De Los Santos, a Texas Ranger, who had helped solve many cases. I called him and told him about my ex-husband's case and the cruel way that he had been poisoned to death. As fate would have it, the commander not only knew about Jerry's case but he had actually helped out on the case when he was stationed in the Wichita Falls area. De Los Santos recalled the arsenic murder investigation and remembered some of the details. He informed me that the squad needed permission from the officials who had prosecuted or investigated the murder. He advised me to contact the DA and see if he or the Clay County sheriff would allow the squad to review the murder case.

So I then had another task at hand. I needed to get Tim Cole to allow the cold case squad to take a look at the case. In the past, Cole had informed me that more evidence of some kind was needed in order for him to have a solid case against the other suspect, Lou Ann Sternadel. I felt the cold case squad could possibly find the additional evidence or something that had been overlooked. I contacted the DA and asked if he knew about the cold case squad and would he consider letting them take a look at the case.

On January 15, I received an e-mail response from Cole.

Cold case squads come in two categories. Those that are truly dedicated to finding new evidence and solving a previously unsolved case and those that are in place for political purposes to the benefit of some person or agency. I do not object to a true attempt to locate new evidence. I will object to some agency simply reshuffling the evidence that has been in place for many years and re-interviewing all the same witnesses and then offering it up as a solved case. Which quite frankly is what many cold case squads do. You see, cold case squads only continue to exist if they can justify their continued existence by showing some results. What many of them want to do is show an extremely high clearance rate, which they can do by declaring the case solved, even if it isn't to the satisfaction of the district attorney who must actually prosecute the case.

So the answer is, it depends. I have no problem with talking to someone about it. I will tell you, Jeannie, that I personally believe every possible stone in this case has been turned over. This case has been investigated and re-investigated numerous times. I think something new is going to have to happen before any new evidence turns up ... something like Debbie Baker or Lou Ann Sternadel telling someone that they did it. There obviously is no physical evidence that could be found at this point, unless someone can figure out where that bottle of poison was bought and who bought it. We exhaustively looked into that in the past, as did the private investigator that you hired. Neither was able to trace the bottle of poison to the point of purchase. I don't think anyone can. But, again, I am open to any new ideas but will be skeptical of cold case squads until I trust their motives.

Tim Cole

After I received Tim Cole's e-mail, I contacted Commander De Los Santos and told him about the DA's response and sent him a copy of the e-mail.

On February 6, I received an answer from Commander De Los Santos.

Just to let you know, I got your message as well as Tim's e-mail to you. Very interesting take by Tim on cold case squads. I think I understand his point and his views or experience with some cold case squads. I cannot speak for how others investigate cold cases, but I can speak for our team. Reshuffling evidence is not what we do. We look at the evidence to see what new technology, if any, can be utilized. We do re-interview witnesses to ascertain if what they said then is what they are saying now. Maybe the right question wasn't asked and maybe they didn't tell all they knew then but now are willing. New witnesses could come out of the woodwork by conducting another investigation. Maybe the suspects have told someone about the murder! Who knows! We will not submit now or ever the same case and try to disguise it to make it look like it's new. Cold case squads do only continue to exist if they are solving cases. Why would any agency commit resources, money, and time if it is not working? We don't consider a case solved until we make an arrest, an indictment, and conviction. I have never submitted any case with poor evidence and risk losing the case and therefore never again be able to take the suspect back to court. I would rather wait until such time that enough evidence is found to successfully convict a suspect. I respect Tim's opinion in regards to his views that everything that could be done on this case was done. I know Tim and he is a damn good prosecutor. He is probably right that everything that could be done has been done. I do not want to leave the impression that there is something else that we can do. We don't make promises of any kind that we will solve this case or any other case. I will e-mail Tim in regards to our squad, but I will not force ourselves on him to submit the case to us. If he did, we still would screen the case to see whether or not we would even accept the case for future re-investigation. Like I said, I can only offer our assistance and nothing else. Believe me, we don't have a bag of magic tricks or claim to be better than any other investigator or agency out there. The only thing we got is "time" to possibly look under every rock! That's all. Talk to you later.

De Los Santos

I called Tim Cole and gave him the telephone number for the cold case squad commander, De Los Santos. Cole said he would call De Los Santos but couldn't promise anything.

Approximately one week later I received e-mail from Cole.

I spoke with Gary via e-mail and told him that I would be willing to talk to him about his squad getting involved in the case. Since then I have not heard from him. As I told him, I have no problem with his group looking at the case and trying to uncover new evidence that could make the case against Lou Ann Sternadel better. What I do not want, and will not accept, is a review of the existing evidence and then an opinion by Gary or someone else that enough evidence exists without finding something new. I think you and everyone else knows my opinion on that point. So if the squad wants to take the case and attempt to locate new evidence, then I will give my okay.

Tim

A few days later Cole called me. He said he was declining to let the cold case squad take a look at the case. "I'm afraid it would jeopardize the case and might contaminate the evidence. I don't want Lou Ann Sternadel's defense attorney to say outsiders looking at the file tarnished the evidence. But I have not given up on charging and trying Lou Ann for the murder of Jerry Sternadel!"

I thanked Tim for considering the squad, and told him I appreciated the fact that he did not want to jeopardize the case.

It was a long time coming, but I decided to find out more information about Jerry's accountant, Andrew Coker, who was found dead six months after Jerry's death. The accountant's blood-covered body was discovered behind a flea market on December 11, 1990. His death was ruled a suicide.

I flew to Texas to speak with the accountant's widow. I found the now sixty-seven-year-old woman living in an independent living community complex in Wichita Falls.

Coker's widow said she had never looked further into her husband's death, but she still did not understand why he would kill himself. She told me almost the same thing she had told Sheriff Jake Bogard back in 1990. "Andrew wasn't despondent or depressed, and we didn't have any money problems. We were planning a nice Christmas with our family. He always picked me up at work. But, that day he didn't show up. That wasn't like my Andy. The flea market where they found his body was only a few blocks away from our house on Hanover. I didn't even know he owned a gun."

I asked, "Could you tell me what the note said that your husband left?"

"What note?"

I replied, "The police said a note was found on your husband's body."

"That's the first I've heard about any note. I don't know anything about a note. The police didn't even notify me about my husband's death. I had to find out myself what happened to my husband that day. When he didn't pick me up from work, I asked a friend to find out what happened. The friend had found out my husband was dead and told me. The police didn't contact me. Another friend had identified Andy."

"Can you tell me a little about your husband?"

"He was born in Saint Jo, Texas, in 1935. He graduated from Saint Jo High School where he was valedictorian. He had lived most of his life in Wichita Falls. He had been in the army and served in Korea. He was on the board at First United Methodist Church and had volunteered in the Lions County Fair. He had worked for Parker Square Bank before he became self-employed. He kept books and prepared taxes. He was a good accountant, a good husband and a good father."

"Your husband had called Sheriff Jake Bogard on the morning of December 11, 1990, saying he had information about the Jerry Sternadel murder case. That afternoon, he was found dead behind the

Cross Roads Flea Market. He had made arrangements to meet with the sheriff the next morning on December 12. The sheriff had never believed your husband's death was a suicide."

I got permission from the widow to get a copy of her husband's death certificate, and written authority to speak with the Wichita Falls police. All the records indicated the fifty-five-year-old accountant had died from a self-inflicted gunshot wound to the head. I believed he knew too much, and was murdered in such a way that his death would appear to be a suicide. I thought, *I might never find out what really happened to Jerry's accountant or what he was going to tell Sheriff Bogard. But ... I would not give up.*

On February 18, I found out a major network was interested in doing a documentary on the arsenic murder case. The Oxygen Channel was starting a new series about women who killed. Jupiter Entertainment out of Knoxville, Tennessee, was going to produce the upcoming shows for Oxygen. *Snapped* was set to premiere on August 8, 2004. Jupiter Entertainment contacted me and said the producer who would be working on the documentary would be in touch with me shortly.

On April 4, I learned that Gary De Los Santos was promoted to the rank of captain in the Texas Rangers.

On May 6, Ray Ramirez, the victim's advocate who had helped us, was honored at the Crime Victim Clearinghouse Conference in Dallas with the Ellen Halbert Award from the Texas Crime Victim's Association, for which I had nominated him.

On May 20, I learned Kevin Barry would be Jupiter Entertainment's producer for the *Snapped* series. I called and talked to him. He asked me if I could contact people who were involved in the case to see if they would do interviews for the show. I said I would be glad to do so.

One of the people I contacted was Jerry's foreman, Jim Sigafus, who agreed to be interviewed for the show. He said he wanted to clarify his relationship with Jerry Stenadel and e-mailed me the following statement as to the facts.

My life crossed paths with Jerry Sternadel many times in the twenty-five or so years that we knew each other. Before I met Jerry, I was a friend of his brother, Bobby Sternadel. I was with Bobby only minutes before he died in a tragic one-car accident.

In the late 1960s, I began working for Jerry Gamble Plumbing Company. This is where I first met Jerry Sternadel, who was the company supervisor. I was a skinny kid, just out of high school. Jerry put me on one of the most strenuous phases at one of the plumbing jobs. By noon, I could barely stand up. Jerry commented to the rest of the crew that I wouldn't make it to quitting time or wouldn't be back the next day, which was exactly what I was thinking. However, it gave me new life to prove him wrong, and I was able to continue. I've often wondered if that was not exactly what Jerry Sternadel was trying to do.

Jerry Sternadel was a much-misunderstood person. I believe he felt he must put up a strong and resolved front or be perceived as weak. He was a very competitive person in all aspects of his life. He had a considerate and compassionate side of his personality that he worked hard to keep hidden, but it would occasionally come out. Jerry did many things for me and other people that often were not recognized properly. We had hunting trips to Colorado, fishing trips, and spent time at horse races, all of which I enjoyed.

Jerry had an uncanny ability to win at many things—from pool hall games to golf to horse racing, as well as in the financial world. This often caused a lot of jealousy and hatred toward him (by others).

After working with Jerry at Gamble Plumbing, I went on to work for him in his own business for some years. We drifted apart for a few years, but in 1989 Jerry approached me to come to work as his foreman, which I did. Jerry told me just before he became ill that he had some big plans for me and wanted us to work together to advance and expand his business, which I was very much looking forward to.

Now, I will move on to explain my views of his terrible
death. These are the facts as I best remember them. On the
occasion of Jerry becoming sick the first time, he and I arrived
at his office at around 12:00 noon. He stated that the girls,
meaning Lou Ann and Debbie, had gone to town and picked
up some Mexican food. He invited me to eat with them. I
declined, because I was busy and went on into town to the
plumbing supply house. When I arrived back, I found Jerry
nauseated and very weak. I asked him what was wrong. He said
he was poisoned and felt it was the Mexican food that was bad.
He went home to recover. The next morning, he looked much
better. He said he was able to eat some toast and scrambled eggs.
I went to work on a couple of jobs. Sometime in the afternoon
that day, Lou Ann called me and wanted me to send a couple of
men to the house to help her get Jerry to the hospital. I called a
couple of guys, and we took Jerry to the hospital. I went to the
emergency room where I spoke with Dr. Humphrey, who told
me he was afraid Jerry had toxic shock syndrome. The doctor
admitted Jerry to the hospital for observation. He spent a couple
of days in the hospital. Then he was sent home feeling better.

When he arrived back at the office, he was very energetic
to get things rolling on the plumbing jobs as usual. I observed
Debbie Baker trying to get Jerry to drink some apple juice she
said she had prepared for him. Jerry told Debbie the apple juice
tasted awful and declined to drink it. He took the juice and
poured it out on the gravel driveway. After a short time back
home, Jerry started feeling sick again and had to go back into
the hospital. He was afraid he would lose his business and said
he needed me to keep it going. I assured him he had nothing to
worry about except getting well and I would protect his interest.
During this time, I was having a lot of problems with Debbie
Baker not wanting to leave the hospital to help me out in the
plumbing office. Debbie and Lou Ann seemed obsessed with

staying right by Jerry's side in the hospital. When I visited Jerry in the hospital, I often observed Debbie and Lou Ann giving Jerry ice from a cup with a spoon. Some days after this, Jerry slipped away and painfully died.

Upon Jerry's death an autopsy was ordered. I was in the office by myself when the Clay County sheriff and investigator arrived. They asked me if they could look around. I told them sure. That was when the sheriff told me that Jerry had been poisoned to death. I paged Debbie Baker and Lou Ann, who were supposedly in town making funeral arrangements. Lou Ann called me back. She became furious when I told her the sheriff was there and wanted to take a look around. Lou Ann told me to run him out of the office, since he did not have a search warrant. I felt this was inappropriate and asked Lou Ann if there was something to hide. Lou Ann did not comment, and the sheriff decided to leave and come back with a search warrant.

A few days later, I decided to leave Jerry's plumbing business. Since Jerry had held the master's plumbing license for his company, it was no longer a legal plumbing business. I had a master's plumbing license and could have put it up to continue the business for Lou Ann, but I was very apprehensive to do this. Upon talking with Bill Gerth, the Texas Ranger assigned to the case, I discovered I was listed as a suspect. I was absolutely devastated by this news and felt I must stay for at least a while to exonerate myself as a suspect and because I did not trust Debbie Baker or Lou Ann Sternadel at all. However, I did put up my master's license for a short period of time just to keep Jerry's plumbing business going. As the investigation went on, I grew more and more suspicious of Lou Ann and Debbie. Debbie even tried to get me to drink some tea she had made and I would not. She asked me if I trusted her. I told her no.

A few weeks into the investigation, the sheriff came out and wanted to look through the trash pit for a Cran-Apple juice jar.

I gave him permission. I felt they did a halfhearted attempt to locate the jar in the trash pit. After the sheriff left, I appointed a man to empty out the trash pit, if necessary, but to find the jar that seemed so important. He did find the jar and commented it had clear liquid in it. I called the sheriff. He came out quickly and took the bottle.

Some days later I heard about a boy who had spent the night with Holly Maag (Lou Ann's daughter) during Jerry's last hospital stay. I learned from the Texas Ranger that this boy had to be rushed to the clinic after drinking Cran-Apple juice from Jerry's refrigerator. I confronted Lou Ann about this and asked why she had not told me about the boy getting sick. Lou Ann said the boy only had the flu. She appeared very nervous when I asked her about the boy. I later found out that Lou Ann had paid the boy's medical bill.

Events began to make me extremely concerned, and I was looking for a way to leave. After a few weeks, the Texas Ranger told me I was no longer a suspect. I moved on to another job at that time.

I will probably never know if Lou Ann had any part in the murder of Jerry. I don't know if she was a part of it from the start or attempted to cover it up, but a lot of things happened to make me one hundred percent sure Lou Ann was involved in Jerry's murder.

Knowing Jerry Sternadel changed a lot of things in my life for the better. I feel he was cheated out of justice in his death and his character was demeaned during the trial. Half of the time at the trial, it seemed like Jerry Sternadel was on trial, not Debbie Baker. I wish you and Jerry's family all the best and I grieve with you in his death.

Sincerely,

Jim Sigafus

Jim's statement touched my heart and brought back memories of guys who had worked for Jerry. They were all decent and honest, like Jim. And a lot of them went on to start their own plumbing business and became very successful.

A few days later, the producer for the *Snapped* series called and asked if I could e-mail him the names and phone numbers of the people who had agreed to be interviewed. I told the producer that Jerry's foreman had agreed to an interview and also gave me a statement. I sent him the following e-mail.

> Dear Kevin,
>
> Here's some info and names and phone numbers.
>
> Harold Newton agreed to be interviewed. He was a salesperson where Jerry bought plumbing supplies. Harold testified at the murder trial in 1994. He knew Jerry for a number of years and worked at Morrison Supply where Jerry purchased much of the equipment that he needed for the plumbing business.
>
> Dr. Thomas Kurt said he would be willing to do an interview on the condition that identifying credentials and proper identification were produced. Dr. Kurt will be out of town until Wednesday, June 2, at which time I told him you would be contacting him.
>
> Tambra Thornton's connection to the case/story: She helped Jerry Sternadel with the horses at the ranch. She also went to visit Jerry at the hospital. Tambra said that Jerry told her the two women had stolen money from him and were trying to kill him. She relayed this information to one of the doctors. Tambra saw the two women trying to force Jerry to drink something when he was in the hospital. She said on the morning before Jerry died, Lou Ann and Debbie were adamant that she come out and clean the house. Tambra refused, because she had heard that arsenic can be absorbed through the skin.

Henrietta is where the Clay County sheriff's office and courthouse are located. Clay County has jurisdiction over the poisoning murder case. The late sheriff Jake Bogard is the sheriff who worked the case along with Sheriff Paul Bevering and Texas Ranger Bill Gerth.

After I talk to some more people, I will give you their names and numbers. I'll be glad to fill you in on any other information you might need. God bless!

Sincerely,

Jeannie

After talking to everyone I felt would agree to an interview for the show, I called Kevin and gave him their names and phone numbers. I also sent the producer a brief summary of the story I was working on about the Jerry Sternadel murder.

On May 22, I received an e-mail from Kevin Barry.

Wow, Jeannie. What a story! It really sheds a lot of light on all that happened. I will do my best to bring attention to what happened and what injustice has been unaddressed. The truth is very powerful, and we'll do all we can to put it into this documentary.

Kind regards,

Kevin Barry

On May 24, I was contacted about being interviewed for the show.

Jeannie,

I will call the office in the morning and find out if they want to talk to you this week, so you can plan your week. I finally talked to District Attorney Tim Cole. He politely declined to be interviewed. He said he couldn't talk about this case because he's trying to build a case against someone else. He was very nice. I confirmed interviews with both Jerry Gamble and Jim Sigafus. Debra Baker's defense attorney, Roger Williams, was very nice, but he says he has to think about it a bit. Spoke to Tom Bradley. He's in Houston, so will be unable to come to Wichita Falls and be interviewed. But he said we could speak to his mom, Shirley O'Neal, instead. The reporter Dan Bartel said he would do an interview, but his knowledge is limited on the case, so I will look for another journalist just in case we need one.

Thanks, Jeannie,

Kevin

I e-mailed the producer back and said I would talk to Jeff Hall, who was another journalist who wrote articles on the case and was also knowledgeable about the trial and case.

Producer filming segment for *Snapped* series

Kevin Barry said he would be flying into Wichita Falls either the first or second week in June to begin conducting interviews.

On May 28, a film crew came to Long Island to interview me for the show. The producer, Mike Hart, was a friend of Kevin Barry's who had agreed to help Kevin out while he was busy on another story. I gave them videotapes, news stories, photos, and general information for their perusal.

I heard back from Jeff Hall that he was willing to do the interview.

Producer Kevin Barry and his film crew flew to Wichita Falls. On June 12, they began filming interviews with the people I had lined up.

Kevin received a surprising telephone call from Debra, who said she would grant a video interview from jail. He and his film crew rushed to Gatesville Prison.

On June 16, 2004, the Texas Board of Pardons and Parole denied parole to Debra Lynn Baker. The board set Debra's next parole review date for June 1, 2008. The board gave two reasons for denying the parole.

> (1) Nature of Offense: The records indicates that the inmate committed one or more violent criminal acts indicating a conscious disregard for the lives, safety, or property of others, or the instant offense or pattern of criminal activity has elements of brutality, violence or conscious selection of victim's vulnerability such that the inmate poses a continuing threat to public safety, or the record indicates the use of a weapon.

> (2) Adjustment during periods of supervision: The record indicates unsuccessful periods of supervision or previous probation.

When I heard the news of Debra Baker being denied parole, I immediately called Kevin Barry and left the news on his answering machine.

The episode about the arsenic murder of Jerry Sternadel was aired on the Oxygen channel's *Snapped* series on February 17, 2005.

I discovered a letter online that was written by Debra Lynn Baker complaining about her treatment in Gatesville Texas Women's Prison. Debra said she was entered into the Woodman Unit on December 1, 2003, and was being mistreated in prison. She stated she suffered from posttraumatic stress disorder (PTSD) and major depression and had been suffering from severe chronic pain for over eight years. She complained of being denied pain medications and other medications. She stated her left hip had been replaced twice. She said she fell and was accused of faking the fall and was refused help by the commanding officer. She also complained that the water at the prison unit where she was housed was contaminated with atrazine.

A short time later, I came across an online article about a problem with the water in the Hobby Prison Unit where Debra was being housed in Gatesville, Texas. According to the article, the water at Hobby Unit was contaminated with atrazine, a synthetic compound used as an agricultural herbicide.

It seemed if the water was contaminated with atrazine where Debra Baker was housed, then it was due to bad karma. Every act done eventually returns with equal impact. Good will be returned with good; evil will be returned with evil. Debra Baker put a toxic compound into the food and drink she fed Jerry Sternadel. Now she was being exposed to a toxic compound in her food and drink. Jerry Sternadel was virtually a prisoner strapped down in the hospital and died from the effects of arsenic. Now Debra Baker was a prisoner in a Texas Women's Prison and couldn't get away from the effects of atrazine. What goes around comes around!

But the battle for justice wasn't over yet.

In January 2008, I was notified by the Texas Department of Criminal Justice that Debra Baker had once again been put into the parole review process.

In February, my family and I, once again, began writing protest letters. We asked others to write letters of protest to TDCJ.

My granddaughter sent me a copy of her protest letter.

Dear Parole Board,

My name is Shana Perkins. I am the granddaughter of Jerry Sternadel. Debra Baker is being considered for parole. When I heard this, my heart was crushed. My family has been through so much and to hear that the woman who caused all this grief and heartache for my family might be let out of prison and put on parole kills me inside.

I am sixteen years old. All of my friends have their grandpa come to their lacrosse games and school awards to cheer them on. I see my friends' grandpas come out onto the field and hug them and tell them how good they did. I don't have a grandpa sitting in the bleachers at my lacrosse games. I don't have a grandpa watching me get awards from school. I don't have a grandpa to watch me grow up. I can thank Debra Baker for taking my grandpa away from me.

My grandpa was murdered one year before I was born. I was not even able to meet my grandpa.

I learned how my grandpa was strapped down to a bed in the hospital while the person who was killing him with poison was pretending to care about him. Nobody should suffer a horrible death like my grandpa did.

Please don't let a cold-blooded murderer out of prison. Debra Baker put my grandpa through this horrible death, and it has had a lasting effect on my family.

Please deny Debra Lynn Baker parole. Please keep her in prison as long as you can. Thank you.

Shana Perkins

My granddaughter's letter tore through me like a dull knife.

The poisoning death of Jerry was like a deep wound that wouldn't heal.

Good news came on May 28, 2008. The Texas Board of Pardons and Parole denied parole to Debra Baker. She is TDCJ inmate

#01201529 and is incarcerated in the Texas State Women's Prison at Gatesville, Texas.

Making sure Debra Baker remained in prison for the full term of her sentence was a relief and a blessing in my long trek for justice.

But there was still at least one more suspect who had not been brought to justice. I knew all too well that Jerry Sternadel could not rest in peace until everyone involved in his murder had been arrested and tried.

However, I found solace in knowing Debra Baker would not be allowed another parole review. My prayers had been answered.

It was a dream come true!

Afterword

Debra Lynn Baker tried everything to stay out of prison, even after she was convicted of the first-degree murder of Jerry Sternadel. On December 1, 2003, she was incarcerated at the Women's Prison in Gatesville, Texas. Parole has been denied to her twice. She is housed in the Hobby Unit at the Women's Prison in Gatesville, Texas. She is TDCJ Inmate #01201529. Her release date from prison is June 24, 2013.

District Attorney Tim Cole was elected district attorney for the 97th Judicial District on the Demoratic ticket in 1992 but later switched to the Republican Party. He had high hopes for a political career. In 2004, he was reelected. On July 7, 2006, Cole resigned as president of the Texas District and County Attorneys Association. On September 1, 2006, Tim Cole resigned as district attorney and established his own law practice in Nocona, Texas.

Jack McGaughey was appointed district attorney of Texas's 97th Judicial District on September 5, 2006, by Texas Governor Rick Perry after Tim Cole's resignation. He had been the assistant district attorney. (Cole and McGaughey had run against each other in the Democratic primary in 1992 with Cole winning the election. Cole later appointed McGaughey as assistant district attorney.) In 2008, McGaughey was elected district attorney of the 97th Judicial District Court.

Texas Ranger William R. Gerth retired from the Texas Rangers in 1993 after having been in law enforcement for thirty years. He keeps his copy of the Sternadel murder case file safe and sound.

Sheriff Paul Bevering retired after twenty-two years in law enforcement.

Thomas Bradley suffers from shingles, a side effect of the arsenic poison. He is currently the athletic trainer at Clear Creek High School in League City, Texas. He has a master of science degree in kinesiology from Midwestern State University in Wichita Falls, Texas; a bachelor of science degree from Central Methodist College in Fayette, Missouri; and an associate's degree from Kemper Junior College in Boonville, Missouri. He holds the following credentials: ATC (certified athletic trainer), LAT (licensed athletic trainer), and LMT (licensed massage therapist). He married his sweetheart, Jaime, on June 26, 2005. He has infertility issues that may or may not be the result of having ingested arsenic poison. After infertility treatments and a lot of prayers, in 2009, he and his wife were blessed with a beautiful baby boy, Beau David.

Lou Ann (Ford) Sternadel has remarried and lives in Sulphur Springs, Texas. She is still a suspect in the arsenic murder of Jerry Sternadel. There is no statute of limitations on murder. Her arrest hinges upon having sufficient evidence to prove guilt beyond a reasonable doubt. (The Criminal Justice Standards are for a conviction to be able to stand up upon appeal.)

Becky Sternadel continues to grieve the loss of her dad.

Sandy Sternadel is trying to get on with his life the best he can without his dad.

Jeannie Walker is continuing her search for justice. She has dedicated her life to seeking justice in the arsenic murder case, so that hopefully, one day soon, her ex-husband can rest in peace. She still feels the "presence" of Jerry Sternadel.

Glossary

ARSENIC: Arsenic is an element, which means it cannot be broken down further into different chemicals. Arsenic in its pure natural state is a gray metal. Most often it is found as arsenic trioxide—a white powder. Traces of arsenic are present in all human tissues. It is the twentieth most commonly encountered element of 103 known elements.

Ingestion results in poisoning and typically affects the digestive system. The fatal dose for arsenic trioxide is about 120 mg. In homicidal or suicidal cases, arsenic is generally swallowed. It can also be inhaled either as a dust or as arsine gas, with the gas producing somewhat different symptoms than the dust. Historically, arsenic was the murderer's most popular tool, primarily because it was found in so many household items—from wallpaper and paste to paints and pesticides.

Most experts believe that arsenic interferes with the function of vital enzymes in the body. Symptoms begin as early as half an hour after ingestion. In acute conditions, death may occur in a few hours or take as long as twenty-four hours.

The best known symptom of arsenic poisoning is severe gastric distress. Other symptoms include esophageal pain, vomiting, and diarrhea with blood. The skin becomes cold and clammy to the touch and the blood pressure falls so that the victim becomes dizzy and weak. In cases where death is not immediate, the skin is jaundiced and the victim becomes restless and has headaches, dizzy spells and the inability to void. Occasionally, there will be moments of paralysis. Because arsenic is an element and does not break down, it remains in the victim's hair, fingernails and urine. Red blood cells are destroyed. If death is delayed by several days, arsenic will show up in the liver and kidney. After long periods of ingestion, the victim develops a rash that flakes away, called exfoliative dermatitis. Convulsions and coma are the final signs, and death usually comes from circulatory failure.

Chronic arsenic poisoning causes the victim to experience burning pains in the hands and feet, numbing sensation throughout the body, localized swelling and skin irritations, hair loss, cirrhosis of the liver, nausea, vomiting, cramps, weight loss, visual impairment and finally cardiac failure.

Inhalation of arsenic dusts may cause acute pulmonary edema, restlessness, dyspnea, cyanosis, cough with foamy sputum and rales.

CARDIOMYPATHY: Cardiomyopathy is a serious disease in which the heart muscle becomes inflamed and doesn't work as well as it should. There may be multiple causes including viral infections. It is often associated with inadequate heart pumping or other heart-function problems.

CYANOSIS: Cyanosis is a bluish or purplish tinge to the skin and mucous membranes. Cyanosis can occur when there is not enough oxygen in a person's blood or tissues.

DYSPNEA: Dyspnea is difficult or labored breathing; shortness of breath. The word dyspnea comes from the Greek words *dys* (difficulty) and *pnoia* (breathing).

EDEMA: Edema is a condition characterized by an excess of watery fluid collecting in the tissues and cavities of the body.

ENDOTRACHEAL TUBE: An endotracheal tube (ET), or breathing tube, is a plastic tube that is inserted through the patient's mouth or nose. One end of it is placed into the windpipe (trachea) and the other is connected to a breathing machine (mechanical ventilator). The ET provides an airway so that air and oxygen from the breathing machine or breathing bag can be provided to the lungs of the patient. The breathing tube goes through the vocal cords and prevents them from moving. This means the patient cannot make sounds.

ENTERITIS: Enteritis is an inflammation of the intestine, especially the small intestine, usually accompanied by diarrhea.

GUILLAIN-BARRÉ SYNDROME: Guillain-Barré Syndrome is an uncommon disorder in which the body's immune system attacks the nerves. Weakness and numbness in the extremities are usually the first symptoms. These sensations can quickly spread, eventually paralyzing the entire body.

HALDOL: Haldol is an older antipsychotic used in the treatment of schizophrenia and in the treatment of acute psychotic states and delirium.

LARYNGOPHARYNX: The laryngopharynx is the bottom part of the pharynx and the part of the throat that connects to the esophagus.

NASOGASTRIC TUBE: A nasogastric tube (NGT) is a flexible plastic tube that goes through the patient's mouth or nose into the stomach. It is designed to remove stomach contents or provide a route to give medication or food to a patient who cannot swallow.

PANCYTOPENIA: Pancytopenia is a medical condition in which there is a reduced number of red and white blood cells as well as platelets.

PERIPHERAL NERVES: Peripheral nerves are the nerves outside the brain and spinal cord.

POLYNEUROPATHY: Polyneuropathy is the simultaneous malfunction of many peripheral nerves throughout the body.

PULMONARY EDEMA: Pulmonary edema is a condition caused by excess fluid in the lungs. This fluid collects in the numerous air sacs in the lungs, making it difficult to breathe.
Pulmonary edema is usually caused by heart failure.

SINUS TACHYCARDIA: Sinus tachycardia is a fast heartbeat caused by rapid firing of the sinoatrial (sinus) node.

CPSIA information can be obtained at www.ICGtesting.com
Printed in the USA
LVOW062058040412

276206LV00004B/156/P